BRITISH INDUSTRY AND THE NORTH SEA

BRITISH INDUSTRY
AND THE NORTH SEA

State Intervention in a
Developing Industrial Sector

Michael Jenkin

First published 1981 by
THE MACMILLAN PRESS LTD
London and Basingstoke
Companies and representatives
throughout the world

ISBN 0 333 25606 9

Printed in Hong Kong

To Phyllis

Contents

List of Figures

List of Tables

Preface

The relations between British Government and industry are frequently the subject of heated debate in many forums, but relatively seldom the object of detailed investigation and analysis. There are many reasons for this, among which are the difficulties of treating a topic that demands familiarity with two seemingly very different spheres of activity and the research problems presented by the confidentiality surrounding almost all government–industry transactions. None the less, the increasing importance of government within the British economy in recent decades warrants augmented efforts to characterise the process(es) whereby government becomes involved with industry and the type of relations which result. To this end, the present book explores the emergence during the 1970s of British Government support for the development of a domestic industry to supply goods and services to the oil companies exploiting the oil and gas reserves of the North Sea. The offshore supply industry, as this new entity has been designated, is in part a product of government industrial policy and, thus, the study provides an opportunity to examine the circumstances in which government is induced to promote industrial capacity and the means it currently has at its disposal to accomplish this. In addition, by comparing government involvement in support of the offshore supply industry with other documented instances of government involvement in industry, the study yields insights into the way in which government capabilities in the industrial sphere are evolving.

Considerable attention is devoted in the chapters which follow to the economic structure of the offshore supply industry, but the study does not dwell either upon the economic performance of the industry or upon the contribution of government policy to that performance. As will be demonstrated, government offshore involvement was not characterised by ends and means which were single and discrete. Instead, ends and means in this context were multiple and subtly integrated, and the present investigation is focused upon establishing both why and how this was the case by examining in depth the processes of policy formulation and implementation in the offshore field. This implies, however, that there is little point, for example, in addressing the question of the economic 'effectiveness' of government industrial policy until the relations between ends and means in this sphere are much more clearly understood than they are at present.

Some of the difficulties of conducting research in the field of industrial policy and government–industry relations have already been mentioned. Sources of information about the structure of particular industries or specific aspects of government industrial policy are often extremely diverse and, at times, scarce. In addition, not only is government generally closed about its relations with industry, but firms, and their trade association representatives, are also frequently reluctant to discuss their transactions with government openly. I was particularly fortunate in the degree of co-operation which I received from politicians, civil servants and industry executives directly associated with offshore supplies policy, but much of this was given on the condition that several aspects of the policy and its impact remain confidential. In deference to the wishes of some of those individuals who contributed information for the study certain details associated with the policy and its implementation which might have been included in the text under other circumstances have been omitted. Furthermore, many of the interview sources for material in the text have been given anonymity in the references. However, in my estimation, these omissions have not been substantially detrimental to the account of government involvement with the offshore supply industry.

A book such as this is never completed without the assistance of a great number of people. I am especially indebted to the civil servants, trade association officials and industry executives who took the time to discuss offshore supplies policy with me. Certain civil servants reviewed and commented upon early drafts of a number of the following chapters, and I am grateful for the corrections and clarification which they supplied. I have also benefited from many discussions with staff and postgraduate students in the Department of Government, University of Manchester. Special thanks are extended to Dr Maurice Wright who provided many insights into the intricacies of policy-making in Whitehall and commented extensively on earlier drafts of this book.

I would also like to express my appreciation to the

Commonwealth Scholarship Commission in the United Kingdom and the Canada Council for the financial assistance necessary to undertake the research and writing of this book. Mrs June Maddocks of Manchester and Mrs Christine DuBois of Ottawa, typed various drafts of the manuscript and I am very grateful to them both for their efforts. In addition, Mr Leo Fahey provided invaluable assistance in drafting the many diagrams and figures which appear in subsequent pages.

Finally, I would like to thank my wife, Phyllis, for her moral support and editorial skills. She has been not only a companion, but a colleague, and much of what follows has benefited from many hours of discussion between us. Naturally, I alone am responsible for any errors or weaknesses in content and argument which remain.

Ottawa,   M.J.
December 1978

1 Governments, Industry and Intervention

Since the early 1960s it has been fashionable among a wide variety of writers to designate the role of government within the economy as *state intervention*.[1] The term has gained such currency in the literature that it is difficult to avoid using it. However, unfortunately, it also presents a number of problems. Among the most important is that the word 'intervention' tends to imply a mechanistic understanding of the political and social relations associated with government involvement in economic affairs. In particular, it suggests that government is engaged in a series of 'push – pull' confrontations with elements of the private sector with the object of expanding its sphere of economic influence. Moreover, there is also the implication that if the state succeeds in pushing back the boundary separating public from private, it enters realms in which it has no natural place. Intervention generally refers to the entry of something extraneous into an arena of interest. Thus, when applied to the position of government within the economic sphere, it infers that the use of political or administrative criteria in areas formerly governed by the market is intrinsically inappropriate, inefficient, counter-productive and perhaps ultimately conducive to loss of freedom.[2] Here, and in the following chapters, it is argued that this understanding of government involvement in the economy misrepresents both the process whereby government becomes engaged in new economic arenas and the relations which result between government and various 'private-sector' groupings. The term 'intervention' is employed in what follows, but in a sense very different from the one outlined above.

If, then, mechanistic analogies are unsatisfactory in characterising government involvement in the economy, the question of alternatives arises. Based upon a survey of the relevant literature and the results of the present study, it is maintained that, at least in relatively stable Western societies such as the United Kingdom,

France, West Germany and the United States, government intervention is predominantly a product of large-scale structural economic change within advanced capitalism and the local or general instability which accompanies it. When confronted with this type of change Western governments act to minimise disruption. In some cases, new developments within the economy appear on balance to enhance economic prospects, but also threaten certain established economic patterns, and governments respond by deploying their resources to ensure an orderly transition from one economic regime to another. In other cases, change is synonymous with industrial decline or growing shortages of energy and crucial raw materials, and governments respond by attempting to restore some semblance of economic equilibrium. (The term 'crisis' is apt when change of either type is rapid or prolonged.) The object in both situations is to maintain a stable, growing economy, and it is in this sense that government intervention complements rather than opposes the economic *status quo* broadly defined. This is not to argue that one can identify the interests of government with those of the private sector, largely because the latter are by no means homogeneous. Yet intervention, whatever the circumstances which produce it, is concerned with mediating change so as to ensure the survival and development of the economic system as a whole.[3]

There is also another side to government intervention. Its nature and direction are primarily determined by the nature and direction of structural economic change, but the form which it assumes is also a product of national, political and social history as reflected in the political and institutional commitments of the members of Cabinet and civil servants involved in responding to change. Of course, these commitments are not static. Along with other things, they are shaped by experience which government accumulates during the course of each intervention in economic affairs. As one instance of intervention succeeds another, ministers and officials adopt different views of the manner in which the economy functions and, hence, different views of the way in which intervention should proceed. Over time, these views are tested in the political and economic arenas; some are found wanting in the face of the economic changes which precipitate intervention; others are to some degree legitimated, and are, therefore, incorporated into an evolving body of opinion about the appropriate role of the state in economic affairs. Some of the specifics of this process in Britain are the subject of this book.

GOVERNMENT IN SUPPORT OF ADVANCED CAPITALISM

In order to provide a context for the foregoing description of government intervention, the following pages review the way in which the intervention process has been understood by a number of authors writing from different national perspectives. The focus is upon industrial intervention, although other types of government involvement in the economy are mentioned.

Most of more recent writers who have addressed the issue of the relationship between government and industry have directed their attention towards the way in which Western governments have accommodated *positive* structural economic change. The writings of J. K. Galbraith, for example, are representative of this approach. In *The New Industrial State*[4] Galbraith argued that the major structural change characteristic of post-war American capitalism has been the rise of very large, bureaucratically organised corporations involved, more often than not, in the more technically advanced areas of industrial production. These new corporate entities and the men who run them (Galbraith's 'techno-structure') place heavy demands upon the social and political system. Unlike the 'entrepreneurial corporations' which preceded them,[5] they operate on such a large commercial scale and monopolise so many of the nation's resources that were they to fail the consequences would in many cases be momentous. Galbraith contends that it is this type of corporate concentration which has induced a variety of types of state intervention in America since the war. In particular, he cites the role of government in developing and maintaining social and physical infrastructures of the kind necessary for engaging in large-scale, technically sophisticated industrial enterprise. Thus, state investment in advanced education, welfare programmes, manpower services, communications and transport has complemented corporate requirements for a skilled and stable workforce and facilities in keeping with nation-wide, if not international, production and distribution. What Galbraith has described is the integration of government interests with those of the dominant corporations in the American economy as a result of the consequences which would follow for the economy as a whole if they were to collapse. The locus of American economic activity is no longer the entrepreneurial corporation, which required little more of the state than to 'hold the ring' by providing a favourable legal environment for the operation of business. Rather, economic stability is dependent upon the fortunes of corporations whose organisational requirements are such as to encourage state intervention, especially in cases such as defence production, where state and corporate objectives are in large measure conflated.[6]

Galbraith was not the only writer to analyse intervention in these terms. For example, a few years after the appearance of *The New Industrial State*, R. Heilbroner, another American economist, indicated that he basically concurred with the foregoing analysis, especially as it applied to government support for research and development.[7] Moreover, in Britain Andrew Shonfield's *Modern Capitalism*[8] confirmed the general thrust of Galbraith's work. In particular, Shonfield's book demonstrated that European governments were also supporting industry in the wake of various forms of structural economic change. In some instances intervention followed upon corporate concentration; in others it was an extension of post-war reconstruction aimed at high growth levels. However, while there were similarities in the pattern of intervention between the United States and Europe, there were also differences. The latter related to the *form* which intervention assumed in European economies. For example, there was a greater emphasis in Europe upon planning and the 'corporate' integration of government and industry in organisations such as social and economic councils. Shonfield attributed this to differences in political traditions and social conditions between Europe and America.

The importance which Shonfield assigned to the political and social 'environment' in determining intervention patterns is particularly significant in the British case, for it is clear from his analysis of intervention in this country during the 1950s and 1960s that British experience is not in the European tradition. The salient feature of this experience is the continued importance of commitments to the free-market ethic within government circles well into the 1960s. The challenges presented by the Depression, post-war reconstruction and the balance of payments crises of the 1960s weakened, but did not eliminate, these commitments. Thus, for example, in response to post-war exigencies the 1945–51 Labour Government substantially extended the role of government in economic affairs through Keynesian demand management, nationalisation and physical controls over resources, but, as Shonfield notes, each of these actions tended to be isolated and limited in intent. According to Shonfield,

The assertion of public authority in new places was wholeheartedly approved; there was, and is, a constant demand from the British Left that the Government should intervene in more and more things. But the nature of this intervention is assumed to be of a strictly limited kind. It is in this sense that the traditional ideology continued to assert itself in the period immediately following the war. Old-fashioned *laissez-faire* had gone; but the old instinctive suspicion of positive government, which purports to identify the needs of the community before the community itself has recognized them, remained as vigorous as ever.[9]

The same kind of commitments continued to shape intervention in the early 1960s when, in the face of consistently low economic growth rates, the Macmillan Government adopted the mechanisms, if not the substance, of Continental indicative planning. The effort to establish a planning system was a significant departure from established British practice, but the exercise foundered on political assumptions which were at odds with the nature of planning. The National Economic Development Council (NEDC), which was to be the focus of planning in central government, borrowed the French example of corporate representation from government, industry and labour, but it failed to evolve the means necessary for giving effect to decisions or bargains struck by the participants because of traditional 'liberal' commitments. Writing in 1965, Shonfield observed,

> the truth is that there is no natural place in the British [planning] system, as it has developed to date, for the contractual relations between the government and individual private firms covering the objectives of the plan which have from the beginning been a feature of French planning. . . . [Discrimination between firms in the French style] would have to overcome a powerful contrary tradition in the British civil service. Planning by this method could not just be conveniently left to ministers making occasional political decisions; government officials would also be called upon to exercise their personal judgement from day to day in meting out unequal treatment to people with theoretically equal rights; and the officials would not like it.[10]

The planning attempts of the 1964 Labour Government were also conditioned by liberal commitments. Before entering office Labour had promised that, in accord with the French planning model, government dealings with firms would be geared to their contribution to the fulfilment of national economic objectives, but the planning system did not, in fact, develop in this manner after Labour assumed power. Rather than exploiting the possibilities which the NEDC offered for striking bargains with firms or sectors of industry concerning investment targets, production levels and the like, the Labour Government took the planning process out of the NEDC, and assigned it to the newly-created Department of Economic Affairs (DEA). Using civil service expertise, the DEA developed a National Plan which relied in large measure upon expenditure and fiscal policy to ensure its implementation. As is well known, the National Plan failed, partly because its reliance upon expenditure and fiscal policy became largely inoperative as a result of the 1965–6 sterling crises, and partly because DEA planners had no means of ensuring that firms and industries would respond to the targets established in the Plan. However, by the mid 1960s the 'liberal' arm's length approach to industry which had served to precipitate the collapse of planning was under challenge as a result of a number of serious structural changes in the British economy.

RECENT STRUCTURAL CHANGE IN THE UK ECONOMY

In the late 1960s the development of the British economy was characterised by several tendencies which were eventually to prompt government intervention of a kind different from that outlined above. In the first place, a number of prominent mergers in the late 1960s drew attention to increasing levels of corporate concentration within British industry. Between 1950 and 1970, for example, the 100 largest firms in Britain increased their share of total manufacturing output from about 20 per cent to about 50 per cent, and estimates suggest that this figure may rise to over 65 per cent by the mid 1980s.[11] Moreover, industrial concentration was accompanied by an expansion of foreign investment in key sectors of the economy. In the years from 1960 to 1970 the value of direct foreign investment in the UK increased by approximately 225 per cent, which was *double* the growth of UK investment abroad in the same period.[12] In particular, Britain became the beach-head for many US multinationals seeking expansion in European markets. Finally, during the same years there was a marked decline in the competitiveness of a large number of domestically owned manufacturing industries, culminating in the collapse of a number of well-known companies. Indeed, the high levels of foreign investment in Britain during the 1960s and 1970s were associated in part with the American and European exploitation of the local market opportunities presented by the decline of domestic manufacturing. The consequence has been that many areas of the UK economy are now dominated by foreign-owned firms. To illustrate, three of Britain's four major car-makers are foreign-owned, and foreign-owned firms play a leading role in such industries as oil, pharmaceuticals, electronics and food processing.[13]

As in America, industrial concentration in Britain prompted government interest because of the pivotal role which large firms were coming to play in the economy. The 100 largest firms were central to exports, employment and inflation, all traditional concerns of government, and particularly so in the 1960s in the wake of stop–start growth patterns and a number of balance of payments crises. Furthermore, the issue of industrial concentration was given added prominence in government circles because of the decline in domestic competitiveness. Within many parts of the business and financial community it had become common to argue that without mergers leading to increased concentration of enterprise British manufacturing would continue to lag in world markets. This understanding of economic tendencies was rapidly translated into government policy. In 1966 the Labour Government established the Industrial Reorganisation Corporation (IRC) to encourage industrial restructuring through the promotion of mergers and consolidations within areas in which British industrial capacity was weak.[14] Significantly, merger promotion, if it was to be undertaken at all, required an extension of government capabilities beyond those characteristic of early post-war policy or indicative planning. To begin with, the IRC's mode of operation was decidedly firm-oriented. Although in most instances of merger promotion its role did not extend beyond that of a catalyst bringing together willing partners, [15] in this process IRC officials gained greater access to the management of individual firms than was ever the case in the planning exercise. Moreover, the IRC's operations constituted a testing ground for many, often subtle, methods of cajoling firms to act in ways they otherwise might not have, methods which were especially effective when the Corporation became involved in rescue operations in the latter part of its life. Traditional liberal commitments were, of course, still manifest. The IRC was separated from the Whitehall apparatus and, therefore, in some measure symbolically divorced from the main activities of government. In addition, its mandate was very clearly premised upon business approval, as indicated by the fact that the first and many of the subsequent series of merger negotiations involving the IRC were launched when business sought the Corporation's advice. Finally, even the relatively limited nature of the Corporation's activities violated the sensibilities of certain sections of the business community and of ministers within the 1970 Conservative Government concerning appropriate relations between government and the private sector. The result was that the IRC was disbanded in 1970. Nonetheless, the IRC's activities constituted a breach, if only a partial one, of the liberal tradition.

Changes which threatened liberal commitments were also occurring on other fronts. For example, on a number of occasions in the latter half of the 1960s the British Government was obliged to take an interest in the impact of foreign multinationals on certain sectors of the economy. In 1967 Chrysler of America assumed ownership of Rootes Motors after having been involved in gradually taking over equity within the British company for some years previously. Recognising the potential impact of the takeover of one of the two remaining British-owned car manufacturers on the structure of the UK motor industry, the Government intervened with the object of obtaining a number of written undertakings from Chrysler concerning the manner in which the American company would manage its new acquisition. The final agreement between the Government and Chrysler covered aspects of the company's operations such as levels of investment in British productive capacity, the place the UK subsidiary would occupy in Chrysler's overall export strategy, the operation of its assembly plants in Britain and the composition of the subsidiary's board of directors.[16] As in the case of the IRC, this attempt to prevent a multinational company from adversely affecting exports, investment and employment brought government into close contact with executives at the level of the firm, if only for a short period of time.

During the same period multinational investment in the computer industry by such US giants as IBM and Honeywell prompted government action. This industry was judged to be of major significance not only because of the importance of computers for defence purposes, but also because of its high technological component. Hence, government intervened to ensure the development of a domestically owned company capable of competing effectively with the American multinationals in the field. It did so by promoting the merger of a number of small British computer manufacturers into a single large firm, International Computers Ltd (ICL), and then providing the new company with equity capital and research and development assistance. Government also supported ICL by guaranteeing a market for the company's products within government agencies.[17] Again, this intervention brought government into immediate contact with individual firms and further reinforced official capabilities in the realm of industrial sponsorship.

However, perhaps the most serious threat to traditional liberal commitments resulted from the rapid deterioration in the competitive position of British industry during the 1960s and 1970s, culminating in the collapse of a variety of domestically owned concerns. Government became involved in rescue operations following industrial failure in pursuit of a number of objectives ranging from employment maintenance (shipbuilding and the motor industry) to the preservation of certain technological capabilities (aerospace and electronics). Yet in all cases industrial collapse challenged previous assumptions about industry and industrial policy. Not only was government forced to react quickly with policy instruments tailored to the particular requirements of single firms, but each failure also highlighted the general 'inadequacy' of the liberal, 'arm's-length' approach to industrial problems. Moreover, the challenge which industrial failure presented was so serious that even the 1970 Conservative Government, which was elected on a platform emphasising industrial 'disengagement', was soon forced to become deeply involved in industrial affairs at the level of the firm.[18]

Thus, by the beginning of the 1970s government intervention had assumed some new qualities. Industrial concentration, the increasing role of foreign multinationals in the British economy and industrial decline had forced government into relations with specific firms, often in circumstances (e.g. rescue operations) which encouraged it to take a large measure of responsibility for the future development of the firms in question. Moreover, gradually the stress on single firms characteristic of the interventions described above came to be extended into every area of industrial policy-making. As Young has noted, this emphasis on the firm constituted one further stage of the progression towards policy instruments with a more and more micro focus which has been characteristic of the post-war history of British industrial policy. Just as Keynesian demand management failed to yield adequate growth rates and, in the light of French experience, was replaced by indicative planning, so after the collapse of the National Plan and in the light of the economic tendencies described above, indicative planning came to be replaced by firm-specific policies.[19]

Yet traditional liberal commitments lingered on even in the very micro approach to industrial policy which was evolving. Except in cases in which it could rely upon business approval, government remained reluctant to intervene in the affairs of firms unless dramatic changes in economic circumstances (e.g. industrial collapse or ownership transfer) demanded it. Furthermore, commitments to maintaining the independence and integrity of the firm continued to have a central place in the formulation and implementation of policy, although in some cases (e.g. rescue operations) ministers and officials felt able to exercise more pressure on firms than in others. Thus, policies directed towards specific industries and specific firms tended to be non-regulatory in character. This was true even of policies directed towards foreign multinationals operating in Britain. For example, the Government had no means of enforcing its 'gentlemen's agreement' with Chrysler. Moreover, when IBM and Honeywell threatened the hegemony of domestically owned firms in the British computer industry government responded, not by limiting the activities of these multinationals in Britain, but by supporting alternative British-owned capacity. Finally, when taken together, all of the firm-oriented, yet non-regulatory interventions of the late 1960s and early 1970s present little direction, little pattern. To use Young's words, they tended to be *ad hoc*, and therefore, erratic in their impact upon industry.[20]

THE CURRENT STUDY

Government – industry relations in this country are never static. The study which follows of government intervention in support of the offshore supply industry illustrates that during the 1970s the character of industrial intervention has altered yet again in response to structural economic change. The commitments of ministers and civil servants involved in intervention have changed, as have the policy instruments which they are prepared to use in the industrial field, and the next chapters investigate both why and how these changes have come about. However, before embarking upon this investigation, I shall briefly indicate why intervention in the offshore case deserves such attention.

Although it does not command the degree of public notice accorded to other areas of economic endeavour, the offshore supply industry is a large and strategic component of the UK economy. For example, in 1977 British offshore suppliers provided approximately £800 million worth of goods and services to oil companies operating in the North Sea, and government estimates for the same year place offshore related investment at about '25 per cent of total UK industrial investment (all industries) and about 10 per cent of Gross Domestic Fixed Capital Formation'.[21] Of course, in addition, the industry has been and continues to be of great significance in ensuring the relatively rapid exploitation of the North Sea oil fields.

Apart from its present economic importance, the offshore supply industry combines several characteristics which are of interest in the study of intervention. To begin with, government support for the industry was initially prompted because firms with the capacity to expand into the field of offshore supplies in the wake of the oil discoveries of the early 1970s failed to do so. Thus, offshore intervention is in the same tradition as a variety of other industrial interventions prompted by declining competitiveness, with the difference that it was addressed to a new (one might say, undeveloped) industry composed of firms which were obliged to adapt in a number of ways in order to cater to the requirements of the oil companies. In addition, offshore intervention provides a means to gauge current government responses to the influence of multinationals upon the British economy, for, with two exceptions, all of the major operators with commercial discoveries in the North Sea have been American-owned multinational oil companies. As the exclusive purchasers of the goods and services produced by the offshore supply industry these companies have had a major impact upon the industry's development. This has obliged government to come to terms with the problems presented by attempting to encourage a domestic industry dependent for its commercial viability on foreign-owned multinationals. Finally, offshore intervention is noteworthy because it was undertaken in the absence of an immediate industrial crisis. It therefore prompts questions concerning the present status of the 'liberal' tradition within the realm of industrial policy-making.

In summary, then, while it is still a case study, the investigation which follows provides an opportunity to assess many aspects of industrial intervention and, therefore, to describe the character of industrial policy-making in the mid to late 1970s more fully. As subsequent chapters indicate, in the offshore area intervention strategies have progressed beyond the firm-specific, yet non-regulatory, policies of the early part of this decade. Slowly, and often hesitantly, government has evolved a panoply of administrative devices which enable ministers and officials to have a highly selective, and frequently very direct, influence upon the commercial actions of a variety of firms without resort to the expropriation of property rights. Given the costs associated with nationalisation and the acquisition of state equity holdings in commercial enterprises, administrative devices of this kind may assume an increasingly important place in the intervention strategies of the 1980s. This book is, therefore, an exploration of the potential offered by this 'new phase' in the history of industrial intervention.

2 A New British Industry: Offshore Supplies

INTRODUCTION

Like Concorde, the North Sea platforms located off the British coast have become a popular symbol of Britain's industrial capability. North Sea operations are of a scale and complexity resembling the industrial 'gigantism' most frequently found in American and Soviet projects, and as a result they have captured the imagination of the British public in a way matched by few other enterprises in this century. Thus, the achievements of the offshore supply industry are widely recognised. But few people, other than insiders, have an accurate understanding of what this new industry is, or of how it developed both internationally and within the United Kingdom. This is unfortunate, for an examination of the present structure and history of the industry can serve to illustrate many of the dilemmas confronting industry and government in the rapidly changing circumstances of the post-war world economy. For this reason, and because subsequent chapters assume a knowledge of the industry and its workings, this chapter isolates a number of the issues connected with the offshore supply industry's pattern of development. The emphasis in the chapter is on the British industry, but because offshore supply production originated in the United States it is impossible to describe British efforts in this field without referring to 'international' developments.

THE STRUCTURE OF THE UK OFFSHORE SUPPLY INDUSTRY

The first matter we should consider is the meaning of the term 'offshore supply industry'. In the last few years a number of different labels have been devised to designate the industry which supplies the oil companies operating in the North Sea. Some of the more common labels are: 'offshore industry', 'oceanic industry', and especially 'offshore engineering industry'. The term 'offshore engineering industry' is the one most frequently used in the press, but for present purposes it is too restrictive because it refers only to a specific part of the supply operations for the North Sea. In this book the 'offshore supply industry' consists of all those firms engaged in a support role for offshore hydrocarbon exploration and production, be it in the form of services or manufactured products.

The industry can be divided into two broad categories of firms: those which provide services (e.g. air and sea transport, diving, etc.) and those which provide capital goods (e.g. drilling and production equipment for platforms). Table 2.1 gives a breakdown of the types of commercial activities undertaken by firms involved in the offshore supply industry. As can be seen from the table, the largest grouping in expenditure terms is the platform manufacturing sector, which includes firms engaged in the installation of platforms on the sea bed as well those manufacturing platforms and the associated specialised equipment for drilling the oil wells and extracting the hydrocarbon deposits. The next largest sector consists of the drilling contractors. These are the firms which own semi-submersible or jack-up exploration drilling rigs and conduct exploratory drilling programmes for the oil companies to test geological structures indicated in seismic surveys. These drilling companies are very important within the industry, for they are responsible for placing the lucrative contracts for building, servicing and supplying their drilling rigs. Of the sectors listed in Table 2.1, the first two consist of firms engaged almost entirely in exploration work, and the last two of firms engaged almost entirely in production work. Firms in the remaining sectors may be engaged in exploration or production or both.

In order to give some indication of the way in which the various sectors of the industry are involved in the exploration and production phases of North Sea work, Figure 2.1 sets out a possible plan for the exploitation of an oil field, listing the stages when specific types of firms take on contracts. As is evident from this presentation, the development phase of North Sea field exploitation is by far the most costly, providing well over four-fifths of the market for the offshore supply industry.

Figure 2.1 presents a typical expenditure distribution for an oil field development by activity, but it is also important to indicate the

TABLE 2.1 Commercial activities of firms in the offshore supply industry

Industrial sector	Company activity	Source of income	Possible income (excl. current prod. plans) £m. 1972–80*
Seismic companies	Provision of personnel, equipment, seismic information and interpretation	Contracts with oil companies and free-lance work	39 (to 1974)
Drilling contractors	Provision of rigs, equipment and crews, and the operation of drilling assignments	Contracts with oil companies	521
Offshore services	Provision of equipment and services, including catering and diving	Contract fees Sale of materials to oil companies	116
Workboats	Provision and operation of supply/tug vessels to transport materials and equipment from shore to rig	Contracts with oil companies or drilling contractors	77
Helicopter operators	Provision of transport for personnel from shore to rig and vice versa	Contracts with oil companies	89
Material suppliers	Manufacture and supply of mud, chemicals and equipment, such as casing etc.	Sales to oil companies	139
Well logging	Provision of personnel, equipment and well information	Contracts with oil companies	19 (to 1974)
Platform manufacture	Steel supplies, equipment supplies, fabrication and installation	Sales to oil companies Considerable sub-contracting involving sales of equipment and basic materials	2000
Pipeline manufacture and installation	Suppliers of steel, concrete and other reinforcement—pipe fabrication and installation	Contracts and sales to oil companies—considerable sub-contracting	Material 151 Laying 456

Note: *Since these estimates were made the costs of North Sea operations have inflated considerably. See M. Gaskin et al., *The Economic Impact of North Sea Oil on Scotland* (Edinburgh: HMSO, 1978) p. 19.

Source: The North Sea: The Search for Oil and Gas and the Implication for Investment (London: Cazenove, 1972) p. 114.

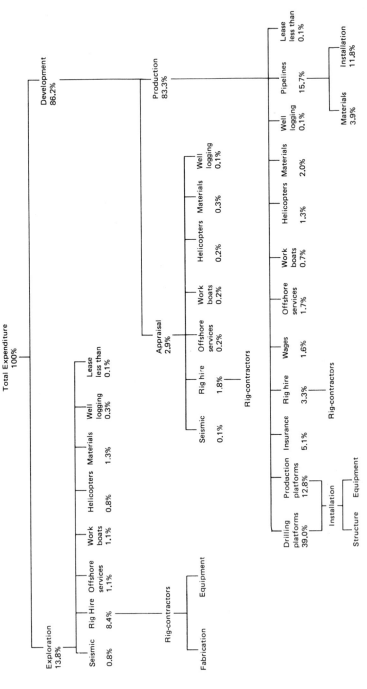

FIGURE 2.1 A possible breakdown of future expenditure

Source: Cazenove & Co., *The North Sea: The Search For Oil and Gas,* p. 50.

total sums involved. The size of the market for the offshore supply industry is vast. In 1978, the largest year to date, orders placed by the oil companies and their contractors for goods and services destined for the North Sea came to £1574 million, of which about £1037 million went to British firms.[1] To date about £8000 million have been committed by the oil companies for North Sea exploration and development work and industry estimates claim over the next twenty to thirty years a further £40,000–50,000 million will be spent on offshore activities around the UK coast.[2] These totals place the offshore supply industry among the more important industries by value in the British economy. Moreover, they represent a remarkable achievement for an industry which prior to 1965 did not really exist in the UK, and only became engaged in the North Sea market in a substantial way in the early 1970s. Estimates of the number of British firms involved in the offshore supply market are variable because the industry is characterised by large amounts of sub-contracting, and many firms which enter the market on this basis are engaged in only a marginal way as a proportion of total turnover. Government estimates in 1974 placed the number of firms in the industry at close to 3000, including 55 major contractors, 800 main sub-contractors and 2000 firms involved in sub-contracting work to varying degrees.[3] Other sources have given the number of firms involved in the industry at close to 1000.[4]

The most detailed analyses of the characteristics of firms in the UK offshore supply industry were surveys conducted by the Scottish Economic Planning Department (SEPD) during 1974–8.[5] The surveys were limited to firms located in Scotland, and a major emphasis of the studies was on the employment-creation effects of firms entering the offshore supply market. The survey results indicate that a total of 38,000 people were employed in 796 establishments in 1976 in work which was directly attributable to sales to the offshore market.[6] Of the manufacturing firms which reported, those building steel and concrete platforms and modules employed the largest number of people (12,550), followed by those supplying industrial plant, steelwork etc. (4750). In the services category, offshore contractors supplying transportation and communications services provided the most employment (3350), followed by distribution and professional services (1600 and 1500 jobs respectively).[7] Manufacturing, not surprisingly, accounted for three-quarters of the oil-related work force and thus the bulk of employment opportunities. Services accounted for the remaining quarter. The 1974 survey statistics indicate that service companies tend to be smaller than manufacturing firms in this field. Service companies employed only a quarter of the workforce, but they constituted 43 per cent of the total number of firms in the market in Scotland.[8]

The 1974 survey also yielded some information concerning the amount of new manufacturing and service capacity that had been established in response to the growing North Sea market. About a third of the manufacturing firms which reported claimed that they were supplying their normal products to the offshore market. In the words of the analysts, this suggests

> that some of the companies (particularly the newly set up ones, but also some existing Scottish companies) have had previous oil industry experience and have simply extended or switched their attention to the North Sea, but it also reflects the fact that a large proportion of the demands from the North Sea comprises standard items of engineering equipment or fabrication work in which Scottish industry has considerable expertise.[9]

The remaining firms in the manufacturing category had modified their products or developed new ones for the North Sea market. However, of all the manufacturing units surveyed, only about a sixth had been set up specifically to meet North Sea requirements. The situation is different for the service category. Eighty per cent of the service companies surveyed claimed that offshore work was a continuation of their normal business activities. This, in combination with information to the effect that about two-thirds of these service companies were newly set up when the survey was launched, led the analysts to conclude that most of the service companies were foreign firms and 'experienced suppliers of the international oil industry'.[10]

Thus, manufacturing firms based in Scotland and engaged in the North Sea market have sold both standard and new or modified products to the oil companies. Few new firms have been created in this category, and most of the industrial engagement has resulted from diversification within existing firms. In the service category the introduction of new firms and units has been much more marked. Oil companies often find it feasible to import equipment for the North Sea from specialised manufacturers abroad, and the pattern of manufacturing activity in the offshore supply industry in Scotland is in keeping with this. Oil companies purchase some of their equipment in Scotland and look elsewhere for the remainder. Alternatively, suppliers of services must be 'on location' near the oil fields. The proliferation of service companies in Scotland is, therefore, in keeping with the logic of the oil industry's requirements, although Scottish firms do not appear to have been especially successful in exploiting their comparative advantage in this respect. It may be that foreign firms have entered this market because Scottish companies engaged in marine services to coastal shipping and fishing were unable to meet oil company needs in the North Sea.

While the SEPD analyses refer only to Scottish firms, the results are probably broadly typical of the situation throughout the United Kingdom, given certain reservations concerning the special features of the Scottish section of the industry. In particular, Scotland has a greater proportion of service companies than the rest of the UK due to its proximity to the oil fields. In addition, Scotland has a higher proportion of platform construction yards than, for example, England. Finally, the offshore supply industry is concentrated in certain well-defined geographical areas in Scotland, while activity is more diffuse in the remainder of Britain. In Scotland, offshore engineering firms are concentrated in the Clyde Valley, although platform-building sites are scattered up the west coast (and there are two on the east coast). Service bases are concentrated in the Aberdeen area and in the Shetlands. In contrast, in England engineering firms engaged in North Sea work are found in all of the industrial areas of the North-West, the Midlands and the South-East. Large fabricating yards and support industries are concentrated in the North-East around Teeside and Humberside. Service industry activity is much less pronounced in England than in Scotland, and most of it is concentrated around Great Yarmouth, the port which serves the southern North Sea gas fields.[11]

Thus, the offshore supply industry is a geographically diffuse collection of diverse elements unified only as a result of the final destination of the goods and services it produces. Such coherence as the industry possesses derives directly from the requirements of the oil companies and their contractors. These requirements are interpreted during the course of continuous inter-company negotiations regarding supply contracts. Unfortunately, the relationships that have evolved between companies during these negotiations are among the most difficult aspects of the offshore supply industry to analyse, for they are always to one degree or another hidden from outsiders for reasons of commercial 'confidentiality'. It is possible, however, to make some generalisations about these relationships on the basis of published information. The offshore supply industry is essentially a huge sub-contracting network. The oil companies are at the centre of this network, surrounded by successive layers of contracting firms such that the firms in each layer accept more specialised supply work than firms in the previous layer. Contrary to what the layman might expect, the oil companies are not extensively involved in the details of purchases from the offshore supply industry. Most oil companies do not have large engineering or purchasing departments to manage their exploration and development activities in the North Sea. Instead, they rely upon the services of specialist engineering contracting firms. These firms take responsibility for supervising the design and specification work for an oil field development, and then tender the work contracts to firms in the engineering and service sectors of the offshore supply industry. They also supervise the progress of work on a field, and act as trouble shooters. While there are variations from one oil company to another, most restrict themselves to reviewing and co-ordinating the different design and contracting decisions made by their engineering contracting firms. However, it is important to note as well that engineering contracting firms also delegate responsibility to the main contractors they select. These contractors, in turn, delegate responsibility to their sub-contractors and so on, with the result that supply chains regularly extend through several sets of firms. Figure 2.2 illustrates the kind of supply networks which emerge from this process. Some indication of the complexity of these supply networks is conveyed in a booklet put out by Shell Exploration and Production outlining the purchasing specifications for a typical field development. The booklet lists a total of twenty-nine categories of equipment for the construction of one production platform. Each category may require anywhere from one to several dozen contractors and sub-contractors.[12] For an average field development with two or more platforms, mooring buoys, pipelines to shore and associated services, the number of supply contractors can easily total several hundred individual firms.

The contracting relationships for exploration work are less complicated than those for the development phase of a project. Seismic exploration, exploration drilling and well analysis are

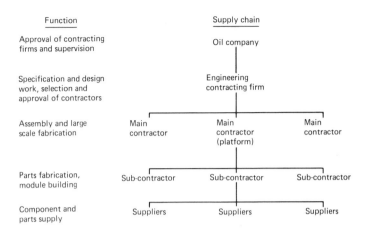

FIGURE 2.2 Supply chain in the North Sea (detail given for platform contracting)

Note: Only part of the network has been shown. There could be several more main contractors in such a network with attendant subcontractors and suppliers. Each contractor could also easily have more than three sub-contractors, and each sub-contractor more than three suppliers and so on. For more complex aspects of a project, supply chains could continue several stages further down the page.

carried out by international specialist firms on direct contract to the oil companies. The exploration drilling companies do make use of a number of service companies during the course of their work, but the scale of operations and the number of firms involved are small by comparison with the scale and numbers characteristic of field development.

Therefore, the lion's share of supply work is concerned with development, and in this field of activity supply chains are long and interconnected. As a result, firms wishing to supply products or services for sensitive areas (i.e. products or services which, if delayed or specified incorrectly, could induce serious disruption in a project and high cost penalties) must be on an 'approved suppliers list'. This is a list of firms which an oil company, or its engineering contractors, judge are competent to bid for certain types of contracts. Firms which are not on an 'approved suppliers list' are not asked to submit bids for contracts, and are thus effectively excluded from entry into the offshore market.[13]

The oil companies have instituted 'approved suppliers lists' in

order to protect themselves against the costs which ensue from
inefficient or incompetent suppliers. However, the existence of such
lists is a reflection of the strengths rather than the weaknesses of the
position of the oil companies within the offshore market. In the first
place, firms in the offshore supply industry have only a limited
number of customers, essentially those oil companies which have
been appointed as operators in the North Sea (in the period covered
by this book there were never more than about a dozen operators
with commercial discoveries at any one point in time). Secondly, a
successful *entrée* into the offshore market can, in time, yield a good
return on investment because of the high value-added in offshore
engineering and service work, and, as a result, any one offshore
supplier usually faces substantial competition in its equipment or
service category both from other British firms and from foreign
firms. Thus, the oil companies are in a position to impose a 'high
entry price' upon any firm wishing to join the offshore market by
making stringent demands concerning levels of service, specifications of products, cost and delivery times. As a consequence of
this, and entrenched foreign competition,[14] it is particularly difficult
for new and inexperienced firms to gain a stake in the offshore
market. Moreover, once in the market, firms often become highly
dependent on the oil companies for business. In some instances firms
make substantial capital investments in specialised areas of production in order to enter the market, and later find that they are
unable to sell their specialised products to anyone in Britain other
than the oil companies and their specialised contractors. Export
markets are the obvious alternative to firms confronting this
problem, but these are frequently difficult to cultivate for firms new
to the business. Given these circumstances, offshore suppliers can
easily become *client* firms of the oil companies.

The dominance of the oil companies within the offshore market is
also reflected in the manner in which they use the 'approved
suppliers lists' to select contractors. British firms wishing to enter the
offshore supply market have to deal with oil multinationals which
are, on the whole, owned abroad and staffed, particularly at senior
levels, by foreigners. These companies have contacts with, and in
many cases commitments to, foreign suppliers of services and
equipment. In addition, the engineering contracting firms which
supervise most development work are foreign-based with branches
in the UK, and have similar contracts with and commitments to
foreign suppliers. Therefore, both the oil companies and their

principal contractors have tended to award contracts to suppliers in their country of origin even when operating in another country. Moreover, in Britain, until recently, they have done this with impunity. The oil companies and their contractors have frequently chosen foreign over domestic suppliers, thereby inhibiting the growth of the domestic supply industry, and few people either within industry or government have questioned their discretion in this respect. Thus, British firms wishing to enter or continue in the offshore market are to a large extent dependent upon the good will of companies which are unfamiliar with, or simply uninterested in, the British industrial system.[15]

How, then, can one summarise the major structural features of the offshore supply industry? First, and foremost, the industry is defined by the destination of its products and services, specifically the offshore gas and oil fields. It differs from, for example, the automobile industry in that firms do not share common methods of production or, indeed, a common product. Some firms are making machinery; others are making structures. Some are providing technical services; others are providing non-technical services and so on. The only characteristic which all of the firms in the industry have in common is some form of contractual arrangement with an oil company or its agent. Firms vary in size, product type, degree of involvement in the market, and, hence, in the commercial interests they have. This variety is a reflection of the many requirements of the oil companies. It is also an obstacle to the articulation of coherent strategies for the industry's further development. As becomes evident in later chapters, the dominance of the oil companies in the market is apparent not only in the manner in which suppliers are chosen, but also in the difficulties the offshore industry has had in representing itself to government and in the problems government has encountered in attempting to construct a policy of assistance for the industry.

THE DEVELOPMENT OF A NEW INDUSTRY

Some of the main structural features of the British offshore supply industry have already been outlined in this chapter. However, a full understanding of the relationships which have evolved between the oil companies and their suppliers requires some reference to the historical development of the offshore supply industry generally and the impact of early events in the US upon the emergence of the UK industry. Offshore supply production is not indigenous to the UK. Instead, it has its roots in the exploitation of American offshore oil, and became established in Britain only recently.

The history of offshore oil production, and hence the history of the offshore supply industry, began in the late 1890s in the US. The first offshore oil came from wells drilled from the end of long piers off the beaches of a town called Summerland on the southern California coast.[16] The first independent oil well – independent in the sense that it was not connected to shore by piers – was drilled in Lake Chaddo, Louisiana, in 1911. These early attempts in the field of offshore production were successful, but they did not involve any departures from the drilling techniques and derrick design used in land-based operations at that time. Serious offshore operations did not begin until the mid 1920s when American engineering companies assisted US oil companies working offshore in Lake Maracaibo, Venezuela, with the design of concrete platforms and the improvement of drilling techniques. However, despite the offshore opportunities in both the US and Venezuela at this time, the 'infant technology did not develop rapidly'.[17]

The first independent oil platforms in coastal areas did not appear until the early 1930s. Then, in 1937, the first productive offshore well at sea was drilled about a mile offshore in shallow waters near Cameron, Louisiana, by a firm that was later to become a leader in the offshore engineering field: Brown and Root. The progress of offshore operations was held up, however, by two problems with severe cost implications. First, there were difficulties associated with drilling exploratory oil wells to determine if promising geological areas had oil deposits. On land, exploratory drilling was a relatively simple task; portable derricks were set up on several locations and bore holes were drilled. In the ocean, however, every time a company wished to drill an exploratory bore hole a platform had to be constructed to support the derrick and drilling equipment. Needless to say, this operation made the drilling of exploratory wells in the sea bed very expensive and, hence, inhibited the level of activity offshore. The other problem which the oil companies encountered in offshore exploration concerned platform construction. The companies did not wish to limit their exploration activities to shallow waters, but as they ventured into deeper areas the costs of building a platform capable of holding all of the equipment required for drilling escalated. This in turn put up the cost and time involved in offshore exploration generally. Both of the problems mentioned above were solved by American engineering firms during the late 1940s. The first breakthrough came in the form of submersible drilling barges which were capable of drilling exploration wells in shallow waters. These were followed by what came to be known as the 'minimum load platform', which carried drilling equipment, storage, power and accommodation in floating tenders attached to a small piled platform holding the derrick and drill.[18] Both of these developments considerably reduced the cost of offshore exploration and production, and by 1948 the offshore oil industry had emerged in something like the form we know it today.[19] In the mid 1950s, with the settlement of jurisdictional disputes between the states and the American Federal Government over sea-bed mineral rights, offshore work in the US surged ahead. By the beginning of 1959 about 2700 exploration wells had been drilled off the coasts of Texas and Louisiana, and these led to approximately 1800 production wells yielding oil and gas. During this period some $2000 million was spent by US oil companies on offshore development in the Gulf of Mexico.[20]

As offshore activities in the Gulf of Mexico increased during the 1950s the oil companies extended the search for hydrocarbons into deeper and deeper waters. At the same time, US engineering companies became extensively engaged in developing exploration drilling rigs which could operate in waters over 100 feet deep. By the early 1960s huge semi-submersible and jack-up rigs capable of drilling in very deep waters were available.[21] There was also an increase during this period in the number of American firms able to build and design offshore production platforms and to cater for the general engineering needs of offshore oil production (e.g. marine drilling equipment). Many of these firms had previous experience in supplying US oil companies in their land-based exploration and development work, and this was useful to them when they branched out into what was becoming a very specialised form of marine petroleum engineering. Finally, other specialised support industries, especially those providing supply and transport services to enable offshore operations to operate continuously, were built up during these years.

The development of the American offshore supply industry was both a logical extension of the activities of the US oil companies and a gradual process. During the 1950s and early 1960s firms in the Gulf states had an opportunity to gain valuable experience of every aspect of offshore operations. Moreover, they acquired this experience at a time when a number of circumstances combined to ease the entry of US firms into the supply field and to lessen the penalties involved in any learning process. In the first place, as this was the first market for offshore services and products, there was no competition for supply contracts from more experienced foreign firms, and this forced oil companies working in the area to seek out local capacity and encourage it to produce goods and services for the offshore market. Secondly, the development of the industry spanned two decades, and production only gradually picked up momentum. Thus, it was easy for firms to enter the market when the industry was young and established patterns of supplier relationships had not solidified. Finally, the level of technology in the industry, and hence the scale of investment and expertise expected of firms, also developed gradually, and this enabled companies to build on established technology in such a way as to lower investment cost and risk.

Thus, when the commercial possibilities in the UK sector of the North Sea came to the attention of the oil industry towards the end of the 1960s the first instinct of most American, and indeed British, oil companies with a stake in this area was to seek products and services from the US offshore supply industry, which at that time was the most highly developed in the world. This was particularly true of the exploration phase of North Sea work when US drilling contractors dominated the market.

INITIAL BRITISH ENGAGEMENT

Until the discovery of natural gas at the inland site of Groningen, Holland, in 1959[22] there was little, if any, interest in offshore petroleum work in the UK. However, the huge Dutch natural gas discovery prompted a number of British and foreign oil companies to consider conducting seismic surveys of the North Sea basin, and by 1962 about twenty oil companies were engaged in such surveys in the international waters of the North Sea.[23] Then, in May 1964, Britain ratified the 1958 Geneva Convention on the Continental Shelf, which recognised the right of states to control mineral exploitation on their continental shelves and committed Britain to negotiate with neighbouring countries over the boundaries.[24] The Government was, thus, firmly committed to control over the resources of the UK continental shelf and the Ministry of Power proceeded with legislation to license exploration and production work in the North Sea. This legislation was passed in the late spring of 1964. The first thirty-five licences for exploration work were awarded in the autumn of that year.[25] The legal and regulatory regime in the North Sea was thereby confirmed, and exploration activity started in earnest with oil companies chartering drilling rigs to conduct drilling programmes in their respective licensed areas.[26] This first round of licensing was followed by a second round in 1965 in which an additional thirty-seven licences were granted, and by a third round in 1969 when a further thirty-seven licences were issued. A much larger fourth round was conducted by the Conservative Government in 1971 when 118 licences were issued.[27]

Before the issue of exploration and production licences in 1964 British firms had been only marginally involved in any offshore work. Two small jack-up exploration rigs had been built, one in 1958 at Redcar and one in 1959 at Southampton,[28] but these were isolated efforts. However, partly as a result of exhortation from the Ministry of Power, some oil companies with North Sea licences placed orders for exploration drilling rigs suitable for operation in the southern North Sea.[29] In the event, a total of nine drilling rigs were ordered from British yards during the period 1965–7.[30]

Yet with the exception of this set of orders, the level of engagement of British firms in the North Sea supply market remained low during the late 1960s. In particular, British firms were slow to become involved in the many engineering and contracting aspects of the development phase for the five gas fields that were discovered in the southern North Sea.[31] Indeed, oil companies complained of not being able to obtain even the most elementary supplies of equipment and materials from UK sources. For example, one oil company engaged in gas field development sent out invitations to bid on contracts to construct the simple steel framework for the offshore production platforms required for gas field development. This work was well within the capabilities of UK contractors, but the company concerned, Shell, received only three replies from British companies, and these three companies in the end declined to tender for the contracts.[32]

Another indication of how marginally British industry was involved in these early developments is the fact that the operator with the largest gas field in the southern North Sea (a British oil company) had spent only 16 per cent of its total budget for developing the field in the UK by the end of 1971.[33] Moreover, during the late 1960s all of the major production platforms for the North Sea gas fields were built in the Netherlands rather than in the UK.[34]

Why British firms did not become more deeply engaged in the early phases of North Sea work is a difficult question to answer. Part of the explanation may lie in the fact that the period during which the gas fields were discovered and then brought into production was a very short one. Most of the gas fields were brought into production within about two years from their date of discovery – a substantially shorter period than that characteristic of the northern oil fields which were discovered in the early 1970s. This short time span between discovery and production was made possible by the relatively mild conditions in the southern North Sea where the waters are shallow and the weather temperate. These circumstances meant that the engineering required for offshore structures was not especially difficult and that, therefore, work could progress quite quickly.

As a result, the time available for British firms to become engaged and tool-up for these early North Sea activities was very limited. Naturally, many of them probably considered the costs of a rapid engagement in the North Sea not worth the consequent diversion of resources from traditional markets. In addition, of course, the short development timetable tended to favour the use of existing specialist suppliers of equipment and services for gas-field work because these firms were most able to provide the necessary products quickly and at a competitive price. As the only firms with extensive experience in this area were foreign-based, it is not surprising that British firms were not heavily involved in this first phase of North Sea work.

There was another consideration which probably also contributed to the low level of British involvement: the scale of the market. Compared with the commercial prospects associated with the later northern North Sea oil fields, the market connected with the gas field developments was small. Total development expenditure on the gas fields was probably no more than £250 million.[35] While this is a substantial sum, it was inevitable that a good proportion of it would be spent outside the country regardless of the efforts of British industry because some of the engineering and service requirements for the development of the gas fields were simply not available in the UK. Even during the late 1960s, it was by no means clear that there would be a continuing market in the North Sea after the gas field developments to justify the level of large-scale investment and risk-taking required of companies wishing to enter the offshore supply industry. This, in combination with the short time span for the development phase of the gas fields, probably discouraged any substantial British industrial engagement during the late 1960s.

Despite these considerations, however, it could still be argued that the lack of initial engagement by British industry simply reflected a lack of entrepreneurial skill on the part of British industrial managers. After all, Dutch firms were able to capitalise on gas platform orders that were on British industry's doorstep when they themselves had no offshore developments and were under the same handicaps concerning entry to the market that British firms faced. Whatever the reasons for British reluctance, the initial performance of British industry in the offshore market can only be described as 'disappointing'.

Another discouraging feature of British industry's experience with the first phase of North Sea developments was that among the small number of firms which did participate in North Sea offshore supply work many lost considerable sums of money. For example, some of the firms which became involved in building drilling rigs for North Sea exploration work lost so much that a few of them were financially jeopardised as a result of their experience. The International Management and Engineering Group (IMEG) Report's summary of British companies' experience in this market during the 1960s is illuminating:

> Although some of the known losses by various builders were very large indeed it is true to say that losses of the same order were being recorded by the same yards on conventional ships, from 1966 onwards. It is also true that some overseas yards entering the rig-building business had daunting financial out-turn at the outset: Halifax Shipyards reputedly lost $4 million on its first two semi-submersibles, but is continuing to take orders in expectation of future profit.
>
> Nevertheless, in some instances it is clear the yards had a very imperfect understanding of what they were undertaking and, with no previous practice as a guide, were widely 'out' in estimating. Unfortunately, either as a result of a traumatic loss or because of order books filled with conventional ships, only John Brown persevered in the market and other dearly bought experience has been largely sacrificed.[36]

Thus, the story of British engagement during the first stage of North Sea development is largely one of opportunities missed and a reluctance to persevere with investment decisions even if pre-liminary results were not positive. It was not entirely unexpected, therefore, that when the first discoveries of oil were announced in northern North Sea waters in late 1969–70 the oil companies proved to be unenthusiastic about seeking British expertise and commercial capacity for the development of the oil resources. It was also not surprising that British firms tended to be unwilling to become engaged in a market which seemed, at least initially, as perilous as that for the southern North Sea gas fields. This was especially the case during the first two years of oil discoveries because the first oil field found in late 1969 (Montrose) was a very small one,[37] and the next discovery, while admittedly large (Forties field), did not occur until late the following year (November 1970). The discovery of the Forties field was followed in 1971 by the discovery of another large oil field and two further small ones.[38] However, it would be fair to say that a general appreciation of the scale of the engineering effort needed to develop the expanding number of oil discoveries did not emerge until the end of 1971.

It was the announcement by BP at the end of 1971 that the development costs for the giant Forties field would be over £300 million (it was later doubled to over £600 million by 1976)[39] which first indicated the true scale of North Sea operations. About the same time, press estimates appeared of the total development costs for the North Sea,[40] estimates that steadily climbed through the first half of 1972 as people connected with the industry began to realise that the rate of discoveries and the scale of market potential characteristic of the first two years of oil exploration work were not likely to drop off in the future.

Thus, the size and commercial potential of the North Sea market did not really become an effective rallying point for British firms until well into 1972. In addition, there were several other con-siderations which discouraged British firms from entering the market. In many areas of offshore work British firms simply did not have the technical and commercial expertise to compete against established internationally based offshore supply companies. This was particularly true in such specialities as offshore drilling contracting and the manufacture of oil production equipment where both the technology and the investment in capital plant were lacking.[41] In addition, in certain sectors of the market firms had to invest heavily before they could compete, but even with such investment the prospects of more than a very few firms surviving in such areas were remote. These sectors included the provision of heavy lift cranes and barges and pipe-line laying barges, sectors in which a few American and European firms had made an early commitment that effectively excluded competitors from the UK.[42] However, there were other areas in which British industry could compete with foreign suppliers with some modification of product line, marketing or specifications. These included the production of prime-movers and power generation equipment, controls, pumps and valves, pipes and fittings, pressure vessels, process plant equipment and steel fabrication work.[43] Yet, while there were many firms capable of manufacturing these types of equipment, and indeed a few which had been in the market from the start, they were hampered by a lack of established contacts, unfamiliarity with oil company standards and operations, and a tendency for oil companies to prefer, and to use, established firms in the field. Furthermore, many of the foreign-based oil companies working in the North Sea were unaware of the capabilities of UK firms in this respect because of their tenuous connections with British industry in general.[44]

The circumstances varied from one firm to the next and from one sector of the offshore supply industry to another, but the central problem seemed to be that when British firms did try to enter the market (and there were many considerations which inhibited them from doing so, as we have seen) they were faced with an unfamiliar industrial environment in which the principal purchasers and users of their products were not British-based. According to the IMEG Report, 'The maximisation of the British contribution to supplying these items of equipment rests, however, not so much on day-to-day matters of detail as on a single key issue. This is who specifies and who buys.'[45] Most of the design and engineering capacity for the North Sea was located abroad, or in the UK subsidiaries of US firms, and many of the companies authorising and supervising the purchases and specifications were foreign oil corporations.[46] Therefore, British firms found the market very difficult to penetrate, particularly in cases in which some degree of risk was involved.

The need for risk capital on a grand scale was especially acute in the heavy engineering side of North Sea work – the building of drilling rigs, production platforms, single-point mooring buoys, etc. Part of the difficulty in this area was that while the potential profits were high, so were the risks. Large-scale capital facilities are a characteristic of this type of supply work, and repeat orders are, therefore, essential for a return on investment. Thus, the products must be commercially viable. However, for firms new to this type of activity the chances are small that their first large capital project will be *both* a technical and a commercial success. This problem is not so acute for firms with previous experience in heavy engineering, or for those that entered the market when 'mistakes' were still possible (e.g. firms in the United States or on the Continent). Yet it did present difficulties for many British firms because the type of capital equipment required for the North Sea oil fields was considerably more complex and expensive than that produced for previous offshore operations as a result of the harsh environmental conditions in the northern oil fields. These problems, in conjunction with the lack of construction sites suitable for platform-building on the east coast close to the oil fields and the poor record of British firms engaged in the early rig building projects referred to earlier, meant that many of the early platform orders and orders for other heavy engineering products went out of the country, as did much of the sub-contracting work connected with these large engineering projects.

The plight of British firms wishing to participate in the offshore market was compounded by the lack of a UK presence in the area of project management. Only a few of the firms engaged in project management work for the oil companies were UK-based (see Chapter 7), and these were in joint partnerships with foreign firms (e.g. Taywood–Santa Fé). The absence of UK companies in this type of work is rather remarkable given traditional British expertise in the field of engineering and the success of a number of British engineering firms in the Middle East. Yet if more of the project management companies for the North Sea had been UK-based and staffed by engineers familiar with, and sympathetic to, UK capacity, it is possible that many more commercial opportunities might have been available in this field to British firms.[47]

Nevertheless, the lack of British engagement in the north Sea cannot be entirely attributed to a hostile market place which discouraged the entry of UK firms. A number of firms had been involved in North Sea operations from the first, and were successfully competing with foreign firms.[48] Indeed, British firms excelled in offshore provisioning and service activities, supply boats and the like, as well as, of course, in some areas of engineering. Even so, many of the firms which did enter areas of the market acquired poor

commercial reputations, apparently because of lack of competitiveness and competence. The oil companies and their major engineering contractors frequently complained that British companies
tended to approach them without any clear idea of what was
wanted, and offered products or services that were unsuitable, thus
displaying lack of market research and 'homework'.[49] Furthermore,
British firms also developed a bad reputation for late delivery and
for not being able to deliver equipment that was 'ex-stock' on
time.[50] These were major failings as far as the oil companies were
concerned. Late deliveries can have serious consequences in the
North Sea because the time available each year to install equipment
on the sea bed is so limited; delays of a few weeks can often result in a
project having to wait a further year before installation can take
place. Consequently, cost penalties arising from late deliveries are
severe.[51] They are the chief reason why oil companies and their
contractors often turn down seemingly cheaper British products;
they are willing to pay a higher price to ensure that the delivery of a
product is on time. This preference is illustrated quite clearly in the
data presented in Table 2.2. The table sets out the delivery and
price quotations given by British, European and American companies for comparable types of offshore equipment during 1973.
While the British companies were often competitive in price terms,
in many cases they were unable to deliver equipment as quickly as
their European and American counterparts and were, consequently, denied supply contracts.

It is arguable whether British firms entirely deserved their initial
reputation. Some of the poor performances with respect to delivery
times can be attributed to the 'learning curve' associated with
companies new to any form of production. Also, many of the firms
who initially had difficulties arising from late deliveries improved
their performance quite dramatically after a year or so in the
business.[52] Furthermore, oil company executives themselves are
divided as to the competence of British firms. Most claim that it is
difficult to generalise about the initial capacities of British firms in
the market. Some were good; some were not so good. Several
executives stated that while there were many British firms which
were not good suppliers, not all foreign suppliers were uniformly
competent either.[53]

Whatever the reasons for the early reluctance or inability of
British industry to become engaged in the market for offshore
supplies, there could be little doubt that at the start of the

TABLE 2.2   Comparative quotations given by British and foreign companies for the delivery of offshore equipment, early 1973

(a) Pumps

UK Bids (£'000)	UK Delivery times (months)	USA Bids (£'000)	USA Delivery times (months)	European Bids (£'000)	European Delivery times (months)
3.0	4	6.5	$2\frac{1}{2}$	4.8	4
5.2	12	5.3	2		
13.0	11				
12.6	7				
10.5	7				
12.8	5				
4.5	8				

(b) Pressure vessels, delivered on site

UK Bids (£'000)	UK Delivery times (weeks)	USA Bids (£'000)	USA Delivery times (weeks)	European Bids (£'000)	European Delivery times (weeks)
10.0	26	10.8	8	10.0	28
9.5	28	11.4	8	10.2	34
8.8	22	12.4	16	10.4	24
9.99	36			9.8	16

(c) Onshore fabrication, specified delivery time

(d) Platform cranes

UK Bids (£'000)	European Bids (£'000)	UK Bids (£'000)	UK Delivery times (months)	USA Bids (£'000)	USA Delivery times (months)
2500	1300	108	14	74	9
1300	1450	80	Not quoted	81	7
1400	2000	76	9	67	6
1700	1300			64	6
1850	1340				
1200					
2200					

Source: L. C. Allcock, 'Britain's Offshore Oil Industry', *Petroleum Review*, Mar 1973, p. 83.

development of the North Sea oil fields, British firms were not doing well, and were suffering from a combination of self-imposed and external difficulties. These difficulties were so severe, in fact, that in mid 1972 the IMEG Report consultants estimated the level of British engagement in the offshore supply market at no more than 25–30 per cent. They also predicted that without changes in the foreseeable pattern of development this share of the market would rise to no more than 40 per cent by 1980.[54] Clearly, this was not a satisfactory situation for a nation possessing a sophisticated industrial structure which was technically capable of occupying a larger share of the market. This consideration, in combination with the likely effects on the balance of payments of the importation of significant amounts of capital equipment and services from abroad to develop the oil fields, and a consequent loss of potential employment opportunities, contributed to a strong case for government involvement in the offshore supply industry. The character of the Government's involvement in the affairs of the industry, and the other circumstances which contributed to this intervention, are the subject of the next chapter.

3 The Foundations of an Offshore Supplies Policy

INTRODUCTION

In 1964 the first serious commercial exploration for hydrocarbons in the North Sea began, followed closely by a series of substantial gas discoveries in 1965 and 1966. With hindsight, one might choose to regard these discoveries as the beginning of an era in which hydrocarbon fuels from the UK continental shelf dramatically altered Britain's status in international energy markets and the future of many national industries. Yet at the time few commentators outside the oil industry recognised the potential importance of the early finds in what is now known to be a major hydrocarbons producing zone. One manifestation of this is that the press and other sources devoted very little attention to the offshore supplies issue, even in the late 1960s when it was common knowledge that British industry had failed to gain a substantial share of the development contracts associated with gas exploitation.

This lack of interest in the fortunes of the offshore supply industry was as marked in government circles as in other walks of life during the late 1960s and early 1970s. However, by 1972 a Conservative Government had taken a number of steps which eventually led to extensive intervention in the affairs of the offshore supply industry and its customers, the multinational oil companies. The present chapter explores the reasons for the lack of interest in the industry's affairs which typified the 1964–70 Labour Governments and the first year and a half of the Heath administration. It also reviews the circumstances which gave rise to the Conservative Government's change of direction in late 1971. As explained in the following pages, the change largely resulted from altered circumstances in the North Sea, which in turn prompted a series of civil service policy initiatives. Thus, this chapter is, in part, a study of the way in which civil servants, in conjunction with ministers, interpret 'national objectives' in the industrial field and translate these into government policy commitments.

THE POLITICAL CONTEXT, 1964-72

Before I describe the first steps in the emergence of government policy in the offshore supplies field, I believe it is essential to review the political context within which those first few steps were taken. In particular, the next pages examine those features of the political situation in the latter half of the 1960s which contributed to delaying substantive government initiative in the offshore supply field until the end of 1971. Despite the gas field developments from 1964 to 1969 government took little interest during this period in firms supplying offshore. There appear to be three principal reasons for this lack of interest. First, industry and the public media at large did not become involved in pressing government to act in the offshore field until the early 1970s. Second, from 1964 to 1972 the industrial policies of successive administrations were not conducive to initiatives in the offshore sector. Finally, the attitudes of ministers and senior civil servants towards the oil companies in their role as multinationals within the domestic economy prevented the marketing difficulties of the offshore industry from being recognised at an early date.

The late 1960s are marked by a lack of public discussion of the offshore supply industry's opportunities, either within the industry or within the political arena. An analysis of both the serious daily press and the industry's trade press during the period 1965-76[1] revealed little or no interest in the offshore supply industry until the early months of 1972 and no mention of a demand for any type of government policy or assistance until the end of that year.[2] Nor was there mention of the level of engagement of British industry in the southern North Sea gas fields during the latter half of the 1960s. As will become evident later, interest in the fortunes of the industry did not, in fact, surface publicly until after it became known that the Government was taking an interest in the issue with the commissioning of the IMEG Report in May 1972. Thus, from 1964 to late 1971 there was little public awareness of the opportunities for British industry in the offshore sector and, consequently, little pressure upon the Government to develop a policy towards the offshore supply industry. This lack of public discussion and pressure may account, in part, for the Government's rather apathetic approach to the affairs of the industry during the late 1960s and early 1970s.

The reasons for this low level of public awareness and discussion are difficult to discern. In part, the public apathy probably reflected a general lack of concern on the part of British industry for the opportunities of the North Sea market. Furthermore, the small size of the original market associated with the gas fields developments, and the problems of adaptation which some British firms had experienced in entering this market (see Chapter 2) probably led to a lack of enthusiasm within British industry for future prospects in the North Sea. Finally, during the 1960s British offshore suppliers were not in a position to lobby effectively. As will be brought out further in Chapter 6, the trade association structure of the offshore supply industry was fragmented in these years, and remained so subsequently. A number of different trade associations served various parts of the industry, and this inhibited the formation and articulation of an 'offshore supply industry view' which could have then been put forward to the public and the Government. Indeed, the absence of a unified offshore trade association not only lessened the likelihood of government interest in the industry, but also slowed the development of an awareness of the market opportunities in the North Sea amongst the many firms with unutilised capabilities in the area. This lack of collective organisation and viewpoint was also reflected in the slow development of a British trade press serving the offshore supply industry. Established petroleum or engineering industry journals such as the *Petroleum Review*, the *Petroleum Times*, *Petroleum Press Service*, and *The Engineer* devoted occasional attention to the offshore supply market. However, journals devoted wholly to the interests of firms engaged in the offshore supply industry did not appear until the early 1970s. For example, the first British journal in this field, *Offshore Supplies*, started publication in October 1972, and the other major journal in the area, *Offshore Engineer*, did not appear until January 1975.[3]

The second reason for government indifference to the offshore sector centres upon the nature of industrial policy in general during this period. In the latter half of the 1960s the Wilson Government was very preoccupied with industrial issues, but for much of its term in office the major emphasis was upon macro-economic strategies such as prices and incomes policy and the attempt at indicative planning embodied in the establishment of the Department of Economic Affairs and the ill-fated National Plan. By the end of the

1960s the emphasis had shifted towards a sectoral approach to industrial strategy, but the new sectoral policies were primarily focussed either upon high-technology industries (e.g. computers) or upon industries in financial difficulty (e.g. machine tools). The offshore supply industry received little attention, partly because the British shipbuilding industry, which confronted considerable difficulties during these years, seemed to dominate the Government's approach towards marine-oriented industries.[4] Moreover, despite the increase in activity in the North Sea coincident with the election of the Heath Government in 1970, interest in the fate of the offshore supply industry remained minimal for the first two years of the new administration. This was due in large part to the Conservative Government's initial commitment to industrial 'disengagement' manifested in the 1971 Industry Act.[5] The future of the offshore supply industry only came under scrutiny after a shift in the priorities of the Conservative Government in mid 1972.

A final feature of the political climate which contributed to the lack of interest shown by government in the development of the industry before 1972 was the line taken by ministers and officials towards the oil companies as multinationals. However, the discussion of this topic requires a few paragraphs by way of introduction.

During the period 1964–71, ministers and officials of both the Labour and Conservative Governments endorsed a North Sea policy directed primarily towards ensuring a high level of exploration activity and the rapid development of any hydrocarbon deposits that were found. This policy was motivated by a desire to alleviate Britain's chronic balance of payments difficulties. It is not within the scope of this chapter, nor indeed of this book, to conduct a detailed examination of government policy with regard to North Sea developments in general.[6] However, a review of licence arrangements and government statements during the 1964–71 period demonstrates that the policies of both governments stressed exploration and development levels and timetables to the virtual exclusion of other issues such as taxation and the participation of British industry in the North Sea market.[7] Indeed, the limited nature of North Sea policy from 1964 to 1971 has been highlighted by the investigations of the House of Commons Public Accounts Committee which surveyed North Sea oil and gas policy in the early 1970s.

The Committee concerned itself primarily with taxation issues, and its investigations both reflected and induced public concern about the taxation and profit levels which would apply to oil companies working in the North Sea. However, ministers in the Conservative Government did not take up this issue, thereby indicating that even in the early 1970s they were reluctant to allow other considerations to interfere with the primary objective of ensuring a rapid development of the North Sea oil fields. Moreover, Conservative ministers did not give any great attention to other issues involving the oil companies, such as the encouragement the companies were giving to foreign suppliers. Even the Public Accounts Committee, which reported in early 1973, failed to pursue this question. In its final report, the Committee gave only four brief paragraphs out of a total of thirty-three pages of text to the subject of the participation of British industry. These paragraphs simply expressed regret that the initiative of the IMEG Report and the establishment of the Offshore Supplies Office (OSO) had not occurred sooner.[8]

Thus, North Sea policy from 1964 to 1971 largely reflected a government preoccupation with speed of development deriving from a wish to improve balance of payments deficits. Other issues, including offshore supplies, were assigned second priority. In some respects this appears contradictory, for the supplies question was so centrally related to the rate of oil field development. In addition, the stakes were so large in the offshore supply sector that the mismanagement of the supplies issue might easily have led to severe balance of payments difficulties. Indeed, the offshore supplies issue was eventually seen as very important to a healthy balance of payments for Britain, and this was one of the primary reasons for government intervention in the affairs of the sector in 1972. The explanation for the early neglect of the impact of North Sea oil exploitation upon the offshore supply industry appears to lie in large part in the attitudes of ministers and senior civil servants towards the multinational oil companies.

Michael Hodges, in his book *Multinational Corporations and National Government*, discusses in some detail the results of surveys conducted during the late 1960s and early 1970s concerning the attitudes of politicians and civil servants to multinational companies and foreign investment in Britain.[9] The surveys indicate a tendency for senior civil servants, ministers in the 1964–70 Labour Governments, and Conservative MPs to look with favour upon foreign multinationals operating in Britain, and upon foreign investment in the country generally. The majority view in all three groups seems to have been that foreign multinationals made a positive contribution to the UK economy (in alleviating balance of payments problems, providing technical and managerial skills and promoting industrial and regional development).[10] Hodges notes that senior civil servants tended to believe that multinationals were more co-operative as corporate citizens than British firms because they were more anxious to avoid confrontation with government than nationally-based firms: this attitude seems also to have been prevalent in the other two groups.[11] Finally, Hodges presents evidence that senior civil servants and Conservative MPs looked upon the UK as the 'home of many international companies', and thus were not in favour of government action against foreign multinationals which might provoke retaliation against British multinationals.[12]

Hodges does not present information concerning the attitudes of Conservative ministers after 1970, but it is likely, given the Conservative policy record in office, that Conservative ministers joined in the consensus about multinationals described above, at least for the early years of the Heath administration. The only group which was not part of this consensus was the Labour backbenches, particularly Labour MPs with trade union affiliations. However, the influence of these backbenchers was never substantial, and the foreign investment issue only received intermittent consideration in the House from 1964 to 1971.[13] Rather, the mood prevailing during this period is reflected in the fact that there were no instances of Labour or Conservative ministers advocating control of the behaviour of multinationals, with the possible exception of those cases involving the specific takeover of British companies (e.g. Rootes), and the creation of government-sponsored competitors to multinationals in strategic industrial sectors (e.g. ICL).[14]

The ruling consensus on multinationals during this period led to the depoliticisation of the issue of the impact of foreign multinational investment on British industrial capacity[15] – including the impact of the oil multinationals on the prospects for the development of a British offshore supply industry. The tendency to view the multinational oil companies in the ways outlined by Hodges probably delayed the realisation that the presence of so many foreign oil companies in the North Sea market could have a damaging effect upon the commercial prospects of those British firms with the potential for participating in the development of the oil fields. It is perhaps indicative of the impact of the consensus on multinationals in government circles that as late as 1970–1, when a group of senior civil servants was asked to name examples of industries with a high foreign component in the UK, only a third of the respondents mentioned oil.[16]

To summarise, then, the lack of an industry 'view' in the offshore supplies field, the nature of the emphasis of economic and industrial policy between 1964 and 1971, and finally, the widespread tendency to view the effects of a number of foreign oil companies on the country's industrial structure as beneficial, contributed to lessening the likelihood that government would take an active interest in the supplies issue. The next section of this chapter reviews the first hesitant steps in the development of government offshore policy during the late 1960s and early 1970s in order to demonstrate the manner in which events within the North Sea industrial arena gradually drew attention to the inadequacies of early British oil policy – inadequacies which in large measure derived from the concatenation of the three sets of circumstances discussed above.

THE OFFSHORE SUPPLIES ISSUE, 1964–70

The years from 1964 to 1970 are marked by a series of scattered and ill-defined attempts to encourage the development of a viable offshore supply industry in the UK. Some of these attempts involved the implementation of licensing regulations which imposed conditions on the manner in which the oil companies could conduct their exploration and development activities on the Continental Shelf.

The first licensing round in April 1964 under the Conservatives did not embody any specific provision relating to offshore supplies. Nevertheless, government was not entirely idle in this regard. Even at this early date the Ministry of Power put pressure on prospective licensees to ensure that they made informal commitments to use specified British capacity in the conduct of their exploration drilling programmes. Moreover, this type of informal administrative pressure was continued after Labour took office in a somewhat more explicit form. During the second round of licensing in 1965 the Labour Minister of Power introduced several new criteria which were to be applied in the selection of applicants. One of these[17] demanded that applicants present proposals which would contribute to the country's 'economic prosperity, including the strengthening of the United Kingdom balance of payments and the growth of industry and employment'.[18]

Officials negotiating licence agreements had some success in pressing the oil companies to buy British. For example, between the first and second rounds oil companies placed orders in Britain for eight drilling rigs (about £17 million) and eight supply boats (about £3 million) as a result of official prodding.[19] Yet these early efforts to promote British suppliers remained unsystematic. There was no formal monitoring system to determine to what extent British firms were becoming involved in North Sea work; nor were there any attempts by the Government to encourage British participation in the development of the North Sea gas fields.[20] Indeed, until 1972, the Department of Trade and Industry, and its predecessor, the Ministry of Power, had 'no precise figures of the total cost of exploration and development'[21] for work performed in the North Sea. The Ministry had restricted its activities to ensuring that the work programmes agreed between the licensee and the Government (i.e. the drilling of a specified number of exploratory wells) were, in fact, carried out.[22]

Given this early lack of information about the offshore supply industry, it is hardly surprising that the Government did not make any efforts to assist the industry directly during this period. However, there was one early attempt to remedy government ignorance regarding the industry and the offshore market. In 1967 the Ministry of Power asked a prominent American oil executive to write a confidential report assessing the level of British participation in the southern North Sea gas developments and any problems which British suppliers had encountered in that market. The report, which the author claims uncovered many of the problems revealed five years later by the IMEG Report, found that British firms were often reluctant to become engaged in the offshore market.[23] Despite these findings, the Government took no action. Ministers and officials may have reasoned that, if industry was reluctant to participate, little could be accomplished by a political initiative. In 1967 the benefits to be gained from British engagement in the offshore market were not as obvious as they were at the end of 1971.[24]

Not all government offshore initiatives during this period were concerned with the engagement of British firms in the offshore market. Some thought was also devoted to the development of British technical capabilities in offshore engineering and marine matters in general. Unfortunately, much of this early work was buried in a series of unfocussed debates embracing many aspects of what may be loosely designated as 'oceanic policy'.

In 1967 the Ministry of Technology's Chief Scientific Adviser, Ieuan Maddock, called a three-day conference on the Technology of the Sea and the Sea-bed. It was clear from Mr Maddock's opening address that the Ministry was primarily interested in using the conference to gain information for use in drafting a national policy on ocean engineering and ocean technology.

Some of the papers prepared for the 1967 conference dealt with offshore petroleum engineering, although none focussed upon British engagement in the offshore supply industry.[25] Furthermore, three of the thirty conclusions emerging from the conference had a bearing upon the offshore market. One dealt with deep-water civil engineering tasks, a second with the safety of rigs in operational conditions in the North Sea, and a third with diving. However, as is evident from the general tone and content of the conference report, these conclusions were isolated contributions to a debate that failed to anticipate many of the major issues which were to dominate sea and sea-bed policy in the 1970s. Fishing and general mineral exploitation were discussed at length, but comments on oil and gas extraction were limited. There was some recognition that Britain was heavily dependent upon foreign experience in undertaking large, deep-water civil engineering tasks. Yet the editors of the conference report did not anticipate that this might bode ill for future British competitiveness in the offshore market. Instead, they felt confident that British industry would respond to the opportunities presented by the North Sea and the Channel Tunnel.[26] Finally, the participants at the conference do not seem to have appreciated the relative economic significance of the subjects within their brief. At a time when North Sea gas was beginning to revolutionise Britain's energy balance, the conference report stated: 'Our most important marine mineral at present is gravel.'[27] In fact, the report contained no mention at all of the importance of hydrocarbons in the North Sea to the British economy.

In the following year (1968) a committee of civil servants was set up under Sir Fergus Allen at the Ministry of Technology to report upon the development of government policy in the area of ocean engineering.[28] The committee's *Report on Marine Science and*

Technology[29] was completed in the autumn of 1968 and published the following April under the auspices of the Lord President of the Council, Mr Fred Peart. This document referred to the offshore supply industry, but, again, the references were buried in a wide-ranging discussion which covered topics varying from fishing to geological surveys. Of the forty pages in the main body of the report, only two were addressed to the development of British offshore engineering and supply capabilities.

The explanation for this is not difficult to discern. Peart recognised in his introduction to the report that the Government wished to 'promote the commercial development of general equipment for sea-bed operations'.[30] He also recognised that the opportunities for UK industry to exploit undersea technology were increasing. However, the report was not optimistic about the prospects of British industry exploiting these opportunities.

> The latest and best equipment for drilling for, and extracting oil and natural gas, is available to the oil companies operating in the North Sea. A great deal of it is of American design and manufacture, which is only to be expected since the techniques of offshore drilling were largely pioneered and developed by American designers and manufacturers for the United States Gulf Coast. However, no fewer than ten mobile drilling rigs specifically designed for North Sea operations have been built in the United Kingdom, and there *may* be opportunities for British firms to compete in the supply of other equipment as offshore drilling expands in the eastern hemisphere. The scope for industry to develop new techniques of offshore oil and gas exploration and production appears to be limited.[31]

This excerpt indicates that, as of 1969, the Government had more or less written off the offshore supply industry. Ministers and officials appeared to agree that with the end of development work in the southern North Sea gas fields, the offshore supply industry's future was bleak. The committee concluded by recommending further geological and geophysical surveys of the Continental Shelf and co-operation between the Ministry and the industry in the development of subsea equipment, particularly submersibles, underwater power tools and diving equipment.[32] These recommendations were useful to certain specialised sections of the offshore supply industry, but taken together they had little impact upon the industry's future development. Not surprisingly, the report, in the words of one commentator, 'struck outside observers as a "monument of complacency" '.[33]

Nonetheless, in some respects the committe's efforts were constructive. For example, one of the report's recommendations led to the establishment of a Committee on Marine Technology (CMT), which was the forerunner of later bodies with responsibility for research and development (R and D) in the field of offshore supplies. The CMT was composed of civil servants from the Ministries of Defence and Technology and the Natural Environment Research Council (NERC) with a mandate to identify and promote the development of undersea technology with commercial applications.[34] However, the Committee had no funds of its own to spend on technological projects; instead, its purpose was to advise the research division within the Ministry of Technology regarding the granting of R and D assistance.[35] Just before the creation of the CMT, the Government had also established a Marine Technology Support Unit (MATSU) at Harwell to provide specialist advice to the CMT regarding technical matters and to undertake research in the field of marine technology on a contract basis.

The CMT had little effect in the field of offshore supply R and D. The Committee published several reports on marine technology, but the funds which it recommended to support R and D in this area were very small. During the period 1970–3 the CMT (and its successor, the Ship and Marine Technology Requirements Board) recommended that the Ministry of Technology, and later the Department of Trade and Industry (DTI) should devote some £150,000 *per annum* to research contracts for offshore equipment.[36] Given the cost of research in this area, this yearly sum was very small, especially when compared with the sums spent by other countries.[37] Furthermore, the greater proportion of the CMT's recommended and approved expenditure was directed to safety and scientific work rather than to projects of a specifically commercial nature.[38]

Thus, apart from the informal attempts by the Ministry of Power to influence oil companies' purchases of capital equipment for the North Sea during the early phases of gas exploration work, and the ineffective efforts of the Ministry of Technology to develop a research and development policy in the field of undersea engineering, one can conclude that during the 1960s government took only a minimal interest in the affairs of the offshore supply industry. Moreover, ministers and officials did not envisage any future circumstances in which the industry might play an important role. The fundamental reasons for this lack of interest and foresight have been indicated earlier. These were compounded by a number of other considerations. Officials appear to have taken the industry's historically poor performance and the lack of any clear expansion of hydrocarbons exploration and production work after the completion of the development phase of the North Sea gas fields as indications that the industry's prospects were bleak. In addition, it is apparent that during this period government did not succeed in developing a coherent and realistic policy framework relating to the exploitation of ocean resources as a whole. Hence, the various facets of ocean technology and ocean engineering, including the supply of equipment and services to oil companies searching for and exploiting hydrocarbons, were not pursued in any depth.

THE BEGINNINGS OF A COHERENT POLICY, 1970–2

When the Conservative Government came to power in 1970 it was not an administration disposed to formulate new industrial strategies. For the first year and a half of its existence the Conservative Government took no action in the field of offshore supplies policy, but by mid 1971 a number of sets of circumstances were converging which encouraged ministers and officials to take a greater interest in the affairs of the offshore supply industry.

In the first place, by the latter half of 1971 it was clear that the Conservatives' experiment with general industrial disengagement had failed. The collapse, rescue, and then nationalisation, of Rolls Royce and Upper Clyde Shipbuilders prompted a fundamental re-evaluation of government–industry relations within the Heath Cabinet. Moreover, the necessity for a change in direction in policy was confirmed by rising levels of unemployment throughout 1972. The period of reassessment culminated in the passage of the 1972 Industry Act which firmly committed the Government to regional assistance and financial aid to industry. Thus, by the end of 1971 the Heath administration had abandoned strict disengagement, and was taking an interest in policies which could stimulate the economy as a whole. It was also losing some of its initial hostility to industrial financial assistance.[39]

More specifically, government was prompted to give increased attention to offshore supplies as a result of the public interest in the oil discoveries which had developed by the end of 1971. Headlines such as 'North Sea Oil will Cost £1000 Million to Develop' and 'Scotland Should Share in £450 Million Oil and Gas Support Industry'[40] in both the serious daily press and the trade press indicated that there was a new enthusiasm for the industrial opportunities which the North Sea offered, and ministers began to respond to this. In a speech given in Aberdeen in December 1971, Sir John Eden, the Minister for Industry in the DTI, underlined the tremendous extent of the market for equipment and services which the oil discoveries had yielded. However, he also sounded a warning:

> The response of British industry to date in providing equipment for offshore operations has been frankly disappointing. Perhaps people have found it difficult to realise that on our own doorstep we have a major oil and gas find. The waters under which the oil fields lie are deep and difficult; very costly equipment is required to produce and deliver the oil. This is where British industry in general stands to gain so much. But we must move. This is a highly competitive business – it will not be handed to anyone on a plate. If Scottish firms want to get in on the act then they must get cracking now. It is business which has to be fought for and won by energetic and imaginative commercial effort. Companies engaged in the same type of activity should not hesitate to pool their resources so as to be able to guarantee the production and the delivery on time of the materials required. The opportunity is immense; we must grasp it now.[41]

This was the first statement by a minister to indicate government concern for the later oft-repeated theme that British industry might not react quickly or dramatically enough to the opportunities opening up in the northern North Sea oil fields.

Eden's concerns were reiterated early in the following year at a major conference held at Aviemore on 'Oil and Scotland's Future' sponsored by the Scottish Council.[42] Many Scottish businessmen attended the conference, and some of the discussions were concerned with the opportunities for Scottish and British industry engagement in the North Sea. A large number of businessmen were critical of the difficulties which the oil companies had placed in their way when they attempted to enter the offshore market. In addition, some noted the many uncertainties connected with offshore investment, uncertainties which often prevented firms from taking a stake. However, many of the non-industry representatives at the conference, particularly those associated with the oil companies, pointed out that Scottish industry did not seem to be especially interested in becoming engaged in the market. One Scottish Council official, who had had extensive experience in trying to encourage Scottish firms to participate in offshore developments, stated: 'Quite frankly, much of the reception we got from Scottish industry was not too encouraging; it verged from the incredulous to none at all.'[43]

Thus, by the beginning of 1972 the offshore supply market had become a topic for public debate, and the Government had joined in the discussions. In addition, those involved in the debate generally agreed that some action should be taken to ensure that British industry participated fully in the offshore market. However, the nature of the required action was still far from clear, and ministers had not yet indicated their intentions, if any. In the event, it was an initiative on the part of civil servants in the DTI and the Central Policy Review Staff which translated Eden's 1971 statement of concern about the offshore supply industry's prospects into a series of government policy commitments a year later.

THE INITIATIVE OF THE CIVIL SERVICE

In late 1971 it was apparent that ministers in the DTI were aware of the problems arising from the lack of UK engagement in the offshore supply industry, yet it was by no means certain that they were in favour of any policy initiatives. However, early in 1972 the DTI was reorganised with the establishment of an Industrial Development Unit (IDU) and the fusion of the industrial sponsorship divisions and the regional development division into a new Industrial Development Executive (IDE).[44] The reorganisation heralded a change of ministers; Peter Walker replaced John Davies as Secretary of State, and Christopher Chataway replaced Sir John Eden as Minister for Industry. The new structure and the new ministers reflected the more activist approach to industrial policy in general which the Government was then pursuing.

Even before the administrative and ministerial changes had

occurred, however, senior civil servants within the Department's Industrial and Commercial Division were developing an interest in promoting the offshore supply industry. Late in 1971 they were disturbed not only by the British industry's lack of interest in the new market, but also by the fact that neither ministers nor officials had received any representations from individual firms or trade associations regarding government action to assist the industry.[45] Early in 1972 they became convinced that the one way of correcting the problem would be for the Department to sponsor an inquiry into the opportunities for British industry in the offshore supply market and to use the ensuing report as a device to create interest in, and also provide information on, the nature of the market. At that stage they were uncertain whether to give responsibility for the enquiry to departmental staff or to engage outside consultants.[46]

At the same time, senior officials in the Central Policy Review Staff (CPRS) were in the process of planning a research programme focussed upon the long-term prospects of British industry. They, too, were impressed by the potential opportunities the offshore supply market presented for British firms. As a routine measure the CPRS officials contacted their opposite numbers in the Industrial and Commercial Division of the DTI to inform them of their developing interest in offshore supplies, only to find that the Department was also contemplating a study of the offshore market. After some preliminary discussions, officials in the two agencies decided that the CPRS and DTI would share the costs of a study of the state of the offshore supply industry. They also agreed that the study would be undertaken by a group of outside consultants with specialist knowledge of the subject.[47]

The concerns which had prompted both CPRS and DTI officials to take action centred not only upon the increase in employment that industrial engagement in the North Sea could generate, but also upon the longer-term implications of engagement for the economy and for industry. Many of the firms with the capabilities to enter the offshore supply market were engineering firms tied into industries in historical decline (e.g. component supply to shipbuilding in Scotland). The offshore supply market offered these firms a way of using established expertise creatively in a high-growth area. In addition, the opportunities for technological development open to firms who entered the market at an early stage might provide a lead for British firms in deep-water offshore technology, and thus create a future export industry. Furthermore, officials were concerned with the balance of payments implications for the economy if, as seemed likely at the time, most of the supply contracts were to go to foreign firms. With a North Sea development bill estimated in 1971–2 to be in excess of £1000 million, the implications for Britain's current account were serious.[48]

Following the decision to sponsor an external inquiry, officials issued tenders outlining the requirements of the study to four consulting firms. Subsequently, ministers were informed of the initiative to commission a study.[49] When the bids were received CPRS and DTI staff decided to place the contract with the International Management and Engineering Group (IMEG), a London-based engineering consultancy with branches in several countries and extensive experience in oil-related engineering work, particularly in the Middle East. The consultants started their work on 1 May 1972,[50] and on 24 May Mr Christopher Chataway announced the establishment of the inquiry in a written reply in the House of Commons. He outlined its terms of reference in the following manner:

> The study will be concerned with the equipment, materials, components and contracting and other services required for the exploration, development and production of hydrocarbons on the Continental Shelf up to 1985 and beyond, and will assess the potential scope for British industry to participate in this market. The desirability of encouraging the manufacture of the equipment, together with the setting up of appropriate contracting facilities, in Scotland and the other assisted areas, will be borne especially in mind.[51]

As is evident even from this brief announcement, the inquiry was to be more than a simple exercise in industrial exhortation. The reference to 'encouraging' contracting capacity clearly indicated that government was anxious for the consultants to provide guidance as to the steps which it might appropriately take in the offshore supplies field.

The IMEG consultants worked on the study for about four months with a staff of ten, including three economists, four procurement engineers and various other personnel, some of whom were employed for only a part of the study's duration. Most of the research consisted of company interviews and a series of rapid surveys.[52] The consultants' work was supervised by a steering committee made up of civil servants from the DTI and CPRS and representatives from the IMEG.[53] The study was completed by September 1972,[54] when a report was handed to ministers. With the omission of commercially confidential information, it was published in an abridged form in January 1973.

THE IMEG REPORT

The report of the IMEG consultants provided the first comprehensive description of the state of the British offshore supply industry and the first projections of the likely demand for its products and services. The report also made specific recommendations regarding how to improve various sections of the engineering and contracting side of the industry, the provision of services and supplies, government manpower and training policy, and research and development policy. Thus, in many respects, it constituted a blueprint for government policy and action. Moreover, a number of the proposals contained in the report were adopted outright or implemented with modifications. For this reason, the content of the report merits discussion.

The IMEG consultants' primary policy recommendation suggested the establishment of an independent Petroleum Supply Industries Board (PSIB) with a mandate to foster the development of an internationally competitive British offshore engineering and contracting industry capable of obtaining a substantial share of offshore oil and gas markets.[55] The consultants envisaged a body with its own legislative identity and budget, working independently of the Civil Service, but reporting to the Secretary of State for Trade and Industry through the DTI. The PSIB was to be responsible for assisting firms in the offshore supply industry to make the most of their existing capabilities and to expand into new fields of endeavour. This could be accomplished, the report suggested, by encouraging the formation of joint ventures between foreign companies and British firms so that UK-based companies could gain access to managerial and technical expertise in areas in which UK capabilities were weak.[56] In addition, the PSIB was to be able to disburse a number of types of financial assistance to firms in the industry. In particular, the consultants mentioned (a) Industry Act assistance, (b) special insurance coverage against high-risk projects and (c) government purchase of capital equipment which could then be loaned to contractors to assist them in entering new areas of activity (e.g. heavy-lift crane barges).[57] All of the above forms of sponsorship and assistance were to involve PSIB officials in discriminating between firms and backing those which seemed likely to have the commercial potential to exploit specific markets. Moreover, the consultants had a number of suggestions for areas of the market in which such selective assistance and sponsorship was most needed. For example, they recommended that the Government or the PSIB should give financial assistance to a selected British shipbuilder to enable it to become involved in the construction of semi-submersible and jack-up drilling rigs.[58] Also, the report contained proposals for encouraging the establishment of a British-based drilling contractor.[59]

Another important IMEG recommendation was the suggestion that the Government should establish administrative controls to prevent the oil companies from discriminating against British suppliers in awarding contracts.[60] The consultants obviously felt that there was reason to believe the oil multinationals were rejecting British bids for other than strictly commercial reasons. One remedy for this, they suggested, would be to require the oil companies operating in the North Sea to submit quarterly returns listing the nature and destination of supply contracts so that government could 'audit' oil company purchases to determine whether British firms were being asked to compete for business and the specific areas in which British capacity was weak. The report also advocated that the assessment procedures for granting North Sea licences should contain criteria which would make it clear to the oil companies that their applications would be reviewed in a more favourable light if they gave British suppliers a 'full and fair opportunity'. Finally, the consultants urged DTI officials to launch detailed investigations into the management practices of the oil companies in order to determine to what extent purchasing decisions were being made by parent companies abroad.[61] If such an investigation showed an unsatisfactory state of affairs, then, the consultants urged, pressure should be brought to bear upon the oil companies to change their ways, and more stringent and explicit requirements concerning the location of operational decision-making in the UK by licensees should be written into the licensing regulations.[62]

The IMEG Report also reviewed and made recommendations in several other areas of government policy. The consultants suggested an increase in the level of information services for the industry, which they hoped would accomplish two objectives: first, it would give British companies a clear idea of what the immediate requirements of the oil companies were for field development projects; and, second, it would 'publicise prospective trends and new developments which will affect the market for the future'.[63] Furthermore, the report proposed that an information service should be made available to the oil companies which would put the purchasers of offshore supplies into contact with potential British suppliers.[64]

Proposals were also put forward in the report concerning the development of education and training to serve the offshore supply industry. In particular, the consultants suggested that the Government purchase a jack-up drilling rig 'to be run as the central facility of a training programme to include both drilling and other offshore skills such as diving'.[65] At the professional level, the report suggested that the two universities with some expertise in petroleum geology and marine engineering (Imperial College, London, and Aberdeen University) should join with other interested universities, the Government and industry to consider the establishment of chairs and undergraduate courses in petroleum engineering, drilling engineering, oil production engineering and other related subjects. The consultants also advocated the establishment of a permanent organisation to supervise the implementation of the report's education and training proposals and to review and coordinate the industry's training and education requirements as time went on.

In the field of research and development the report stressed that if British industry was to benefit not just from North Sea offshore activities, but also from international opportunities, it was important 'for British enterprise to be among the leaders in the development of new equipment and techniques for offshore operations, with particular reference to the requirements of very deep waters'.[66] In particular, it recommended the funding of research in eight specific areas of technical development connected with drilling technology, platform design, subsea completion systems, submarine pipe-lines, submersibles and offshore mooring systems. Most of the research and development proposals emphasised the importance of existing technology and 'state of the art' development. The report warned against attempts to make up for British industry's slow start in the offshore market by leaping into the forthcoming generation of offshore technology.[67]

Finally, the consultants presented a number of miscellaneous recommendations regarding matters such as infrastructure in Scotland, the necessity to expand the UK oil and gas processing industry to accommodate increased flows from the North Sea and the employment-generating potential of offshore supply industry in west central Scotland. They were especially anxious to highlight the 'value added' possibilities arising from the used of North Sea oil and gas as feedstocks for the petrochemical industry. In particular, they suggested that the Government encourage a British liquified natural gas (LNG) capacity, including LNG tankers, to take advantage of gas reserves in the smaller fields, which could not be exploited on a commercial basis without LNG technology.[68]

In many respects the IMEG Report was an exceptional document. The consultants obviously believed that without immediate government action the tremendous opportunities of the offshore market for British industry might well be lost to foreign enterprise.[69] For this reason, the report contained a larger than average number of policy recommendations which, if implemented, required both a major change in government policy and a substantial role for the state in directing the development of a new industry. In the consultants' view, government had to provide leadership and initiative in the efforts to establish a viable British offshore supply capacity.

However, the report also broached the question of intervention in a politically astute manner. Thus, the consultants couched recommendations for increased financial assistance to industry and firm-specific industrial promotion within an institutional framework (the proposed PSIB) which was likely to appeal both to industry executives and a Conservative Government just emerging from 'disengagement'. According to the consultants, offshore supplies policy did not belong within the civil service sphere. They argued instead that the policy should be implemented by an independent executive body which was to be industry-oriented, entrepreneurial in style and technically and commercially informed.[70] It was these latter themes which eventually eased government acceptance of the high levels of industrial intervention which were also implicit in the report.

Two recommendations in the IMEG Report deserve special note. The first of these is the auditing proposal.[71] A close reading of the report provides no indication about its origins or rationale. Yet, according to its editor, the consultants did not receive any representations from industry about government supervision of oil company purchasing.[72] This accords well with information obtained from the senior civil servant in charge of the IMEG Report steering committee to the effect that officials, rather than the consultants, were responsible for drafting the auditing proposal. Apparently, officials were attracted by the auditing concept for a number of reasons. In the first place, if effective, an auditing procedure promised to have a very rapid impact upon the pattern of demand within the offshore supply market. In addition, officials felt that this could be accomplished with a minimum of effort and expenditure using traditional administrative techniques (although difficulties in ensuring the effectiveness of the procedure became apparent later). Finally, officials were aware that auditing had the advantage of allowing the Government to take action which had a high public profile and would serve as a demonstration of its concern about the fate of the industry.[73]

The other key recommendation in the IMEG Report, and indeed all the other policy proposals, were the responsibility of the consultants alone. According to the report's editor, the consultants did not propose the PSIB as a result of suggestions from their industrial contacts. Rather, the PSIB concept emerged as a logical extension of the type of development strategy which they felt would be most beneficial for the industry. However, the consultants rapidly discovered that officials objected to the principle of establishing a politically and administratively independent policy-making board.[74] Civil servants feared that the creation of a body such as the PSIB would lead to policy conflicts between government departments and the board about the future of the industry. Generally, officials were in favour of the report's recommendations, but the PSIB proposal, including the recommendations about government financial assistance, went far beyond anything they had originally envisaged.[75] Thus, the report's recommendations extended the scope of the debate about government options in the offshore supplies field, but senior officials in the DTI were opposed to at least one of the key recommendations which the consultants advanced.

Nevertheless, the interaction between officials and the consultants was a productive one. The consultants were not able to persuade officials of the value of the PSIB concept, but the latter did come to accept the need for some type of agency to encourage the industry. In addition, during the IMEG Report's preparation officials were prompted to propose an unorthodox policy option (auditing) which proved to be a significant innovation in government–industry relations. Thus, while there were differences in emphasis, in that officials focussed upon government supervision of oil company purchasing operations and the consultants were primarily concerned with increasing financial assistance to industry, both groups recognised a similar objective, namely substantial change in the Government's relationship with the offshore supply industry.

The IMEG Report was released to the public in January 1973,[76] and the response which it elicited was mixed. Generally speaking, the industry and the public at large welcomed the new emphasis which the consultants brought to the debate about the future of offshore supply capacity. In particular, most commentators endorsed the PSIB proposal as a sensible suggestion which would ensure an independent and consistent administration of the industry's development.[77] However, the trade press also noted that the consultants had made little attempt to assign priority to their recommendations or to ensure their full coherence.[78]

These latter criticisms were amplified in later press reports. For example, a number of reviews contained comments to the effect that the report's recommendations were overly general and not sustained by sufficient detailed analysis of the state of the industry and of the market.[79] Thus, the manager of the Underwater Engineering Group (UEG), an industrial research association with over seventy member companies in the offshore supply industry, had this to say:

> A fault of the report lies in the greatly varying depths of detail which are provided, ranging from generalised statements to, at the other extreme, an equation for weldability of steels in terms of the chemical constituents. *Such variation naturally raises doubts as to the validity of the conclusions.*[80]

The report was also criticised for failing to outline a strategy to ensure the long-term viability of the offshore supply industry. The IMEG consultants had recognised that it was necessary for British firms to become engaged in areas such as deep-water technology in order to acquire a secure standing in the international offshore market. Yet the report contained very few indications of how this was to be accomplished. This *lacuna* caused the *Financial Times* to comment:

Since other countries with some experience of offshore exploration are presumably thinking along similar lines, this implies
that the Government should define clearly the direction in which
U.K. underwater research and development is to be concentrated. The IMEG Report fails to meet this requirement – it is
more a collection of the many different ways in which industry
hopes to attract Government financial assistance.[81]

An evaluation of the IMEG Report which appeared in the Institute
of Petroleum's journal, *Petroleum Review*, contained similar
statements.[82]

Criticisms of the report like those reviewed above have also been
voiced by oil company executives during the course of interviews
with the present author. They, too, mentioned the uneven and
overly general nature of the report's findings and recommendations.
One oil company executive noted that in reading through the report
he found himself agreeing with a recommendation on one page and
then violently objecting to another recommendation a few pages on.
After checking with colleagues in other companies, he discovered
that the recommendations with which he agreed were actually
suggestions he had made to the consultants when they interviewed
him, while the ones with which he disagreed were recommendations
his colleagues had made to the consultants. In a sense, this executive
claimed, the report was a compilation of views on the industry's
prospects rather than a thorough and independent analysis of its
present state and likely future.[83]

Some of the above criticisms of the IMEG Report were justified,
and some of the recommendations which commentators found
wanting (e.g. the purchase of a drilling rig for training purposes)
were never taken up by the Government. However, to be fair to the
consultants, four months is an extremely short period of time to
produce a report of wide dimensions. Indeed, given the limitations
imposed upon the report's authors, the document attracted a
remarkable level of support within the industry for its principal
recommendations: the creation of an independent PSIB and the
extension of financial assistance and other government services to a
beleaguered offshore supply industry.

CONCLUSIONS

With the publication of the IMEG Report, civil servants achieved their original objectives in commissioning the document, and more. The report both stimulated interest in the offshore market and provided information about its conditions for firms wishing to participate. Beyond this, it advanced a series of specific policy options which demanded a government response. Senior officials disapproved of some of these options, but it must be assumed that in allowing these to go forward they believed they would provide a framework for a major government policy initiative in the area. Indeed, as is apparent from the next chapter, the report's recommendations served as a reference point in the initial development of an offshore supplies policy.

The reasons for the report's eventual impact are not difficult to discern. Part of its effectiveness stemmed from the fact that the consultants' sense of urgency was shared by the relevant senior civil servants. At the same time, the report was not an internal civil service proposal, and thus it carried little intellectual baggage which the Cabinet would find objectionable. In fact, coming as it did from an independent, private-sector organisation with a high level of technical expertise, the report was to command a substantial degree of acceptance within the higher echelons of the Conservative Government. Finally, the IMEG consultants prepared their recommendations in such a way that the Government could not avoid taking a view of the offshore supply industry and its prospects, especially given the rising tide of enthusiasm for North Sea opportunities coincident with the report's appearance. By January 1973, few doubted the economic analysis which served as a foundation for the report's proposals, and consequently there was no possibility of the Cabinet postponing action without political penalty. In the event, government policy was far from a carbon copy of the report's recommendations, but the consultants did define the general areas for government action (e.g. financial assistance, the need for a specialised agency to deal with the problems of the industry, etc.) and, through their proposals for a comprehensive policy, forced the Government to respond comprehensively.

Civil Servants as Policy-makers

While it cannot be said that the contents of the IMEG Report were all that senior DTI officials might have wished for, the initiative to commission the report is a demonstration of the manner in which civil servants are able to elicit government action in selected policy areas.

The evidence presented in this chapter indicates that prior to mid 1972, when commentators in the press began to give some attention to the work of the IMEG consultants, there was little overt political pressure on ministers or civil servants to introduce policy measures in the offshore supplies field.[84] Rather, during the course of reviewing a number of industrial issues and their implications for the economy as a whole, civil servants and ministers apparently came to perceive that the offshore-supplies question was directly relevant to a number of central government objectives: the maintenance of a 'healthy' balance of payments; enhanced employment opportunities in the regions; and adequate orders and revenue for British industry.[85] Thus, beginning with Sir John Eden's Aberdeen speech in December 1971, the government initiated an offshore supplies debate reflecting a conviction in government circles that the supplies issue had too many national dimensions to remain solely the concern of the private sector. However, the question of what stance government could most appropriately adopt in the area was still open.

This latter issue was resolved, in part, through the commissioning of the IMEG Report. Early in 1972 civil servants in the DTI and CPRS took it upon themselves to launch a study of the offshore market and the British offshore supply industry. The original intention was to assemble information about the opportunities latent in the North Sea developments which could be used by British firms in preparing to enter the market. However, the scope of the study expanded rapidly, with the result that officials and consultants became involved in drafting policy proposals with serious implications for the level of government intervention in industry.

The fact that the IMEG Report initiative was carried virtually to the point of implementation (i.e. to the final award of the contract to an outside consultant) without reference to ministers does not signify that civil servants were usurping political prerogatives in this instance. On the contrary, this is an example of how senior civil servants function in their capacities as policy advisers and formulators by acting 'within the minister's mind'.[86] However, in this case civil servants were especially effective both in anticipating the political predilections of their ministers (i.e. by hiring an independent set of private-sector consultants to prepare the report) and in formulating administrative strategies (i.e. auditing) to answer the requirements of British firms in the offshore market. The result was a significant and novel initiative by the state in a new and growing industry.

4 The Early Progress of Intervention, 1973–6

INTRODUCTION

Government intervention in industry rarely proceeds according to any specific master plan. Rather, once circumstances have produced a commitment to intervene, the character and progress of intervention are dictated by developments in the economy at large as they impinge upon the specific political and bureaucratic structures of British government. This implies that as economic conditions change and novel situations requiring a government response proliferate, intervention 'strategies' frequently become more and more meaningless. It also implies that economic circumstances beyond government control are dominant in the determination of the character and progress of intervention as of other developments in the state sector. Thus, while, for example, different approaches to intervention arising from different types of political commitments can be distinguished, these differences may be overwhelmed depending upon the pace and gravity of economic events in the larger arena. This, of course, is not to argue that there is no pattern to government intervention in industry, only that in recent years this pattern has been more clearly a product of the manner in which national and international economic developments affect the state as a whole rather than of divisions within the state or changes in its complexion over time.[1]

Such has been the case with government intervention in the affairs of the offshore supply industry. This chapter traces the early progress of intervention in this area from the first actions of the Conservative Government in 1973 through to 1976 when many of the important functions of the present OSO were in place. As is evident from the following pages, coherent 'strategies' played only a minor role in determining the character of intervention in the offshore supply industry. Instead, under both the Conservatives and

Labour, the 'objectives' of intervention became less and less distinct as OSO functions proliferated in response to national and international developments with a bearing upon the offshore supply industry. In addition, the policies of both governments demonstrate that conventional analyses which portray Labour Governments as collections of *dirigiste* planners and Conservative Governments as champions of free-market orthodoxy are both dated and inappropriate. Each of the two governments intervened extensively in the affairs of the offshore supply industry. There were, of course, differences in emphasis and form between the two regimes which broadly reflected their respective philosophical stances concerning the role of government in economic affairs. However, these differences pale by comparison with the range and variety of policy instruments which *both* governments developed and employed as successive 'crises', at times large, at times small, engulfed the offshore supply industry.

CONSERVATIVE GOVERNMENT POLICY AND THE ESTABLISHMENT OF THE OFFSHORE SUPPLIES OFFICE, 1973-4

Upon publication of the IMEG Report in January 1973, the then Secretary of State for Trade and Industry, Peter Walker, made an important policy statement which outlined the Conservative Government's response to the offshore supply industry's problems. He revealed that the Government was about to establish an Offshore Supplies Office (OSO) to oversee its policies towards the industry. He also indicated that the government intended to introduce a system of quarterly returns or audits whereby the oil companies would report their offshore supply purchases to government officials. Further, he reported that ministers would give 'urgent and sympathetic study to possible ways of meeting the needs of industry' through the provision of financial assistance.[2] Significantly, in providing a rationale for the new policy initiatives taken by the Cabinet, Walker emphasised the importance of the offshore supply industry to the Government's regional development programme. In the Secretary of State's own words,

The opportunity is of particular importance to the nation's regional policies in that the main oil fields discovered so far lie off our Scottish and North Eastern coasts thus providing these regions with all the potentialities of being the natural base for the operating companies.[3]

It is very likely that even in 1973, after the reversal in Conservative industrial policy, the Cabinet only accepted the OSO and auditing proposals because they were presented as a means of contributing to regional objectives.

The most important of the new measures announced by the Secretary of State was the establishment of the OSO. This measure was inspired by the IMEG Report, but rather than setting up an independent policy-making board (the proposed PSIB) as the IMEG consultants had suggested, the Conservative Government opted for the creation of a specialist division within the Industrial Development Executive (IDE) of the DTI. In doing so, it rejected the concept of an independent agency designed to promote the offshore supply industry's development. Instead, the Government approved an addition to the traditional administrative structure within an existing department. Mr Walker's rationale for this centred upon the need for effective administrative integration:

> The off-shore supplies office will be able to commence operations immediately and will have all the advantages of working within the Industrial Development Executive. There will, therefore, be no overlapping, no indecision and the substantial powers available under the Industry Act will be able to be used to benefit the fast expansion and growth of our supplies and contracting industries.[4]

As is obvious from the above comment the Government was anxious to avoid the creation of a 'hived-off' executive agency of the type that had been advocated in the IMEG Report and that had emerged in other areas of policy-making during this period.[5] Clearly, on this issue ministers had decided to follow the advice of the senior officials in the DTI who had cautioned against the establishment of an independent board for fear that conflicting objectives might develop within the industrial policy sector.[6] The Government did, however, accept the IMEG Report's suggestion that the OSO should be staffed with outside experts familiar with the offshore supply industry.[7]

Despite Walker's statements to the effect that the OSO would be simply another division within the DTI, there were early indications that official statements did not convey a full picture of internal developments. For example, the OSO had a distinctive organisational style which was reflected in its nomenclature. The new unit was called an 'office' rather than a 'division', and the head of the OSO was referred to as a 'Director-General' rather than an Under-Secretary. The reasons for these departures from standard practice are now clear. According to the minister in charge of the OSO at the time, the Government wished to create an organisation patterned upon the Industrial Development Unit (IDU). Thus, the Government intended that the new body should report directly to the Minister for Industrial Development rather than through the civil service hierarchy. In addition, the Government wished to have a substantial part of the OSO's staff recruited from industry as was the case with the IDU (see Fig. 4.1).[8]

About ten days after the announcement of the creation of the OSO, J. P. Gibson was named as the first Director-General. Gibson was recruited from industry, and at the time of his appointment was the managing director of Lummus Co. Ltd, an American-based engineering contracting company. Previous to this, Gibson had worked as a manager of New Products in ICI's Heavy Organic Chemicals Division, and before that as a manager with Rolls Royce. He was to head the OSO for the first four years of its existence.[9] The Government obviously intended that Gibson's extensive industrial experience should inject a private-sector bias into the operation of the new OSO.

In his announcement of the creation of the OSO Peter Walker was remarkably vague about the functions of the Office. Information about these only came to light in an interview which the new Director-General of the OSO gave shortly after taking up his appointment. At that time, Gibson said the OSO would attempt to ensure that 'UK companies which have the capability to take part [in the offshore supply market] do not miss the opportunities'. On the other hand, he did not envisage any direct role for the OSO in 'seeking and enforcing that UK industry took any particular set share in the market'.[10] Gibson stated that he was primarily concerned with the effectiveness of the audit function because an efficient audit operation was a prerequisite for change in established supplier–customer relationships. He also expressed a concern with the fact that a number of British companies requiring venture capital for offshore projects could not obtain funding from City

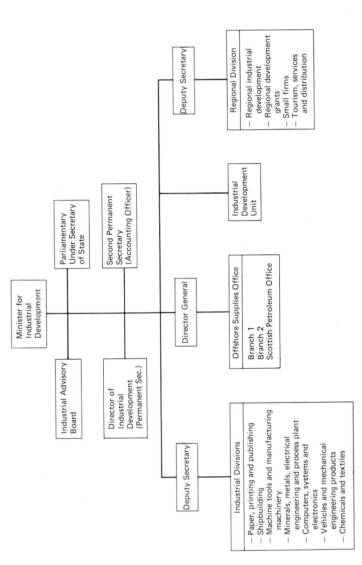

FIGURE 4.1   The Offshore Supplies Office in the Industrial Development Executive, 1973

Source: Industrial and Regional Development, Cmnd 4942 (1972), Annex D; and Chataway interview. For a description of the functions of IDE, see Cmnd 4942, pp. 5–6. Used with the permission of the Controller of Her Majesty's Stationery Office.

institutions. The IMEG Report had contained proposals for financial assistance programmes designed to overcome difficulties of this kind, and Walker's statement announcing the creation of the OSO had referred to ministerial deliberations concerning these proposals.[11] Gibson made it clear, however, that the Government had developed doubts about many of the IMEG proposals relating to financial assistance,[12] and in a later interview he confirmed that the Government did not have a strong interest, for example, in the 'risk insurance' programmes which the IMEG consultants had advocated.[13] From the Conservative standpoint, 'assistance' as interpreted in the IMEG Report presented the danger that government could become involved in substantial and continuing outlays to the offshore supply industry. In short, according to this view, 'assistance' in the IMEG sense meant 'subsidy'. However, this did not imply that the Government was opposed to all forms of financial assistance. For example, some months after the creation of the OSO Gibson indicated that the Government was prepared to provide financial assistance for specific projects with major once-off development costs, but only in circumstances where government expenditure would not lead to a continuing commitment.[14]

The Government's growing doubts about the value of the IMEG financial assistance proposals were also reflected in the one major announcement which Gibson made during his first press interview. The Director-General stated that in order to rectify the venture capital 'shortage' the OSO was about to acquire another role. This was the venture management function in which venture managers on the OSO's staff would assist offshore suppliers to identify commercial opportunities in the offshore market and to find private venture capital for new products and services. Gibson described the venture managers as catalysts who would spark the interest of British firms in viable projects by encouraging joint ventures and arranging attractive financial packages. However, he was careful to stress that the OSO venture managers would not be involved in industrial restructuring (like that which had been fostered by the Industrial Reorganisation Corporation). In doing so, he rejected yet another of the aspects of the IMEG proposals for an independent PSIB.[15] Indeed, while the Conservatives acknowledged that government might play a part in remedying certain 'anomalies' in the capital markets of the City, they did not envisage a major role for the OSO in building up domestic offshore capability. At the time of the establishment of the OSO ministers and senior officials were convinced that government could be of most assistance to the offshore supply industry by endeavouring to change oil company purchasing patterns. Accordingly, most of the OSO's efforts during the first months of 1973 were directed towards negotiations with the oil companies concerning the offshore supplies purchasing audit.[16]

To summarise, then, in creating the OSO the Conservative Government recognised that a number of types of institutional and policy innovation would be required if government were to play an effective role in assisting British industry to gain a larger share of the offshore market. This is evident in the recruitment of a private-sector head for the OSO, in the slightly unorthodox organisational style of the Office and in the decision to establish a procedure for registering oil company purchasing patterns. Venture management was also a departure in that it served to introduce the ethic of the merchant banker into a civil service department. In short, the Conservative Government could not ignore the difficulties confronting the offshore supply industry which the IMEG Report had highlighted, with the result that the state's role in the industry's affairs expanded considerably.

During this early period in the history of the OSO the Conservative Government's actions were in large degree determined by ideological considerations. Thus, the IMEG Report was interpreted in light of Conservative sensibilities regarding government involvement in industrial affairs, and ministers tailored their measures accordingly. For example, the Conservatives readily accepted the IMEG recommendations concerning the use of private-sector people in offshore policy and more 'commercial' approaches to government–industry relations.[17] Both stances were in keeping with the 'business like' approach to the management of government affairs which typified the Heath administration generally. Alternatively, the Conservatives did not condone the consultants' suggestions concerning financial assistance and industrial 'restructuring', again for ideological reasons. However, later in the history of the OSO ideological considerations became much less prominent in the determination of offshore policy, as the Government confronted a number of economic crises with a bearing upon the offshore supply industry. Indeed, it is possible to argue that the introduction of the venture management function was symptomatic of future changes in offshore policy, for the Conservatives only became involved in venture management because of a 'mini-crisis' in North Sea financing arrangements, and then only reluctantly. In the process certain ideological stances were weakened. Members of the Heath Government obviously had no intrinsic objections to 'merchant banking', but as is evident from the next sections of this chapter they were never very comfortable with the notion of civil servants engaging in 'private-sector' functions. Nevertheless, they condoned the practice in the face of 'anomalies' in the City, and thereby considerably extended the scope of government involvement in the offshore supply industry. Thus, just as the IMEG blueprint fell victim to Conservative ideological selectivity, so the 'consistency' of the Conservatives' early approach to offshore policy was short-lived as developments in the larger economic arena obliged ministers and officials to contemplate increasingly radical departures from conventional regional development and industrial policies.

Public and press reaction to the Government's new interest in the offshore supply industry was unenthusiastic. In particular, many commentators were quick to point out that the IMEG proposals had been abandoned in large degree. The trade associations in the offshore field were disappointed that the Government had decided not to proceed with the IMEG Report's main proposal for an independent PSIB. They regarded the creation of the OSO as a second-best alternative, and feared that it indicated a lack of government commitment to a unified approach to the problems of the industry. The trade associations felt that the OSO would be unable to provide the type of industrial leadership that might have been achieved with an independent, industry-oriented board.[18] As for the general press reaction, the *Economist*'s comments are typical:

The action the Government is actually taking is hardly exciting. The Department of Trade and Industry is merely setting up an office of unspecified size to sponsor the development of an internationally competitive industry. Mr. Peter Walker, the Secretary of State for Trade and Industry, said that further action will be taken as the problems are more precisely defined, which hardly suggests a great sense of urgency. Yet this is one area in which the Government could lash out money with some profit. If it can find £1.2 billion [i.e. £1200 million] for the coal industry, whose prospects are hardly bright, it should be more than generous towards Britain's biggest opportunity in decades.[19]

Clearly, then, although auditing, venture management and the organisational style of the OSO were unusual by civil service standards, government actions did not meet public expectations in 1973. The IMEG Report had served to focus public attention on the offshore supply industry, and after its publication the media were not reluctant to criticise any government lassitude in responding to the problems of the industry, particularly given the 'positive' image which it had acquired. From the publication of the IMEG Report onwards the press was to be instrumental in highlighting the opportunities available in the offshore market as the scope of the North Sea discoveries became more apparent and in urging ministers to greater efforts on behalf of UK firms.

CONSERVATIVE POLICY INITIATIVES OUTSIDE THE OSO

The publication of the IMEG Report and the creation of the OSO in early 1973 represented the chief thrust of government offshore policy. But there were a number of other changes in government policy during the first two years of the Heath administration which were to have an impact upon the offshore supply industry.

Outside the OSO, the government commitment to the offshore supply industry was most apparent in the provision of research and development assistance. There were several interrelated developments in the Government's R and D policy which had an impact on the industry. The first of these was the reorganisation of the entire government R and D structure based upon the recommendations contained in Lord Rothschild's 'Think Tank' report of November 1971, and set out in full in a White Paper issued by the Government in July of the following year.[20] The new R and D policy emphasised the need to inject a more commercial element into the funding and administration of government research work. This was to be achieved through the use of a contractor principle in awarding and supervising contracts and of more specifically industry-oriented criteria in developing research projects. One outcome of this approach was the creation of a number of Research Requirements Boards catering to specific industries and staffed by industrialists as well as civil servants. The members of these boards were charged with reviewing existing projects and making new proposals which simultaneously reflected government policy and the commercial requirements of industry. The new boards also had responsibility for

supervising research, contracting out research projects and reviewing overall research strategy.[21] As a part of this new research policy
framework, on 16 October 1972 the Government announced the
creation of a Ship and Marine Technology Requirements Board
(SMTRB). The SMTRB was given responsibility for interpreting
and implementing government policy regarding research in the
shipbuilding and marine (including offshore) industries. It replaced
the Committee on Marine Technology (see Chapter 3), and was
assigned a substantial budget.

The SMTRB was set up at the end of 1972, and therefore its
approach to R and D problems in the marine industry was heavily
influenced by the conclusions of the IMEG Report which came out
a month after the SMTRB's first meeting.[22] However, the new
board had also inherited a number of marine technology programmes (concerned mainly with geological surveys and safety
research) which had been originally sponsored by the CMT.
Consequently, there was little *immediate* emphasis on industrially
applied marine research. In fact, the SMTRB's first budget in 1973
allocated only about £1 million of a total £4.5 million to research in
sea-bed engineering, and of this only about £400,000 was directed
towards industrially applied marine research.[23] The following year,
however, in response to the IMEG Report, the SMTRB increased
the allocation for industrially applied marine R and D to £625,000,
and this figure was doubled during the 1974–5 financial year.[24]
These sums were directed to such areas as diving, exploration
drilling, platform construction, underwater tools, pipe-lines, sal-
vage techniques and submersibles development.[25]

The new research arrangements were, however, far from ideal.
While they fostered a more industry-oriented approach to policy-
making in the R and D area and some increase in funding levels,
there were fundamental problems. In the first place, the sums were
still very modest by international standards, particularly as research
in the areas covered by the SMTRB tends to be very expensive. In
addition, the Board was obliged to divide its attentions between the
shipbuilding industry and the offshore and marine industries with
the result that its commitment to the latter industries was partially
diluted. Indeed, most of the independent (industry) members of the
SMTRB came from companies or organisations with shipbuilding
interests.[26] These problems were reflected in a statement by the
Underwater Engineering Group (UEG – an industrial research
association) to the Select Committee on Science and Technology

shortly after the Board's creation was announced by the
Government in October 1972:

> The UEG Committee believes that, despite the significant
> overlapping of interests in offshore technology and ship tech-
> nology, the two should not be combined within one
> Requirements Board. Indeed, the UEG Committee are con-
> vinced that the case for a single Board is more than outweighed by
> the dissimilarities which exist between a new rapidly developing
> advanced technology on the one hand, and on the other hand a
> well established industry. The organisation of the systems, and
> the experience and qualities sought from personnel in the two
> industries differ significantly.
>
> Accordingly, and with all possible stress, the UEG Committee
> submit that the proposal to establish a single combined Ship and
> Marine Technology Requirements Board be re-examined by
> H. M. Government.[27]

While less strident than the UEG, British Petroleum was also
critical of the newly established SMTRB in its evidence to the Select
Committee on Science and Technology given in late 1973:

> Nationally there appears to be no definitive overall policy and
> there is a lack of an adequate independent agency funded by
> Government for planning and development in the marine field.
>
> The recently established Ship and Marine Technology
> Requirements Board has a relatively small budget for research
> and development and this has to be divided between the
> requirements of the shipping industry and offshore technology. It
> is arguable whether these requirements are themselves com-
> patible in view of the fact that one is an industry of long standing,
> and the other a development yet in its infancy.[28]

Thus, although the Government had attempted to strengthen
support for the offshore supply industry's R and D efforts, these were
still highly fragmented and rather modest.

THE EXPANSION OF THE OSO, 1973-4

By the end of its first year the OSO had expanded to include some forty members of staff.[29] They were divided into two branches: a policy and finance branch, and an engineering branch which was responsible for implementing the offshore purchases audit. In addition, the Government created a Scottish Petroleum Office in Glasgow as an adjunct to the OSO to assist in encouraging the development of offshore supply capability in the west central region of Scotland (see Fig. 4.2).[30]

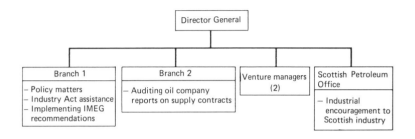

FIGURE 4.2   OSO organisation, 1973

Source: Select Committee on Science and Technology, *Minutes of Evidence*, HC 41 i–iv, Session 1973–4, pp. 46–7. Used with the permission of the Controller of Her Majesty's Stationery Office.

During these initial months OSO staff were primarily preoccupied with establishing and developing the audit function. Auditing constitutes a significant departure in the history of government intervention in industry in that for the first time civil servants acquired a detailed knowledge of the purchasing patterns of a group of large multinational companies operating in Britain. Moreover, auditing allowed civil servants to participate in deliberations with the oil companies on the basis of access to privileged information about purchasing. The importance of auditing is such that it was decided to discuss the evolution, operation and significance of this OSO function in a separate chapter (Chapter 8).

In addition to the work on auditing, OSO staff endeavoured to clarify the Office's role on a number of other fronts. For example, as already mentioned, shortly after it was created the OSO assumed a venture management function. The reader will recall that the venture capital 'shortage' which Gibson referred to in his first interview with the press provided the immediate impetus for the formation of the venture management group within the OSO. This 'shortage' highlighted a number of interrelated problems. Ministers and officials were anxious that British companies with the capabilities to enter the market should do so. But they were also concerned that companies with an interest in the market were aware of the resources which could be tapped to ensure a *successful* entry. These included sources of risk capital in the City, the expertise accumulated in other companies which might be tapped through joint ventures, and information which the OSO was then in the process of gathering concerning oil industry attitudes and work patterns.[31] From a Conservative standpoint, the venture capital shortage of 1973 indicated that British companies required advice about how to present their commercial proposals to City institutions and how to take advantage of expertise already available in the offshore supply industry. The OSO's venture management group was established to provide this type of advice.

The group was composed of officials recruited from outside the Civil Service with backgrounds in areas such as engineering contracting and merchant banking. The venture managers' task was to facilitate the entry of British companies into the offshore market by acting as financial and industrial brokers. Their work had several aspects. They encouraged firms with complementary commercial characteristics to engage in joint ventures. They introduced prospective suppliers to the relevant oil company purchasing managers. They assisted companies in seeking financial assistance for commercial projects either from government or from private sources. And finally, they provided marketing advice to British suppliers.[32]

The work of venture managers and their impact upon UK industrial engagement in the offshore market is discussed in the next chapter. However, there are several points concerning their work which should be stressed at this stage. In the first place, the venture management function was relatively innovative in that it required civil servants to abandon their conventional role as impartial arbitrators and become 'initiators' within the industrial arena. For this new task, they needed the skills of the merchant banker and, to a lesser degree, of the entrepreneur. Secondly, this innovative function was introduced by a Conservative Government which in so doing further extended direct government involvement in industrial affairs, especially at the level of the firm. Nevertheless, there were limits to the Conservative commitment to venture management. For example, during most of the Conservative period in office there were only two venture managers on the OSO's staff, and these two were unable to obtain any Industry Act assistance for their clients (see Table 5.2).

During the first year of the OSO's operation a few other modest initiatives were taken with the object of lending greater coherence to government offshore policy as a whole. The impetus for these new initiatives came largely from the IMEG Report.

The first of these initiatives concerned training. Late in the spring of 1973 the OSO organised an inter-departmental committee to study training, and this committee produced a report in August of that year.[33] The inter-departmental report, which was essentially a detailed assessment of the IMEG training recommendations, put forward a number of proposals, all of which were adopted over the following two years. The proposals included the establishment of a Drilling Training Centre in Scotland to train oil rig drilling crews,[34] the financing by the University Grants Committee of a number of postgraduate and 'post-experience' courses in petroleum engineering and geology, and finally improvements to diver training and safety programmes.[35] As recommended in the IMEG Report, the Department of Employment agreed to assume overall responsibility for co-ordinating training programmes for the offshore supply industry, a task which later fell to the Training Services Agency when it was created in 1974.[36]

In research and development policy the OSO's role was initially quite limited, although its responsibilities in this area expanded substantially after mid 1974. In 1973 the SMTRB set up a sub-committee on offshore oil and gas technology. The members of this committee recognised that much of the Board's work would be of direct interest to the OSO,[37] and, consequently, by the autumn of the same year the SMTRB and the OSO had established a joint working party chaired by Gibson to work out a long-term R and D strategy for the offshore supply industry.[38] Despite these initiatives, however, the OSO's involvement in the Board's work remained quite limited during 1973. Indeed, Gibson did not become a member of the SMTRB until early 1974.

These latter initiatives, however, pale in comparison with other events. Even in the first year of the OSO's operations developments in the economy at large led to an expansion of the OSO's activities in directions far removed from those originally envisaged in the IMEG Report. The first development to have a major influence on policy was the growth in market demand for oil production platforms during 1973. The size and number of the oil fields discovered by the end of 1972 had encouraged a number of civil engineering consortia to put forward design proposals for what looked like a substantial, and potentially highly profitable, market. Most of these proposals involved the building of the newly popular concrete platform design which the Norwegians had so successfully pioneered, and as such, the proposals required coastal construction sites with deep harbour channels.[39] As it turned out, most of the sites with these characteristics were located on the west coast of Scotland in areas of profound natural beauty. The locations identified by the contractors for platform building sites pleased neither the local Highland tourist industry nor the national conservation organisations. The result was open conflict between conservationists and the platform contractors.

The OSO had become involved early in 1973 in encouraging contractors with the appropriate design and contracting capabilities to come forward with proposals for platform building yards. This was done in order to ensure that British industry garnered as many of the orders as possible, not only because of the sheer magnitude of the work involved (and the consequent benefits to the balance of payments and employment), but also because if the principal platform contractors were located in Britain the opportunities for British firms to obtain contracts for the supply of the ancillary equipment needed to complete the platforms would be greatly increased.[40] The OSO became much more involved in this problem when the first proposals for the construction of a concrete platform site at Drumbuie in north-west Scotland encountered considerable local opposition and the Secretary of State for Scotland was obliged to set up a public inquiry on the merits of the proposal.[41]

The Government became concerned that difficulties raised at the public inquiry could seriously delay the start of work on the platform sites, and might result in British firms losing valuable orders. Consequently, the OSO decided to participate in the public inquiry on behalf of the contractors. In supporting the contractors, it stressed the importance of the sites to the national North Sea effort. However, the OSO's role went further than this; in anticipation of possible further objections by protest groups at the inquiry, OSO officials met with the two companies seeking to build on the Drumbuie site, and persuaded them to combine their plans so that the environmental impact of the projects would be reduced and

the strength of their application would be consequently increased.[42]
A senior official at the DTI described the OSO's role in getting the
two companies together in the following way:

> It is fair to say, I think, that it was partly at least due to their
> discussions with us that they probably came together, because
> their attitude to begin with – and an understandable one, I
> suppose – was to say: 'Surely the Government must realise this is
> terribly important and they must give approval for these sites?
> We cannot understand why it is so difficult.' We obviously
> explained to them it was not an easy decision for a Government to
> take. There were perfectly legitimate arguments on both sides of
> the case, and I think we made it clear to them it would be rather
> surprising if the Government were to allow a complete free-for-all
> and litter these sites all over the place without any regard to
> environmental considerations whatever. As a result of their
> discussions with us, they came to the conclusion that instead of
> two of them having applications in for the same site, and one of
> them for another site as well, that it was likely they would be more
> successful if the two of them threw in their lot together as far as the
> site is concerned.[43]

OSO interest in the Drumbuie inquiry continued into 1974, and
gave rise to close links between the OSO and the Scottish Office
over matters of land use planning and the location of platform
sites.[44] This latter development was also significant in that it
involved the OSO in a number of further proposals for platform sites
throughout 1974. As a result, the OSO was given a major role in the
new Labour Government's platform sites policy late in that year.

Another development which contributed to the growth of the
OSO (although in this case, in an indirect way) was the general
increase in the interest expressed by British companies in the
offshore market during 1973. Both in the serious daily press and in
the trade press there was a marked increase in the discussion of the
commercial opportunities for British industry in the North Sea
market.[45] This was partly as a result of the 'fall-out' from the
publication of the IMEG Report in January 1973, and partly
because several of the development programmes for the larger oil
fields (Beryl, Forties, Brent, etc.) were well under way by mid 1973.
The orders placed with UK industry as a result of these development programmes were of great interest to British firms, especially

engineering firms anxious for work. This new interest by industry led to greater pressure on OSO services such as venture management and market research. During 1973 very little in the way of Industry Act assistance was given out by the OSO,[46] but the demand from industry for financial assistance was growing, particularly to meet increased competition from foreign suppliers who could take advantage of cheap export credit finance provided by their home governments. The difficulty facing UK suppliers at this time was that shipments they made to the North Sea oil fields, while outside UK territory, were not landed in a foreign country. Thus, British firms could not qualify for Export Credit Guarantee Department (ECGD) assistance in financing their deliveries, and hence were not as cost-competitive as their foreign rivals.[47] This situation was complicated by the fact that foreign suppliers could send equipment to the UK via a bonded warehouse for later delivery to the oil fields without liability to tariff, which made their prices even more competitive. In response to this problem in November 1973 the Government announced an Offshore Supplies Interest Relief Grant Scheme to be funded under Section 8 of the 1972 Industry Act.[48] The scheme, which was administered by the OSO, paid grants towards the costs of borrowing money in the UK commercial market, and effectively cut the annual rate of interest for money borrowed to finance North Sea purchases by about 3 per cent, thus bringing the UK domestic commercial rate into line with the cheaper export credits rate available to foreign suppliers.

In addition, two political events in 1973 had a very substantial impact upon the OSO's role within the framework of North Sea developments. The first of these was the 1973 Arab–Israeli war, and the second, the 1973–4 national coal miners' strike.

The 1973 Arab–Israeli war and the resulting OPEC boycotts and oil price rises had a deep impact on the Government's North Sea development policies. The dramatic increase in the price of Middle East crude with its implications for the UK balance of payments and security of oil supplies made the Government even more determined to accelerate the pace of oil development.[49] This new urgency concerning timetabling for North Sea oil production had a direct effect on the OSO's policy of industrial encouragement, for in the words of the minister in charge, 'the objective of the encouragement of British industry came a poor second to the speedy recovery of the oil'.[50] In particular, the oil crisis had an impact on the OSO's fledgling venture management role because the

Treasury became anxious that Section 8 financial assistance given out by venture managers be allocated to projects which would speed the recovery of oil. As the provision of financial assistance to British firms to establish new capability in the offshore market to compete with foreign firms seldom materially altered speed of development, it was difficult to obtain Treasury approval for such assistance. This was particularly true at the end of 1973 when the international recession was beginning, and there was a good deal of spare capacity internationally in the offshore supply field.[51] In addition, of course, the new emphasis on speed of development (which alone generated many practical problems)[52] made it very difficult for the OSO to persuade oil companies to purchase British goods and services because the switch from established to British suppliers might delay field developments, especially in cases where new or inexperienced suppliers were involved.

Despite the negative impact of the oil crisis on the OSO's venture management policy, the Government's concern with development timetables also meant that the OSO began to play a larger part in ensuring that British suppliers made deliveries on time and that as many obstructions to the delivery of offshore supplies as possible were removed. These new functions, later grouped under the title 'monitoring', received added impetus from the 1973 miners' strike and the subsequent decision by the Conservative Government to declare an emergency which restricted the operation of factories to three days a week so that power station coal stocks could be conserved. In order to prevent the 'three-day week' from holding up the North Sea development timetable unduly, the Government decided to exempt offshore supply contractors from the work restrictions, and assigned the OSO the task of granting the necessary exemption certificates to the 2000 or so firms engaged in North Sea supply work.[53] This exercise gave the OSO an opportunity to learn the details of the supply relationships within the industry and to gain an understanding of the types of problems which were causing delays in the delivery of supplies to North Sea contractors. It also set the stage for a further expansion of the OSO's activities in the field of 'monitoring' when the Labour Government came to power a few months later.

Finally, the twin fuel crises encouraged the Conservative Government to give the energy question a more important place in government policy-making. The result was the creation of a Department of Energy under a Secretary of State (in this case, Lord

Carrington) in January 1974. The new department was very much a policy-oriented ministry. As such, it took over from the DTI the co-ordination of energy policy, responsibility for all North Sea oil and gas matters, and the supervision of the nationalised energy industries (the Central Electricity Generating Board and area boards, the British Gas Corporation, the UK Atomic Energy Authority, and the National Coal Board). The Department of Energy was effectively a resurrection of the old Ministry of Power which had been merged with the Ministry of Technology in 1969.[54] While the twin fuel crises were not the only developments which contributed to the creation of the new department (for example, the growth in the political importance of North Sea oil and gas and the increasing complexity of energy policy would probably have eventually spawned a new department of state), they certainly served to accelerate the process.

When the Department of Energy was created, Lord Carrington insisted, and the Cabinet agreed, that the OSO should be taken out of the DTI's Industrial Development Executive and placed within the Department of Energy in order to ensure that energy policy emerged as a coherent whole, including the industrial side of oil field development. This relocation of administrative responsibility for the North Sea lent a new level of importance to the OSO's work, especially to the energy aspects of its activities. The transfer also increased the OSO's importance as a policy-making unit, for it was no longer simply another industrial sponsorship division within a huge conglomerate department but one of the Department of Energy's principal instruments in its efforts to influence the development of the North Sea and ensure that British industry played its full part in that development. Nevertheless, the new arrangements presented a number of difficulties for the OSO. The OSO had responsibility for the offshore supply industry and direct access to policy-making on the energy side, but it was now separated from DTI (later, the Department of Industry) and was, therefore, cut off from much of the policy-making process with regard to industry. On the operational side, the OSO was still required to use the DTI's industrial assistance machinery, and disputes frequently developed between the two departments over the manner in which OSO applied assistance procedures to the offshore supply industry (see the next chapter). In addition, the new arrangements placed the OSO in a difficult position with respect to the SMTRB and the development of an R and D strategy for the industry. After January

1974, the SMTRB became the only research requirements board with allegiance to two departments (Energy and DTI). This only intensified the above-mentioned split in the Board between shipping and marine technology. Thus, disputes within the Board relating to OSO activities could be amplified by differences of opinion between divisions in the two departments.

In conclusion, what is remarkable about the policies pursued by the Conservative Government during 1973 and early 1974 is that they laid the foundations for a substantially interventionist policy on the part of the incoming Labour Government. All of the significant functions which the OSO had by the end of 1976 were either the direct product of Conservative policies (e.g. auditing, venture management) or were extensions of functions introduced by the Conservative Government (e.g. monitoring, platform sites planning). However, the progress of intervention in 1973 and early 1974 was by no means fully coherent. Indeed, by the end of 1973 a significant dichotomy was apparent in the Government's offshore policy. The main thrusts of the Heath administration's initial attempts to establish an offshore supplies policy had been to promote changes in the purchasing patterns of the oil companies and, secondarily, to provide a measure of technical and financial assistance to British firms wishing to enter the offshore market. Yet the OPEC price rises later in 1973 necessitated an acceleration in North Sea development timetables with the result that offshore supplies policy began to favour rapid oil field exploitation over the ordered development of a domestic offshore industrial capability.

THE LABOUR GOVERNMENT'S OFFSHORE SUPPLIES POLICY, 1974–5

When the Wilson Government came to office in February 1974, its principal North Sea interests were participation and taxation.[55] The commitment to public ownership and a new taxation regime for the North Sea had formed a prominent part of Labour's election campaign platform, and after the election most of the Department of Energy's efforts were taken up with these important issues. In contrast, the offshore supplies issue received little overt attention from the new administration. The Government's White Paper on

UK offshore oil and gas policy published in July 1974 made no mention of the offshore supply industry or of the Government's approach to its future development.[56]

Despite this lack of formal recognition of the offshore supplies issue, the Government did embark on a number of administrative changes and an important legislative initiative which had an impact on the offshore supply industry. The first of these changes came in early April 1974, when Eric Varley, the new Energy Secretary, announced in the House of Commons that there would be an increase in the OSO's staffing complement from 60 to 180 and that the OSO's headquarters would be transferred from London to Glasgow so that it might be closer to the industries supplying goods and services to the offshore market.[57] The details of the OSO's expansion and relocation were given later in a speech by Dr Gavin Strang, the Parliamentary Under-Secretary of State for Energy, at the OSO's Glasgow offices in July. According to Dr Strang the staffing increase would have no dramatic effects upon the OSO's ratio of administrators to professional staff (then about three to one). Strang also stated that the increased staff levels were to be accompanied by a change in the OSO's organisational stracture. Dr Strang announced the creation of two additional OSO branches, one concerned with market research and research and development, and the second with representational and liaison work with other government departments. Furthermore, the venture management group was to be expanded, and the OSO's senior management increased with the addition of a Deputy Director-General. Alan Blackshaw, the man appointed to fill the new senior post, was a civil servant from the Energy Department's Overseas Oil Policy Division who had just returned from secondment in the City with the Charterhouse Group.[58]

There was some ambiguity about the purpose of the OSO's expansion. In his announcement to the House of Commons, Eric Varley mentioned that one of the principal reasons for the changes was the need to overcome the slippage which had occurred in North Sea development timetables.[59] At the same time he claimed that 'It is now our intention that the Offshore Supplies Office, which was set up in 1973, should ensure that British Industry is given full opportunities to supply and equip offshore operations'.[60]

The OSO's industrial development role, as distinct from its role as an expeditor of North Sea offshore supply deliveries, was also stressed by Dr Strang in his Glasgow speech:

This Government attaches the highest importance to the creation of a major British offshore supplies industry. We do not yet possess such a capability. Its creation is, for me, a matter of top priority. And that is why we decided that OSO must be dramatically strengthened.[61]

It may have been that the Government was anxious for the OSO to assume a 'progress-chasing' function in the field of offshore supplies without, however, relinquishing its primary responsibility for encouraging the development of the offshore supply industry. In any event, it is clear that Labour ministers were concerned that the desire for rapid oil development in the North Sea which manifested itself towards the end of the previous Conservative Administration should not dominate policy-making in the offshore supplies field. According to one minister,

Let me put it this way: the OSO was set up to maximise the capability of British industry and there was Peter Walker's original statement which I read on numerous occasions. That was the main object of the exercise. . . . *There should be no misunderstanding that that is the OSO's main objective.* I think what happened was following the oil crisis, the sharp increase in oil prices and the sudden and highly publicised switch in the Government's thinking – in that they became much, much more concerned to get the oil out as quickly as possible, and Lord Carrington, I think, used the phrase of wartime operation – people began to forget what OSO's over-riding objective was. One of the things I have been anxious to do and we all have been anxious to do in this expansion and relocation of the headquarters of the OSO is to get back to the basics and get down on paper once again what are the objectives of OSO and how best do we deploy manpower in OSO to achieve these objectives.[62]

Thus, Labour ministers initially placed a substantial emphasis upon enhancing British capability in the offshore market. However, like their Conservative predecessors, Labour politicians found that they could not postpone the consideration of problems connected with the pace of North Sea development for any great length of time. This is apparent in the nature of two decisions which the Labour Government made in mid 1974. The first of these was the decision to set up a monitoring group within the OSO to check on a variety of

delivery problems which the offshore supply industry had encountered. The second was to create a Platform Sites Directorate
within the OSO to supervise the Government's platform sites
policies. While both decisions eventually enhanced government
contacts with British suppliers and allowed officials to exercise a
greater degree of leverage in attempting to ensure that British firms
did not lose supply contracts unnecessarily, they were primarily
intended to give the OSO an ability to influence the pace of
development in the North Sea.

As indicated earlier, the monitoring function emerged from the
experience of the 'three-day week', especially its adverse effects
upon the pace of oil field development. The monitoring group
within the OSO was located in the same branch (OSO 4) as the
auditing group, and was established to ensure that British firms
supplying goods and services to the North Sea market were not late
in meeting their delivery deadlines. This work involved both
intelligence-gathering to inform ministers of potential delays in the
delivery of supplies and liaison with individual firms in the industry
to overcome bottle-necks in deliveries. The latter part of the
monitoring function was designed to provide whatever assistance or
pressure OSO could muster from the government machine in an
effort to avoid delays.[63] Monitoring is treated in detail in the next
chapter, but even from this brief description it is clear that the
monitoring function was an unusual addition to the range of policy
instruments at the OSO's disposal. In particular, the emergence of
monitoring signified that in the interest of accelerating the pace of
North Sea development the Government was prepared to undertake a deeper involvement in the day-to-day operations of a
multitude of diverse firms.

During the summer of 1974, the Government was also preoccupied with platform construction sites. As a result of the
prolonged inquiry which, in fact, stopped the development of the
joint Drumbuie construction site the Government issued a policy
statement in August 1974 indicating its intention to nationalise a
number of coastal sites in Scotland for the purpose of establishing
platform construction yards. The Government planned to lease
these sites to contractors on the condition that when the work was
completed the contractors would be responsible for returning the
sites to their original state.[64] This proposal eventually led to
legislation (the Offshore Petroleum Development (Scotland) Act)
which became effective in March 1975. The OSO's initial involve-

ment in the Drumbuie inquiry meant that it was the natural organisation to administer the legislation, and consequently, a Platform Sites Directorate was set up within the OSO. The staff of the new directorate consisted of officials from both the Department of Energy and the Scottish Office. They were given responsibility for all aspects of the Government's platform sites development policy, including the supervision of site construction, environmental impact, land use planning, and other technical matters involved in the choice of suitable sites. Soon after the Directorate was formed it participated in taking over two platform building sites, in supervising the construction on site and in leasing the sites to platform contractors. Officials within the Directorate also administered the financial assistance which contractors received in order to ease the transfer of operations to the new sites. Thus, like monitoring, the platform sites policy involved the Labour Government in substantial intervention in another sector of the offshore supply industry for the purpose of accelerating the pace of offshore oil field development.[65]

However, not all government policy at this time centred upon development timetables. The sizeable increase in OSO manpower also led to an expansion in the auditing of oil company purchases, a greater capacity to carry out publicity and promotional work, and a more elaborate market research and R and D policy capability. Government interest in industrial encouragement was also apparent both in the greater number of new projects undertaken by the venture management group and in the higher level of financial assistance given to industry after mid 1974 (see Chapter 5). This emphasis on industrial encouragement accords well, of course, with traditional Labour approaches to industrial policy, in particular a willingness to use the capabilities of government to influence the growth and direction of industry. Offshore policies were particularly attractive to Labour because the offshore supply industry promised to augment the industrial benefits of North Sea oil to the economy as a whole. The industry could also play a part in revitalising the economies of regions which traditionally have high levels of unemployment and where Labour obtains much of its political support, namely the North East of England and West Central Scotland.[66] The Labour Cabinet was particularly anxious that its offshore policies should be seen to be bringing benefit to Scotland in order to counter Scottish National Party claims that industries located in Scotland were not likely to profit fully from

Labour's North Sea oil policies. With an election in the offing (eventually called for October 1974), the relocation of the OSO's headquarters from London to Glasgow and the emphasis placed upon industrial encouragement constituted 'good electoral politics'. Labour politicians were hoping that by stressing industrial spin-offs from the North Sea, especially those which could accrue to strongly Labour Clydeside, they might stem any significant increase in SNP support.

Yet the Government's electoral concerns do not fully explain the Labour interest in encouraging the development of the offshore supply industry. For example, throughout 1974, the Government was under increasing pressure to aid the industry as a result of growing press interest both in the commercial opportunities available to UK industry in the offshore market and in the difficulties some British firms were encountering in trying to take advantage of these opportunities.[67] This media interest reflected a higher level of concern for the development of the offshore supply industry in many commercial and political circles throughout Britain. Another manifestation of this higher level of concern was the decision of the House of Commons Select Committee on Science and Technology to undertake an investigation of the problems of the industry. The investigation began in November 1973 and carried over into the new session of Parliament during the first half of 1974. The Committee produced its report on the industry in July 1974, and, in view of its assessment of government policies relating to industrial assistance, it deserves some comment at this point.

THE REPORT OF THE SELECT COMMITTEE ON SCIENCE AND TECHNOLOGY

The Select Committee held hearings and received evidence from civil servants and ministers, oil company executives, trade associations, research organisations, journalists and executives of engineering companies from October 1973 to July 1974.[68] The Committee's report,[69] which appeared on 25 July 1974, did not limit itself to a discussion of the technological and research and development aspects of government policy as was normally the case with the work of this Committee, but instead dealt with the Government's offshore supply policy in general.[70]

The report reviewed the state of the offshore supply industry, and its conclusions concerning the offshore market and British industry were very similar to those contained in the IMEG Report a year and a half earlier. Committee members were especially disappointed in the failure of British firms to become involved in the development of subsea completion systems (at that time these seemed to have great potential, given the great depths encountered in the North Sea) and the absence of a British presence in such potentially profitable areas as pipe-line laying and offshore construction work (i.e. installing platforms and modules). On the whole, the Committee seemed to favour the *type* of policy initiatives which Government had taken to assist the industry, but they had criticisms to make of specific government attempts to come to terms with the problems of the industry. The Committee's evaluation of a number of aspects of the work of the OSO was typical of this criticism. The committee members approved of the initiative which OSO represented, but they also believed that the Government should provide the OSO with even greater resources than it had at that time. In the Committee's own words:

> We do not minimise the importance of OSO's work. Our view is rather that the scope and size of the Office do not match the scale of its task. The OSO seems to have been tacked on to the existing structure rather than made the focal point for the implementation of Government policy in offshore operation. The impression given by the evidence is that Ministers and Departments have so far been unwilling to make the restructuring of Departments which the establishment of the more powerful Board recommended by the IMEG Report would have involved. We welcome the more constructive approach shown in the evidence of the Parliamentary Secretary which seemed to indicate that the Office was now likely to become much more significant than merely a section of the Industrial Development Executive.
>
> *We are convinced that the functions of the Offshore Supplies Office are essential, but that even with the planned expansion the OSO will be too small and under financed for the job it has to do.*[71]

Criticisms were also levelled at the Government's Offshore Supplies Interest Relief Grant Scheme. The Committee felt that the scheme was too limited to be of substantial assistance, and recommended that offshore deliveries qualify for ECGD credits.[72]

Turning to its normal area of interest, the Select Committee also found faults in the 1973–4 institutional framework for government research and development and the level of financial support which the Government was giving to research projects for marine technology.[73] It recommended that the Government divide the SMTRB into two boards, a Ship Technology Board and a Marine Technology Board. In addition, the Committee felt that the budget for the Marine Technology Board should be expanded beyond what was then being allocated to marine projects under the existing SMTRB.[74] Members particularly wished to see more attention given to the problems the offshore supply industry had in launching large-scale development programmes. Their impression was that under existing arrangements British firms encountered difficulty in obtaining significant government financial support.[75] The Committee consequently called on the Government to become more actively involved in backing high-risk, large-scale projects involving technological developments. It also stressed that R and D policy should be more commercially oriented, whatever structures the Government eventually chose to supervise marine research and development. In the Committee's words,

> We must avoid, too, the mistake of assuming that a re-organisation of Government R and D in marine technology will solve the basic problem, which is to develop policies which will ensure effective industrial participation in offshore enterprise. It is essential to closely relate R and D to the industry it is meant to serve, and to recognise that if the fundamental industrial structure is unsound a massive increase in R and D, however superbly managed, will not make any great difference, at least in the short to medium term.[76]

Finally, the Committee addressed itself to the question of whether or not an overall government policy towards ocean-based industries was feasible. During the Committee's hearings many of the trade associations which presented evidence, as well as some of the industrial companies, had argued for the creation of a national ocean industries policy with an agency to co-ordinate and develop a national strategy for research and industrial development. While the Committee felt unable to put forward such a proposal without further intensive study,[77] it did criticise the proliferation of departmental responsibilities for North Sea matters, and stressed benefits that could be obtained in rationalising departmental responsibilities more effectively. Members cited the case of one industrial research association that was forced to deal with fifteen different divisions within six departments, all of which had an interest in marine affairs. Another witness claimed that "in the diving field alone, there are about four separate Government Departments, all interested in diving, all going their own sweet ways".[78]

The interesting point about the Select Committee's Report is that its criticisms were directed, not at any fundamental misdirection in the Government's policy, but at the need for even greater levels of state intervention in the affairs of the offshore supply industry. It therefore served to reinforce the legitimacy of many of the initiatives which both the Conservatives and Labour had taken in the offshore supply field.

The Government's response to the Select Committee's Report was slow in emerging. A little less than a year after the Select Committee Report was published, the Government released its observations on the report's recommendations in a Command Paper.[79] The Government basically rejected most of the Committee's proposals for increases in the OSO's staff and budget and for the replacement of the Offshore Supplies Interest Relief Scheme by ECGD credits, claiming that the recent expansion of the OSO and the administration of the Interest Relief Scheme met current demands from the industry. It did, however, agree with the Select Committee on the need for a restructuring of the administration of research and development assistance directed towards the offshore supply industry. In the same Command Paper the Government announced the establishment of a new Offshore Energy Technology Board (OETB). The OETB was to take over responsibility for the Department of Energy's offshore oil and gas R and D programme.[80] The new board, in common with the other Requirements Boards, was to be made up of official representatives of government and industry, but in this instance the industry representatives were to be drawn exclusively from offshore supply companies and the oil industry. In order to maintain some co-ordination between the new OETB and the SMTRB the Government decided to institute a number of cross-appointments between the two boards. Significantly, the Government did not establish a board for marine technology in general. Instead, it opted for a board whose responsibilities were limited to technology applied to offshore oil and gas work. Marine technology was thus left within the SMTRB orbit. What the change did ensure was that in future the SMTRB would not have to cater to the needs of two different departments of state.

Why the Government's response to the Select Committee's Report was delayed is unclear, but it may have been due to the length of time required to negotiate the splitting-off of the OETB from the SMTRB and the fact that, during the latter half of 1974, the OSO, and the Department, were concerned with other matters, such as the platform sites policy, Petroleum Revenue Tax, participation and so on. As in the case of the transfer of the OSO to the Department of Energy in early 1974, the Department of Industry was opposed to the involvement of the Energy Department in industrially based research and development policy, and fought the proposal through the Whitehall machine so that eventually the dispute had to be resolved by the Prime Minister.[81]

THE STRUCTURE OF THE OFFSHORE SUPPLIES OFFICE, 1975–6

By the middle of 1975 the structure of the OSO and the complexion of government policy instruments for the offshore supply industry had more or less stabilised.[82] However, during 1975 there were extensive changes in other aspects of government policy towards the North Sea: for example, the establishment of the British National Oil Corporation, the implementation of the participation policy, and the enactment of legislation concerning a Petroleum Revenue Tax. In addition, under the new Petroleum and Submarine Pipelines Act, the Department of Energy was given extensive powers to control the development of oil fields and the operators' development plans and to regulate the production and disposal of petroleum and natural gas. Thus, by 1974–5 the Government had consolidated its position on a number of other policy fronts. Overall, its influence over the pattern of development in the North Sea had substantially increased.

In mid 1975 a much-expanded OSO was implementing offshore supplies policy. The OSO had grown from the small group of about forty staff in mid 1973 to over 150 staff by mid 1975. It had also acquired an elaborate organisational structure divided into seven branches (see Fig. 4.3). In 1975 and 1976, the OSO consisted of a

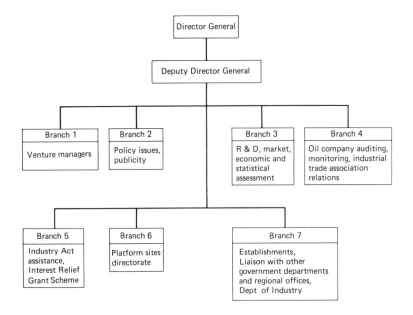

FIGURE 4.3   OSO organisation, 1975–6

Source: 'Offshore Supplies Office Organisation Chart', 19 Nov 1975 (mimeo.).
Used with the permission of the Controller of Her Majesty's Stationery Office.

policy branch, an engineering and industrial affairs branch (com-
bining the auditing and monitoring functions), an R and D and
market assessment branch, a venture management branch and,
finally, the platform sites directorate. Outside the OSO itself, the
Government had established the OETB for offshore R and D policy
development.

By 1975–6 the OSO had also ensured that it would not be isolated
from either energy or industrial policy-making by setting up a series
of inter-departmental links. Apart from its close contacts with the
Energy Department's Petroleum Production Division for technical
advice concerning oil company development plans, the OSO had
also established a working relationship with the Department of
Industry's regional offices. Local officers in these offices handle
representational work for the OSO and assist firms in making
preliminary inquiries regarding assistance and other services. On
the research and development side, the OSO has direct links with
both the OETB and the SMTRB through the Director-General,

who sits as a full member on each board. Finally, there are close ties with the Scottish Office concerning land use and infrastructural questions stemming from the OSO's involvement in the platform sites issue. Thus, not only did the OSO become larger and more complex during its first years, but its unique position as an arm of both energy and industrial policy has also resulted in substantial inter-departmental contact and co-operation. However, as will become apparent in the next chapter, progress in this direction has not always been smooth.

CONCLUSIONS

The previous chapter indicated the importance of the IMEG Report in the development of offshore supply policy, both as a means for civil servants to place the offshore supply industry's future on to the policy-making agenda and as a device to concretise policy options. From the evidence presented in this chapter it is clear that the report also had a part in guiding the development of policy instruments in the offshore supplies field after its publication in January 1973, most notably in the areas of auditing, training and research and development. Yet the IMEG Report was not a blueprint for offshore intervention, and most of its impact was limited to the first year of government involvement with the offshore supply industry. From the beginning, the Conservative Government was not loath to modify the proposals contained in the report to suit Conservative ideological predilections about the appropriate role of government in the affairs of industry. More importantly, after mid 1973, developments in the larger economic arena, such as the OPEC price rises, the 1973–4 miners' strike and the 1973–4 growth in the offshore market came to shape the offshore policies of both the Conservative and Labour Governments.

The relative importance of the forces influencing the progress of intervention in the offshore supplies field is apparent when one compares the policies of the Heath and Wilson administrations. Significantly, it was a Conservative government, and one originally opposed to virtually any form of industrial intervention, which undertook the more novel initiatives in the area of offshore supplies (i.e. the creation of the OSO, the introduction of a venture management function and the auditing of oil company supply purchases). Labour simply extended and amplified these and other initiatives which the Conservatives introduced. Clearly, the similarities in approach between the two regimes cannot be explained on ideological grounds. However, the similarities become comprehensible if due weight is given to the influence of large-scale developments of an economic and political nature upon policy. Both administrations confronted like sets of economic contingencies in the North Sea (e.g. the rising price of imported oil and its impact upon the balance of payments), and responded in like ways. This is particularly apparent, for example, in Labour's failure to reverse the set of offshore priorities which had emerged in the latter months of the Heath administration. Labour ministers may have disliked the emphasis which the Conservatives had placed on rapid exploitation, and may have wished to give more weight to industrial encouragement *per se*. Nevertheless, like their predecessors, these ministers could not ignore the high price which had to be paid for energy after 1973, and in the event, 'speed of development' was almost as central to Labour offshore policy as it was to offshore policy under the Conservatives.

It is in this context, as well, that the impact of the IMEG Report upon offshore policy becomes comprehensible. The work of the civil servants and consultants who participated in preparing the report served to highlight a 'crisis' in the field of offshore supplies. British industry had simply failed to respond in a massive or coherent way to the opportunities of the offshore market. Obviously, this failure did not have the political immediacy of, for example, the Rolls Royce collapse. Yet the importance of North Sea oil to the general health of the economy, and the balance of payments crisis which threatened to ensue if most of the products and services required in the North Sea were imported, meant that even a Conservative government could not afford to remain complacent about the problems of the offshore supply industry (although on occasion action was only taken in the face of direct economic pressures, as in the case of the introduction of venture management). From this followed the Heath administration's willingness to implement a number of the IMEG Report's recommendations. At the same time, however, the IMEG Report did not foresee all of the developments in the 1970s which would be of relevance to the future of the offshore supply industry. Thus, as economic circumstances changed, the influence of the report upon the course of offshore intervention declined.

In summary, then, changing economic circumstances in the

North Sea arena as a whole seem to have been dominant in the determination of the progress of offshore intervention, with the result that Conservative and Labour approaches have in large measure converged in this area of policy-making and the offshore strategy contained in the IMEG Report has declined in importance over time. Yet this is not to deny that there are secondary forces which had a part in dictating the detailed nature of offshore intervention. In particular, ideological considerations seem to explain what one might call differences in 'style' between the Labour and Conservative offshore policies.

As mentioned earlier, the Heath administration was responsible for the introduction of most of the policy instruments which would characterise the OSO in 1976. However, this does not imply that the Conservative Government was fully committed to wholesale intervention in the offshore field. In the first place, the Conservatives were enthusiastic about 'indirect' methods of improving the British stake in the offshore market, such as the auditing procedure. As is evident from Chapter 8, there is no doubt that auditing consitutes a significant departure in the history of government–industry relations, but initially the Conservative Government simply intended to use auditing as a means of preventing 'non-markct' considerations from lessening the opportunities for British firms in the North Sea. Once the latter had been removed, Conservative ministers seem to have expected that the market would allow British companies to obtain the share of the market they deserved.

Secondly, although the Heath Government was responsible for introducing venture managers into the OSO in an attempt to give *direct* encouragement to the development of a domestic offshore capability, during most of the Conservative period in office the venture managers were few in number, and they were unable to obtain any funds under the Industry Act for their clients (see Table 5.2). Thus, the Conservative Government was administratively innovative, but in some instances, notably those involving industrial sponsorship, it was not prepared to provide the staff and financial resources necessary to make these innovations a prominent aspect of government policy. Conservative ministers seem to have retained a lingering belief that government action should be limited to exhortation and traditional forms of financial assistance (e.g. R and D aid).

The Labour Government's approach to the offshore supply industry resembled that of the Conservative Government in many respects. For example, even Labour's innovations in the areas of monitoring and platform sites policy were firmly based on foundations laid by the previous Conservative administration. Where the differences seem to lie is in the willingness of the Labour Government to make use of sizeable amounts of public money to implement industrial policies and in a Labour tendency to have less faith in the ability of industry to function in market conditions once 'non-market' influences have been 'eliminated' by government. Thus, Labour enlarged the amounts of financial assistance for both R and D and industrial investment available to the offshore supply industry. It also expanded the OSO's staff complement in 1974. This expansion was in large part based upon the Labour belief that the offshore supply industry required more direct encouragement than had been provided by the Conservatives, particularly in the last months of that administration; it implied a rejection of the Conservative reluctance to put a premium on industrial assistance. As noted earlier, Labour's policies were also strongly influenced by the 'speed of development' issue. Nonetheless, Labour continued to view the OSO as more than a device to accelerate oil field development while the Conservatives latterly did not. In summary, then, the Conservatives relied principally upon 'market corrections' in the conduct of offshore policy, but Labour also tended to favour increased levels of assistance to domestic industry in the belief that certain forms of industrial restructuring were important in order to achieve greater levels of British participation in the offshore market.[83]

Thus, the traditional ideological stances of both parties appear to have had some bearing upon the 'style' of offshore intervention. On the one hand, the auditing function and a lack of vigour in implementing venture management reflect a Conservative reliance upon market ideology and a distaste for overt industrial assistance, respectively. On the other hand, Labour 'largesse' in the offshore supply field is in keeping with traditional Labour beliefs to the effect that economic 'crises' are structural rather than transitory aberrations in an otherwise stable market system. Regardless of these differences, however, both governments in their respective ways substantially enlarged government involvement in the affairs of the offshore supply industry.

5 Intervention in Operation

INTRODUCTION

As indicated in the previous chapter, the orientation and character of intervention in the offshore supply industry were primarily conditioned by developments in the economy at large impinging upon government. At the same time, neither the Conservatives nor Labour operated from a *tabula rasa* in responding to the exigencies of the North Sea market and the offshore supply industry. In some instances both governments relied heavily upon established or orthodox practice within the Civil Service in developing offshore policy instruments. In other circumstances, they abandoned established practice. However, even the most unorthodox departures constitute novel applications of familiar and, for the party in power, politically acceptable role models. Under the Conservatives, for example, the City's reluctance to finance offshore supply projects was addressed by transposing the activities of the merchant banker into the Civil Service, and the result was venture management. Later, Conservatives and Labour found common political ground in promoting the role of the 'evaluative engineer' within the Civil Service. The policy instrument which emerged has been labelled 'monitoring'.

Whether a policy instrument is orthodox or unorthodox, intervention involves a fundamental tension between the specific demands which originally prompted government action and the limitations of the models and methods adopted in response to those demands. The present chapter examines the implementation of many of the policy instruments introduced in Chapter 4, with the purpose of clarifying both the degree to which demands and policy formats have been congruent and the direction which governments have taken in favouring certain types of unorthodox instruments over orthodox ones. For purposes of exposition the instruments under discussion have been categorised. The Interest Relief Grant Scheme, R and D, market assessment, publicity, general exhortation and, finally, export credits and export policy fall under the heading of orthodox instruments. The Platform Sites Directorate, venture management and monitoring are classified as unorthodox given the history of government – industry relations in Britain.[1] The audit function, which is also unorthodox, is dealt with in Chapter 8. This division does not imply, however, that innovation is confined to the unorthodox category. As the following pages demonstrate, while the OSO's orthodox instruments may not involve institutional innovation nor encompass new subject areas of policy concern, their implementation has frequently given rise to a number of unusual issues and problems.

ORTHODOX POLICY INSTRUMENTS

The Offshore Supplies Interest Relief Grant Scheme (IRGS)

The IRGS was established late in 1973 in order to provide a counterweight to the export assistance schemes which Britain's overseas trading rivals were operating at the time. It was designed to overcome the problem presented by the fact that British firms could not obtain export credit grants for the North Sea. I have discussed some of the aspects of the operation of the scheme in the previous chapter, and here I intend to examine the broader implications of the implementation of the scheme.

The most striking aspect of the implementation of the IRGS was the way its application came to be limited to specific types of firms. When the scheme was originally announced the Government intended that both suppliers and purchasers of offshore supply equipment would be able to apply for assistance under the terms of the scheme.[2] However, upon implementation, civil servants in consultation with ministers decided that only purchasers of offshore equipment should receive government aid, which in this case meant the oil companies. Departmental officials adopted this position for a number of reasons connected with the administration of the scheme. In the first place, officials were concerned that the flow of paperwork would be unmanageable if a large number of suppliers (and there are many in any offshore development project) applied simultaneously for a grant. Consequently, applications to the scheme are accepted only from oil companies, and the grants are offset against the interest paid on sums borrowed for oil field development. According to officials, this arrangement has the added advantage that because the oil multinationals borrow very large sums of money for financing a single project they are able to negotiate more favourable interest terms than a group of suppliers seeking a large number of small loans. Hence, if an interest rate reduction scheme is operated through the oil companies, the grants are utilised more effectively, and the Government is, therefore, able to have more impact with its limited funds.[3]

The application procedures for obtaining IRGS finance are complex. Oil company executives register contracts which they plan to place in Britain with OSO officials. These registered contracts are then vetted by OSO audit engineers to ensure that the goods claimed to be British are, in fact, produced in the UK.[4]

As is evident from the figures presented in Tables 5.1, the sums disbursed to the oil companies under the IRGS have been growing year by year despite a decrease in the number of contracts registered annually. This arises from the fact that many of the contracts registered in the scheme are eligible for grants over several years. Officials estimate that the sums paid out in grants should stabilise at about the level seen in the 1977–8 financial year.[5]

TABLE 5.1   Offshore Supplies Interest Relief Grant Scheme, 1973–8

	1973–4	1974–5	1975–6	1976–7	1977–8
Number of contracts registered	0[a]	193	130	144	90
Value of contracts registered (£m.)	0	128	264	N/A[c]	N/A[c]
Grants paid out (£m.)	0	0.044[b]	1.1	5.4	14.7

[a] No grants were paid out during 1973–4, although some contracts were in the process of being registered under the scheme.
[b] The first grants came due only during the last quarter of the 1974–5 financial year.
[c] Information on the value of contracts registered was not provided for these years.

Sources: Industry Act 1972, Annual Report for the following years: 1973–4 (HC 339, Session 1974), 1974–5 (HC 620, Session 1974–5), 1975–6 (HC 619, Session 1975–6), 1976–7 (HC 545, Session 1976–7), and 1977–8 (HC 653, Session 1977–8). Used with the permission of the Controller of Her Majesty's Stationary Office.

Several interesting policy problems have emerged in connection with the development of the IRGS. In the first place, the scheme has put a heavy emphasis on buyer credits. While this is becoming increasingly common in all types of interest relief support schemes, and particularly those of the Export Credit Guarantee Department (ECGD), *total* reliance on buyer credits as in the case of the OSO scheme constitutes an unusual departure in this field. The structure of the offshore industry (very few buyers, but many sellers) has forced government officials to reconsider the impact of assistance schemes, and the result has been rather remarkable: a policy instrument initially designed to assist domestic industry to become more price competitive has evolved into a device to subsidise the oil companies' borrowing costs for those capital projects which involve the use of British suppliers. Obviously, even if the interest relief grants were paid directly to British suppliers, rather than to the oil companies, the latter would still benefit from the grants through the resulting decrease in the prices charged by their British suppliers. However, the policy as it exists at present does deny domestic firms the benefits of lower borrowing costs in financing their North Sea orders, which, in periods of high interest rates, could have the beneficial effect of reducing a firm's overall borrowing requirements, thereby helping it to cut costs in general.[6] Ironically, the structure of the offshore supply industry, and the Government's desire to reduce its administrative workload, have combined to create a situation in which the oil companies, rather than domestic firms, have become the focus for the application of assistance programmes in support of the domestic industry.

The implementation of the IRGS has also led to administrative difficulties because the scheme's legality has been challenged by the EEC Commission on the grounds that it violates the Treaty of Rome in giving an unfair competitive advantage to British firms when they bid against companies from other Community countries for North Sea contracts.[7] The Commission originally agreed to the IRGS in 1973. However, the Commission's Competition Department subsequently received a number of complaints about the scheme, and decided to recommend to the Commissioners that the British Government either drop the scheme or modify it in such a way that companies from all Community countries can obtain funding. The Government objected to the Commission's position on this issue, and provided it with evidence to the effect that other member countries also supply export credits to their manufacturers for items to be exported to the UK Continental Shelf. Hence, the Government argued, the complaints of member countries about

British practices were not justified.[8] Recently (summer of 1978), the Commission has taken up this issue yet again in response to a further set of complaints from EEC member countries. While the question is likely to reoccur,[9] its solution is difficult as it raises a number of issues about the appropriateness of the industrial subsidies of other Community countries, many of which are covert and contravene the spirit of the Treaty of Rome. However, these altercations with the EEC Commission do illustrate the difficulties which Britain's membership in the Common Market present for government efforts to assist domestically based industry. British industrial assistance policies must now take into account both the possibility of violating Community regulations pertaining to free trade and the political acceptability of such programmes to member governments. Moreover, the international complexion of a market like that for the North Sea makes it more difficult for a national government to pursue programmes to assist domestic industry without incurring 'political' penalties from other Community members.

While it is difficult to specify the exact effect of the IRGS upon the purchasing preferences of the oil companies and, hence, upon the competitive position of British offshore suppliers, it has probably been modest. Officials estimate that the Chevron consortium developing the Ninian Field, which will be by far the largest beneficiary of the scheme, could receive up to £43 million in grants over an eight-year period.[10] This is a substantial sum of money, and does, indeed, represent about 3 per cent of the approximately £1.2 thousand million which the Chevron consortium will spend on field development in the same period.[11] Yet, the IRGS incentive to purchase British products pales by comparison with the other considerations which the oil companies take into account in allocating their huge development budgets over a limited time span. Thus, for example, the ability of a British supplier to meet delivery deadlines and to meet oil company specifications are much greater determinants of an oil company's propensity to purchase British goods than a 3 per cent price advantage.[12] At most, the IRGS could be said to add modest reinforcement to the other administrative procedures which the OSO employs to encourage the oil companies to purchase British goods and services,[13] but it can hardly have more than a marginal influence on total purchases. Nevertheless, it is important to note that the IRGS is but one of a number of policy instruments which OSO uses in the offshore field.

As set out initially, the IRGS concept in many ways derived from a very traditional approach to the administration of financial assistance in that it did not discriminate between buyers and sellers in an industry, and it invoked uniform criteria of assessment for all applicants. However, upon implementation, the scheme has, in fact, discriminated between types of firms on the basis of their commercial roles (customer and supplier), and limited the population of firms which stand any chance of obtaining funds. The original IRGS concept also reflected traditional approaches to government industrial assistance in other ways. For example, one of the original aims of the scheme was to overcome non-market barriers to competition (i.e. the supply of export credits by foreign governments to their national firms involved in the North Sea market) through the provision of a subsidy. Here again, however, a traditional objective was abandoned upon implementation. The scheme places the subsidy with the oil companies, which, in turn, use it to defray general borrowing costs for the British component of developing projects. Even if OSO staff bring this subsidy to the attention of the oil companies when the prices of British suppliers are discussed, it is impossible to review the price level of every item purchased by the oil companies from British industry. For the scheme to have its full effect, oil company purchasing managers would have to be reminded at all times that the quoted price of a British product will eventually be reduced by about 3 per cent. However, this reduction does not show up on the tender documents submitted by a British firm bidding for a contract. The initial effect of the scheme is, therefore, less than might have been the case if the subsidy were given directly to the supplier, who might then translate it into a simple reduction in his selling price to the oil company. The separation which exists between the provision of funds and the pricing of British products encourages the oil companies to regard IRGS simply as a subsidy for their borrowing costs.

Marketing Assessment and Advice

One of the more orthodox of the OSO's assistance policies is the provision of advice to industry. Significantly, of all of the OSO's services to industry, the provision of advice about the offshore market and information concerning how to gain entry seem to be the ones that are most in demand from industry.[14] Ironically, the

OSO is not specifically organised to provide such advice to firms. None of its branches have been given this particular responsibility (see Fig. 4.3). The OSO's R and D branch does do some market assessment work; it conducts studies on 'trends' in the offshore market to pinpoint areas where UK industry might be able to make an impression in the market. These assessments are used by that branch and by the venture managers in order to evaluate the commercial viability of projects presented to the OSO. Yet the OSO does not make these assessments directly available to firms, although no doubt the results from such surveys influence the type of advice firms receive from officials. In addition, the OSO's Engineering Branch provides firms with information concerning the availability of component suppliers. Most advice given to firms takes the form of information about how to approach the oil companies and about who firms should see within the oil companies and their major contractors. The OSO publishes various guides and pamphlets on the offshore market, but beyond this, the advice it gives to firms is limited. Companies wishing for information about overseas markets are often referred to the British Overseas Trade Board for general assessments about export markets.[15]

Research and Development

The evolution of the Government's offshore R and D policy instruments has been discussed in the previous chapter. By the end of 1975 R and D policy *vis-à-vis* the offshore supply industry was entirely the responsibility of the OSO's R and D branch which sponsors projects through the Offshore Energy Technology Board (OETB). The OETB is the central policy advisory body for offshore R and D, and assists the Government in determining the general principles and direction of offshore R and D. It receives research proposals concerning safety or geological and reservoir engineering research from the Petroleum Engineering Division of the Department of Energy and other proposals concerning research of commercial interest to the UK offshore supply industry from the OSO[16] (see Fig. 5.1.).

The research policy of the OETB is based, like that of the SMTRB, on a contractor principle. Organisations are employed to conduct research on the basis of a contract written by the Board on behalf of the Secretary of State which sets out research objectives and timetables in a commercial manner, regardless of whether the

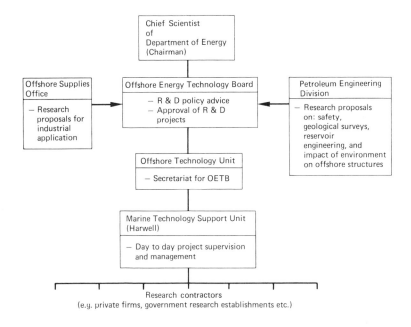

FIGURE 5.1   The Department of Energy's research and development structure
                for the offshore supply industry, 1977

Used with the permission of the Controller of Her Majesty's Stationery Office.

body conducting the research is a government agency or a private
firm. The Board's approach to R and D funding[17] is to assist only
applied research that is also financially supported by viable British
firms capable of carrying the research work into direct commercial
application. In meeting this objective, the Board attempts, as far as
possible, to place research contracts with the firm or combination of
firms that will ultimately make use of the research results.[18]

    The offshore R and D infrastructure is a product of the specific
characteristics of the offshore supply industry and of the contractual
relationships which exist between it and the oil companies. As there
are few customers (i.e. the oil companies) for the products of the
offshore supply industry, ministers decided that the requirements
board structure for R and D in use in the Department of Industry
(where the boards are representative of both customers and

suppliers) would not be suitable in the case of the offshore supply industry. The needs of the oil companies are highly specialised, and the number of customers very limited. Hence, the Department thought it best to concentrate upon involving the oil companies in the new OETB at senior management level rather than attempt to guarantee a representative cross-section of industry and official representatives, as was the case with the industrial requirements boards. By involving executives who had direct senior responsibility for the procurement activities of the oil companies in the activities of the Board, the Department hoped to ensure that the oil companies would come to accept as many of the commercially applicable research projects approved by the Board as possible. The Department also believed that this type of arrangement would be the most effective means to ensure that research would be translated into commercially viable products.[19] At the same time, the Government could not give executive responsibility for R and D in the offshore supply industry to a body dominated by the oil companies for obvious political reasons. Hence, the OETB did not take the form of an executive requirements board. Rather, it emerged as an advisory body chaired by the Department of Energy's Chief Scientist.[20] In theory, the Board is charged with advising the Chief Scientist concerning whether or not specific research projects should be funded. In practice, it is usually the deciding authority, although its decisions are subject to appeal by the proposing organisation (for example, OSO) to the Department's Chief Scientist.[21]

In 1976 the OETB had fifteen members: three were senior executives from companies acting as operators in the North Sea, (BP, Shell and British Gas Corporation), and one was the head of the oil companies' representative organisation. The remaining three industry representatives on the Board consisted of a senior manager of a company with interests in a North Sea consortium searching for oil, a representative from a large engineering firm which was acting as a project manager for several oil companies in the North Sea, and finally a representative from a firm involved in offshore shipping work.[22] Thus, the Board's membership clearly reflected a concern for the customers' needs. By contrast, the domestic offshore supply industry was virtually unrepresented on the Board. Evidently, the Government was seeking a special relationship with a set of large, multinational purchasing companies in its efforts to establish an R and D policy for a domestic industry.

Such an organisational arrangement for R and D promotion seems to be unprecedented.

OETB policy towards support for domestic R and D projects is highly selective in that it actively discriminates between firms in the domestic industry on the basis of their commercial viability and capacity to use and market research results.[23] In the Board's words,

> In the present financial climate we are unlikely ever to have the resources available to support more than a fraction of the necessary activity. *Our approach should always be to complement known commercial initiatives in a highly selective fashion.* This obliges us to make technological and commercial judgements simultaneously and forces an intimate collaboration between research and the main work of the OSO.[24]

By adopting the approach outlined above the Board has acted, at least in part, in the capacity of a risk-taking institution. It serves both to interpret the needs of the oil companies to domestic industry and to select those suppliers with the technical and commercial characteristics necessary to fulfil the oil companies' requirements.

As indicated above, within the OETB the needs of the oil companies in the R and D field have first priority. Nevertheless, the domestic industry is not without representation within government. Both the OSO and the Petroleum Engineering Division of the Department of Energy seek out firms with promising proposals, and 'champion' their projects before the OETB.

Thus, in total, government, and specifically various divisions of the Department of Energy, provides a forum in which, in theory, the technical and commercial needs of the oil companies are reconciled with the plans and capabilities of domestic industry. However, over the long term the effect of these arrangements may not be so simple. The negotiations which proceed between the OETB on the one hand and domestic firms, together with their championing divisions, on the other *may* be of substantial commercial benefit to the domestic industry in the short and medium term. Yet the OETB, dominated as it is by oil company representatives, retains discretion in recommending the award of R and D contracts, and in the long term this may limit domestic industrial benefits, in part because of the conservative approach which the large oil companies traditionally adopt in assessing new technology.[25] The enormous capital outlays involved in oil field development have meant that the oil companies are often reluctant to experiment with unproven technologies and unproven suppliers. Thus, the OETB's structure might hinder the development of the domestic industry in the future if radical new approaches to the industry's problems (e.g. research concerning drilling operations in depths greater than 200 metres) are required in order for the British offshore industry to remain internationally competitive. In addition, in the consideration of viable research projects oil companies are naturally interested in maintaining a development and supply capability in several locations in order to guarantee themselves a maximum number of competitive and flexible sources of supplies. For this reason they tend to favour the development of UK technical capability in areas which are also under development elsewhere in the world in order to ensure that they are not subject to a monopoly supply situation. Needless to say, this may not, in the long term, be compatible with the Government's general offshore R and D strategy, which is designed to promote a technological lead for British industry that will allow it to penetrate export markets.[26]

The outcome of the Government's offshore R and D policy to date has been difficult to discern. This is due partly to the limited time during which the R and D programme has been in operation (beginning May 1975) and partly to the long lead time required in R and D work for the results of policy and research decisions to become manifest. A number of research projects which have a direct application to the offshore supply industry are currently supported by the OETB. In addition, in mid 1976 the OETB, through OSO, invited a number of research proposals from industry covering a total of twelve product and service areas from tethered buoyant platforms to submersibles development.[27] Furthermore, since the establishment of the OETB, the number of allocations for commercially applicable R and D expenditure has been rising rapidly, as is evident from the data presented in Figure 5.2. The 1977–8 research budget called for expenditures of about £15 million, although not all of this was directed towards commercially applicable R and D.[28]

Moreover, even if present and future R and D budgets and project allocations were known in detail, it would be difficult to assess the effect of R and D upon the offshore supply industry as a whole. For example, many offshore suppliers are engaged in activities which do not depend upon access to advanced technology. Even those firms which make use of advanced technology can often

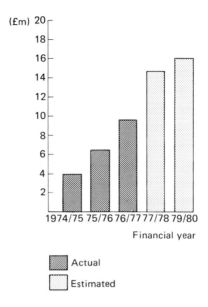

FIGURE 5.2   Offshore Energy Technology Board R & D expenditure (£m.)

Sources: Department of Energy: *Report on Research and Development, 1976–77* (London: HMSO, 1978) p. 8; *Report on Research and Development, 1975–76* (London: HMSO, 1976) p. 32; *Report on Research and Development, 1974–75* (London: HMSO, 1975) p. 29. Also interview with a civil servant at the Department of Energy. HMSO material used with the permission of the Controller of Her Majesty's Stationery Office.

obtain it fairly easily on licence. Indeed, there are only a small number of firms in the industry for whom access to technology ahead of competitors and on an exclusive basis is of substantial commercial importance.[29] These companies are generally in work concerned with the design of offshore structures or with subsea operations (e.g. submersibles, subsea completion systems, other underwater equipment). Thus, government R and D policy is of importance to only a few sections of the offshore supply industry (see Chapter 6). How important the R and D promotion activities of the Government will be to this section, and how important the section is to the prospects of the industry as a whole, remains to be seen.

One point, however, which is reasonably certain is that the effectiveness of offshore R and D policy has suffered as a result of problems associated with the implementation of the programme. Many of these problems centre upon the split within the OETB research budget between commercially applied research and research concerned with other matters such as safety, geological and geophysical questions and reservoir engineering. At present, commercially applied research takes up only a small proportion of the OETB's budget. For example, in 1976–7 only about 15 per cent of a total research budget of £6,368,000 was spent on commercially applied R and D. If one includes basic research on platform design undertaken primarily for safety reasons, but which can be of commercial benefit to platform designers, the figure jumps to, at most, 36 per cent of the total R and D budget.[30]

There is a policy commitment on the part of the OETB and the OSO to divert increasing proportions of the R and D budget to commercially applied research, but there are also considerations which make such a diversion difficult. In the first place, much of the non-commercial research funded by the Board is of a kind which is traditionally conducted by government in the 'national interest' (safety research, research on the geological structure of the North Sea, etc.), and would be unlikely to be undertaken unless funded by the state. Second, according to officials, the number of R and D proposals coming from industry to the OSO has simply not been that large. There have even been occasions when officials have been obliged to urge appropriate firms to submit research proposals which they knew would meet with approval from the Board.[31] Without a high demand for research funds from industry, a dramatic shift in funding patterns within government is difficult to achieve. However, part of the reason for the lack of enthusiasm shown by UK industry for R and D asistance has been the slowness with which government officials sometimes respond to requests for funds.[32] These delays have been disputed by civil servants, and part of the problem may lie in the different views government and business take of the granting procedure. Business executives presenting a research proposal will often want an immediate reply because of the short time scales to which they frequently work. Alternatively, officials will be concerned to examine the proposal thoroughly in order to ensure that public money is properly invested.

A final note should be added about the significance of R and D policy for the character of the state's intervention in the offshore supply industry. As noted previously, the offshore R and D policy discriminates between firms within the market. This is not novel in that discrimination takes place whenever government places a research contract with an individual company. The difference in this instance, however, is that the stated intention of the offshore R and D policy is to ensure that some firms gain a commercial advantage from the research. Some research results obtained with government assistance are released to several firms in the industry. But some are used only by the firm with the research contract on the grounds that this firm is the one most suited to make commercial use of the research results. Thus, government research assistance can enhance the competitive position of a firm within the UK market, and hence give it a commercial advantage over its rivals in the UK.

Exhortation

Exhortation encompasses all of the Government's policy instruments which are designed to encourage firms to enter the offshore market without the use of financial or regulatory inducements. The exhortation devices employed in the offshore supplies policy area have been similar to those used in other types of industrial policy.[33] There have been the usual ministerial speeches concerning the offshore supply market and the potential for British industry, and a number of articles on the opportunities for British industry have been published in various widely circulated government journals such as *Trade and Industry*.[34] In addition, the publication of the IMEG Report in 1973 constitutes what is probably the most significant example of the use of information assembled in the public sector to stimulate interest in the offshore market. Since that time, the OSO has employed a number of other forms of publicity. Officials have distributed information packs to firms, which give details about government services to industry and the nature of the offshore opportunities. The OSO has also sponsored the publication of buyers' guides to the UK offshore supply industry in co-operation with private publishing houses. Furthermore, along with the British Overseas Trade Board (BOTB) and various trade associations, it has assisted in sponsoring offshore supply trade missions abroad and in advertising British capacity at overseas exhibitions. On occasion, the OSO has placed advertisements in the trade press announcing its services to British firms.

Perhaps the most detailed type of exhortation which the OSO employs is undertaken by the network of local representatives operating out of the regional offices of the Department of Industry throughout the country [Scottish Economic Planning Department (SEPD) in Scotland]. The functions of these representatives vary quite markedly depending on the level of offshore supply work in the region and the priorities of the regional office. At the very least, the representatives act as points of contact for local firms with inquiries about the offshore market. The local officers provide firms with information on the state of the market, inform them of the work being done by other firms in the area for the offshore market, and supply them with lists of contacts in the oil companies and their principal contractors. In cases in which R and D assistance is required, in which there are complaints about unfair treatment of firms by oil companies, or in which a new venture is proposed, the representatives make referrals to the appropriate OSO staff in London or Glasgow.[35] In some regions (particularly those with large amounts of offshore work, e.g. the North-East of England) the number of staff working with the offshore supply industry is larger and their activities more specialised. For example, the North East regional office publishes a highly detailed guide for local firms about the state of the market.[36]

According to an official, exhortation has had a considerable effect, to the extent that in some regions, notably the North East and Scottish industrial areas, over-confidence in the industry's prospects 'caused considerable eventual distress'.[37] However, the system does have certain weaknesses. In large part, it relies upon firms to initiate inquiries, and although attempts are made by local officers to 'spread the word' by speaking at business functions and the like, their ability to reach a large number of firms is limited. Also there is some evident unease between the local officers and the OSO, caused by the fact that inter-departmental co-ordination in this area has not always been smooth.[38] Both of these considerations limit the effectiveness of the local officer's work, despite the very obvious advantages they have as a result of their detailed knowledge of local industrial activity and firms' capabilities, knowledge which can be useful both in assessing which firms to interest in the market and which oil companies would be most responsive to direct inquiries from offshore contractors.[39]

Export Credits and Export Policy

A final orthodox policy instrument is the provision of government

export credit facilities to offshore supply companies bidding for
export contracts. The use of this policy instrument assumed
particular importance during the 1975–7 recession in the offshore
supply industry. During this period OSO officials believed that the
crisis might be partially relieved by trying to encourage British firms
to seek export orders and thus compensate for the domestic slump.
In keeping with this new policy emphasis the OSO reinforced its ·
presence at overseas offshore supply exhibitions, and increased its
publicity concerning the benefits of export markets. Officials also
undertook detailed market surveys of potential foreign markets to
determine which UK companies would have the best commercial
opportunities in particular countries. Most of these efforts followed
fairly traditional government practices in other areas of industrial
policy. Yet, as in the case of some of the OSO's other orthodox
initiatives, the attempt to secure further export orders for British
industry resulted in a number of departures from received practice.

A sizeable proportion of the potential export market, and one
which provided British firms with an excellent *entrée* into foreign
markets, consisted of large 'turnkey' contracts[40] for oil field
development. During 1975 the OSO discovered that a number of
British firms had lost major 'turnkey' contracts simply because
several British firms were competing for orders against foreign
consortia which represented the full contracting capacity of each
country involved in the bidding. Consequently, the British competitive effort was fragmented and weakened. The OSO then
approached the leading contracting companies in Britain and
appealed to them to be more selective in seeking business abroad so
that instances of several UK firms competing for the same contract
might be reduced. While the companies were anxious to follow this
procedure, they had no means by which they could collectively
decide which firm should tender for which contract. This function
had to be performed by government. The OSO was willing to take
on this role, but it would do so only if there was clear evidence that
competition between British firms for an overseas contract would
obviously jeopardise the chances of *any* UK firm obtaining the
order.[41] The OSO has now, in fact, intervened in at least one major
project in which there was a clear danger that internal competition
might have caused the loss of a large international contract. In
letting a major contract for a £70 million rig-building yard, the
Soviet Government asked for a single bid from the UK to compete
with bids from other countries. The OSO complied by scrutinising

the potential UK firms for a suitable candidate. It finally decided that the American-based firm, Brown and Root, was the most appropriate contractor, provided that it associated with UK companies in a joint venture. Brown and Root agreed and chose BP and Wimpey as its partners. Brown and Root had collaborated with BP in the design and development of the Forties Field production complex, and had been associated with Wimpey at Nigg Bay. In order to prevent other British firms from bidding, the OSO made it known that the Brown and Root–Wimpey–BP consortium would have preference in gaining access to the line of credit which the Government had negotiated for British–Soviet trade.[42] Thus, by controlling access to export credit finance, in this instance the OSO was able to have a large influence in the way British firms bid for an international contract.

This method of influencing the way major contractors conduct their export business is not novel in the sense that no *new* policy instruments were used, but it does represent a substantial departure in the manner in which the Government chooses to use export credits as a policy tool. In the past, these credits have been used as a non-discriminatory device available to all firms in order to assist them in financing export orders. In this particular instance, an orthodox policy instrument (export credits) was used in an unorthodox way that not only involved the government in discriminating between firms, but also involved it in making commercial judgements about the capabilities of certain firms to win export orders. Officials have been anxious to play down the implications of this latter role. In the words of one senior official: 'We're not going into the business of selecting winners from lame ducks. This is too risky. We will act only when we think a potential British order is at risk.'[43] Despite this reservation, judgements are being made by officials about the commercial potential of different companies, albeit only under limited circumstances.[44] In fairness to officials, it should also be pointed out that while these types of choices are novel within the UK context, practices of this kind have been common for a number years in several European countries, most notably France. It is not altogether unexpected that UK governments should adopt these practices when UK firms start to suffer from a lack of government support in international competition.

UNORTHODOX POLICY INSTRUMENTS

The Platform Sites Directorate

When the Government first decided to take over a number of platform building sites, and then to assist in their development, it was acting on the basis of official forecasts of the likely demand for offshore production platforms of both the steel and concrete type. In 1974 the Energy Department estimated that the demand for production platforms to 1980 was in the range of fifty-five to eighty platforms, with the likely figure closer to the upper end of that range.[45] The Government, in common with most other observers at the time, also estimated that the bulk of new orders from 1974 onwards would be for the newer concrete design. It was therefore assumed that there would be demand for a number of construction sites on the west coast of Scotland, where the geographical conditions were suitable for building concrete platforms.[46] The government estimates, which were made by OSO staff, eventually proved to be overly optimistic.

The estimation of platform orders over a six-year period is indeed a difficult exercise. The number of platforms required per field is often difficult to forecast, due to changes in information about the reservoir characteristics of proven oil fields and improvements in drilling and recovery techniques. In addition, projections for size of field development may change, owing to alterations in internal oil company finances and in the oil market in general. Despite these difficulties, however, there are indications that the Department did not give the platform-order question the thorough attention it deserved.[47] For example, during the period when the Government was framing its platform sites policy (spring of 1974) it had available to it two reports on platform estimates both of which indicated a substantially lower level of projected platform orders. The first was a study carried out for the Scottish Office by the Department of Political Economy at Aberdeen University, published in April 1974. It placed the demand for platforms to 1980 at between forty-five and fifty-five with the likely figure in the *lower* end of that range.[48] The second study was published by the Scottish Council in the same month as the Aberdeen report, and it estimated platform demand to 1980 at between forty-three and sixty-five platforms. It also stressed that the upper limit was unlikely to be reached.[49] Officials claim that there are differences in the assumptions underlying these three estimates,[50] yet for purposes of policy, these alternate assumptions and estimates were not considered in any great detail. Thus, in its August 1974 announcement of the platform sites policy, the Department persisted with its original estimate of fifty-five to eighty platforms. It was not until a year later (July 1975) that the Government officially revised its platform estimates downwards to a likely figure of fifty-three orders to 1980.[51] By that time, it had acquired two platform building sites, and had made a total investment commitment of £23.5 million to them.[52] According to independent estimates in early 1975, the maximum demand for platforms during the peak years of ordering (1977–8) would be a total of eleven platforms, and by then there would be construction capacity for a total of nineteen platforms (eight steel and eleven concrete) in the UK.[53] Despite this predicted surplus in capacity, in July of the same year the Government committed funds for the construction of the second platform building yard at Hunterston. By late 1978, neither of the two government-sponsored yards had obtained a single order to build a production platform.

It is difficult to explain the continued commitment to the platform sites policy long after it had become obvious that the demand for platforms was not going to be sufficient to ensure adequate orders for the government yards. It is possible, despite the North Sea induced growth in industrial activity in Scotland,[54] that the commitment to the platform sites policy after 1974 (and, in particular, to the development at Hunterston) was undertaken as much to show government concern for chronically high unemployment levels on the Clyde as for any other reason. Whatever the explanation, the Government committed itself to a specific forecast of expected demand. There then followed a public ministerial statement of policy based on that forecast. There are also indications that after these two events there was considerable reluctance to abandon a policy initiative based on the forecast, particularly when it had been the justification for bringing forward the Offshore Petroleum Development (Scotland) Act. In addition, according to civil servants, the Government proceeded with the Hunterston site despite a likely over-capacity, partly because officials and ministers expected the yard to win a contract in late 1975 or early 1976 (in fact, none emerged), and partly because the site was close to a pool of skilled labour (in Glasgow) and had industrial potential after platform building had ceased, due to its proximity to a new nuclear power station and a new British Steel development.[55]

The platform sites episode highlights some of the difficulties which officials confront in executing a policy in which commercial judgement is so central. It should first be granted that the offshore market is volatile because of rapidly changing technology and shifting financial conditions. Nevertheless, two independent studies did predict levels of platform demand which were broadly con-firmed by subsequent developments, while the Department of Energy's analysis did not. According to a senior official involved with the preparation of the Department's forecast for platform demand, the figures presented were based on an extensive survey of oil companies and engineering contractors which were asked for their individual estimates of how many platforms their organi-sations would be involved with up to 1980. The individual responses were then aggregated according to their source; this process led to a variety of aggregate figures reflecting the types of industrial firms consulted. Officials reviewed these estimates and chose a range which appeared most probable. Officials seem to have been working on the assumption that by aggregating external opinions on the state of the platform market they could arrive at a viable estimate of demand to 1980. It is likely that the final figures reflected the overly optimistic assessments of the market by oil companies and platform building contractors, assessments which may in part have been influenced by the process of government inquiry. Moreover, it seems that at that time the Department's staff did not have sufficient experience of the market to feel confident in taking an alternative perspective on the demand for platforms. The relative conservatism of the other two studies in their estimates of demand may derive from the analysts having more definite (if not more concrete) beliefs about the state of the offshore market against which to gauge industrial opinion.

The platform sites policy was also weakened by the Government's reluctance to change course after it had become apparent that the initial forecast was inadequate. Undoubtedly, ministers run the risk of political embarrassment in admitting that departmental es-timates may have been faulty. Yet a failure to recognise error and act upon that recognition is a severe handicap in the conduct of an industrial policy, for flexibility in the development and implemen-tation of policy is especially necessary when it is addressed to an industry which is both complex and subject to constant changes in its structure and performance.

Apart from the above difficulties, the implementation of the platform sites policy has involved the OSO and the Department of Energy in a close relationship with the platform building industry. For example, one of the first decisions which the Government made in this area was to choose, in collaboration with the oil companies, seven platform designs which departmental officials believed offered good commercial prospects for orders from the oil companies. The Government then intended to ensure that each of the consortia with an approved design had a suitable site on which to build its platforms.[56] If necessary, the Government knew that it could use its powers under the Offshore Petroleum Development (Scotland) Act to nationalise suitable sites if consortia were unable to find sites where planning permission would be readily given. In fact, the Government did use its powers under the Act to assist in the development of two sites, one at Portavadie on Loch Fyne and the other at Hunterston, west of Glasgow. The Portavadie arrangement involved the OSO in the nationalisation of the site, obtaining planning permission for the site, and hiring the contractors to build the facilities. The site was then to be leased to the platform building contractor, Sea Platform Construction, on that firm's receipt of its first platform order. The total investment by the Government in this case was about £12 million. The acquisition of the second site, at Hunterston, involved a government guarantee of an £11.5 million loan to the contractors (the Andoc Consortium) to purchase land and build site facilities. If the group did not obtain an order, the arrangement was that the Government would assumé the debts the consortium incurred in building the site. If, however, the group did obtain an order, it would be liable for all loans and debts assumed to build the facilities.[57]

The wisdom of making these grants of assistance can be questioned.[58] The decisions certainly did involve the Platform Sites Directorate in substantial supervision of the activities of the platform contractors at both sites. This supervision was intended to ensure that work was carried out to specification and that funds supplied or guaranteed by government were not used to install facilities more properly supplied by the contractors when they did obtain orders. There were, however, expectations that the effort would be worthwhile. The Directorate had specific arrangements with Andoc to the effect that the next platform building order which the group obtained, regardless of its destination, would be built at the Hunterston site.[59] This was despite the fact that Andoc at that time already had platform building facilities in the Netherlands.

The platform sites policy also involved the Directorate in a number of support activities such as the licensing of offshore assembly points where concrete platforms can be 'mated' to their decks and modules,[60] and the commissioning of underwater surveys to determine suitable towing channels for taking the deep-draft concrete platforms out to the North Sea. These operations required the services of marine safety specialists and specialist surveying contractors, and thus obliged the Platform Sites Directorate to take an interest not only in matters concerned with planning and construction, but also in marine affairs. This new responsibility led to the recruitment of further specialist staff. In addition, in keeping with its mandate to minimise the burden of the platform building sites on local infrastructure and the environment, the Directorate proposed the development of a common user facility for all the contractors operating on the west coast (there are two other concrete yards, one at Ardyne and another at Loch Kishorn, both with orders). This operation was intended to lessen the possibility of duplication and waste in platform building capacity.[61] The planning associated with the proposal also meant close collaboration between the Directorate and the contracting companies charged with constructing the facility.

More significant for the implementation of the Directorate's policy than the links it has had to forge with the contractors, however, has been the high degree of inter-departmental co-operation and co-ordination required to carry out the policy. The platform sites policy requires the combination and co-ordination of a number of government functions: land use and environmental planning, financial supervision, civil engineering and marine safety, to name but a few. These functions have required the talents of a varied group of specialists drawn from the Department of Energy, the Scottish Office and several other outside bodies. In addition, as the Directorate was operating in an area that was the administrative concern of two departments (Energy and the Scottish Office), inter-departmental administrative and policy co-ordination has been necessary. Unfortunately, this mix has not been a happy one, and there have been disputes between the two departments over the implementation of the platform sites policy with the result that the co-ordination of arrangements has not been as smooth as it could have been.[62]

Perhaps the most interesting aspect of the whole platform sites policy, however, has been the way in which it has forced the

Government to mediate between the interests of the oil companies and those of the domestic platform contractors. As is evident from the Government's original policy statement of 12 August 1974, the major objective was to speed up the development of the North Sea, first, by ensuring that no bottle-necks developed in the country's capacity to construct production platforms, and second, by ensuring that every competitive design had a British construction yard and contractor so that oil companies would have little excuse for not purchasing their platforms in the UK. Apart from these 'commercial' considerations, of course, officials were concerned that the local environment and infrastructure of western Scotland should not be overtaxed.

The result of the policy was, however, somewhat different from that intended in the original policy statement. In effect, the Government financed the risk factor for two major British consortia in their attempt to enter the platform contracting business, while at the same time subsidising the provision of surplus industrial capacity in the UK to meet short-term demand peaks in the North Sea development programme. Thus, not only did the platform sites policy create benefits for a few potential UK platform builders, it also provided the oil companies with further sources of supply (and subsidised ones at that) from which they could choose a suitable contractor. If the oil companies had had to purchase their platform requirements in the UK without this provision of surplus capacity, high demand would probably have pushed up costs and led to longer lead times for deliveries. Of course, in the normal sequence of events, the oil companies would simply have looked abroad (e.g. to Norway) for alternative contractors to undertake the work, thus relieving bottle-necks in the UK and adding the necessary competition to keep prices down. It is in this sense that the policy imposes some costs on the oil companies by denying them a cause for placing orders abroad and thus limiting their choice of contractors. Hence, while the oil companies benefit from the provision of extra capacity, they do so at some additional cost. Industry in the UK benefits because the 'spin-off' effects of having platforms built in the UK are greater than if orders go abroad. At the national level the balance of payments is improved through the consequent reduction of imports necessary to develop the North Sea oil fields.

However, this policy suffers from a number of major weaknesses. In the first place, despite government pressure, the tendency for the oil companies to purchase production platforms abroad has not been wholly curtailed (see Chapter 8). Second, while domestic industry gains from having its risks underwritten by the Government, and is thus in a position to capitalise immediately on any new flood of orders, if those orders do not materialise, as seems likely, several firms will have been encouraged to divert their energies into markets with few commercial opportunities.[63] On balance, therefore, it seems that the pursuit of the platform sites policy has been of greater benefit to the oil companies than to British industry in that the dependence of British firms on oil company decisions has been reinforced through a misdirected policy.

The failure of the platform sites policy has been due to weaknesses in the manner in which it was formulated. The Department proceeded with a highly speculative investment on the basis of a forecast which proved to be incorrect. This mistake was then compounded by the Government's reluctance to change course when new information had come to light. The result was that an unorthodox policy instrument designed to assist the offshore industry also came to benefit the oil companies through the provision of too much platform building capacity. Had the estimates associated with the decision about whether or not to invest in platform sites been better, the Government might have given less attention to platform building capacity and more to environmental issues and the provision of common user facilities.

Monitoring

The monitoring function in the Government's offshore supplies policy is carried out within the OSO branch which has responsibility for supervising and auditing the oil companies' offshore supply purchases.[64] The monitoring function consists of two basic tasks; first, intelligence-gathering about the progress of North Sea field development so that ministers can be informed well in advance of potential delays in the development programme; and, second, work to ensure that wherever possible the full resources of the government machine are used to attempt to overcome potential delays in the programme and to assist in resolving disputes between contractors and the oil companies. As monitoring has not been the subject of public scrutiny, most of the information in this section comes from interviews with civil servants.

Intelligence-gathering involves officials in building up extensive files on the performance profiles of domestic suppliers (for example, the ability of a firm to meet delivery deadlines). The files are used by monitoring engineers to identify bottle-necks and gaps in the market. They also allow the OSO to rate the commercial performance of individual UK firms supplying the various oil field development projects (particularly the larger firms). This information is helpful if officials wish to check the claims of the oil companies concerning the reliability of specific UK firms when disputes arise about the use of UK suppliers.

The above information-gathering procedure is supplemented by the work of a set of engineers whose primary duty is to work with groups of UK firms supplying particular categories of offshore products to the oil companies. Their role is to attempt to discover through personal contact with company executives and visits to plants the progress being made on existing projects and contracts. In this work the monitoring engineers concern themselves not just with the actual progress on contracts but also with the company's financial position, component and material supply situation and its labour relations record. This information is then used to assess in advance whether a particular company will have problems meeting its delivery commitments.

The second aspect of the monitoring function is that of providing specific assistance to firms with problems meeting delivery deadlines. Most of this work is carried out by the monitoring engineers. The type of assistance which a monitoring engineer can give to a firm depends to a large extent on the nature of the problem and the personal relationship he has with the firm concerned, and is, therefore, usually limited in scope. Sometimes, this assistance will consist of 'moral' pressure by the engineer on delinquent material or component suppliers who are preventing a firm from finishing a contract on time. Frequently, this process involves the official in contacting specific private and nationalised concerns in an effort to accelerate particular deliveries. In addition, wherever delays are due to circumstances over which other government departments may have some control (e.g. planning permission), the monitoring engineers attempt to use the civil service network to overcome these problems.[65] Furthermore, whenever monitoring engineers detect that labour relations difficulties may delay North Sea work they alert the Advisory Conciliation and Arbitration Service (ACAS) and encourage both the company and union officials to seek arbitration before disputes result in work stoppages.

Perhaps the most unusual part of the monitoring engineer's work, however, is the role that he plays in mediating in disputes between contractors and the oil companies. When a UK supplier is accused by an oil company of late delivery, or delivering material that is not to specification, the OSO monitoring engineers often intervene in order to investigate the complaints and to attempt to determine which party is at fault. Sometimes delays in delivery are due to factors beyond the control of UK contractors (e.g. problems of material supply). In addition, at times oil companies impose unrealistic delivery deadlines or specifications on contracts, or mid-contract design changes, all of which can delay a delivery date through no fault of the UK supplier. An independent investigation by OSO officials can often uncover these facts and assist in resolving the dispute. The OSO has embarked on this function in order to ensure that UK suppliers are not unjustly accused of poor performance. Accusations of commercial incompetence, if left unchallenged, may seriously damage the future prospects of UK suppliers. This function has also proved necessary because of the formal relationship which often exists between the oil companies and their engineering contractors, on the one hand, and the supplying firms, on the other. Frequently, a supplier is reluctant to discuss all the reasons for delivery delays with the oil company as they may cause commercial embarrassment to the firm, even though the supplier may not be at fault.[66] In a situation in which neither party can be frank with each other, the OSO's role as an 'honest broker' is often of assistance to both.[67]

Monitoring has not been an easy task. Domestic firms are frequently suspicious of government officials attempting to, in effect, investigate their commercial operations. As a result, it usually takes time to build up a relationship of trust between a firm and a monitoring engineer. In addition, when a company does make the engineer privy to its commercial problems, the engineer is not always able to reciprocate by providing assistance to the firm, due to the limited facilities at his disposal. In these circumstances the success of the policy depends very centrally upon the skills of each individual monitoring engineer and his ability to gain the confidence of the executives of those firms for which he has responsibility.

The relationship which has evolved between the monitoring engineers, domestic firms and the oil companies raises a number of issues. In the first place, the image of the 'honest broker' which monitoring engineers cultivate is not an entirely accurate representation of their activities. In practice, monitoring engineers may act as champions of domestic firms in their disputes with the oil companies. Furthermore, this policy instrument requires officials to maintain very close relationships with individual firms within the domestic industry. Obviously, traditional approaches to industrial policy which emphasise the equality of all actors in the market regardless of their role in the economy, or their importance to government policy objectives, are called into question by these developments.

There are, of course, other areas of industrial policy in which the Government has engaged in monitoring the affairs of individual firms. However, in most of these cases monitoring has been associated with the provision of government financial assistance to firms in financial difficulties. Monitoring has, therefore, usually been directed towards ensuring that firms' financial obligations to the Government are fulfilled. Indeed, in shipbuilding, one of the few other industries in which monitoring seems to have been extensive, monitoring was limited to the firms' financial affairs, and there seems to have been a desire amongst officials to curtail the extent of monitoring for fear that it might lead to even higher levels of government financial commitment to the shipbuilders.[68] This is in direct contrast to the case of offshore monitoring. In this instance, officials have shown no particular reluctance to involve themselves not only in the financial, but also in the commercial affairs of individual firms. This is probably owing to the strategic importance of the offshore supply industry to the fulfilment of oil development timetables. Also in this case, officials have been willing to assume greater involvement with firms because monitoring has not been associated with financial commitment.

Finally, monitoring embodies both a new set of skills and a new 'style' in the conduct of industrial policy. In the first place, intelligence-gathering and the mediation in disputes place a high premium upon technical and commercial expertise. Hence, most of the officials involved in monitoring are engineers, and many of these have industrial experience. In addition, monitoring relies upon the cultivation of highly personal relationships between officials and executives in individual firms. To be effective, a monitoring engineer must gain the trust of his clients, and this is only achieved through a continuous effort to understand the situation of the client and prompt action when difficulties emerge. Taken together, then, the skills and style associated with monitoring indicate that this instrument departs substantially from orthodox patterns within industrial policy, which have emphasised administrative skills and an impersonal or 'arms-length' approach to the relationship between government and firms.

Venture Management

Venture management is another of the more unusual policy instruments developed by the Government in its attempt to encourage British firms to participate in the offshore market. Some of the details of the work of the venture manager have already been discussed in the last chapter. In this section I propose to examine the operation of the venture management policy in greater detail and to discuss its implications for the Government's relations with domestic industry. Like monitoring, the work of the venture management section of the OSO has received little public attention. Hence, most of the information for this section of the chapter has been obtained from interviews conducted with government officials.[69]

The venture management section of the OSO usually operates in the following manner. The venture management group review potential gaps in the offshore supply market, using the OSO's market assessment capability and outside consultants, if necessary. Once a section of the market in which there appears to be a promising opportunity has been isolated the venture manager seeks out UK firms with the appropriate capabilities, and suggests that they seriously consider the market potential. The companies contacted then usually either initiate action themselves to enter the market, or seek further assistance from the venture managers. In general, the policy has been to promote the creation of a British industrial capability in offshore work where the export potential beyond North Sea markets is high. In addition, venture managers tend to concentrate their efforts on firms which could add entirely new industrial capacity to the UK offshore supply effort, rather than on firms whose entry into the market would involve only an adaptation of existing products or services.

Much of the venture managers' work has been of a confidential nature due to the commercial sensitivity of their role, so it is not possible to discuss cases involving specific firms in detail. However, it is known that venture managers have been operating in the following sectors with varying degrees of success: diving services, offshore construction, submersibles, drilling contracting, and offshore maintenance work. Much of this activity consists of a highly specialised form of exhortation in which OSO officials make commercial propositions to companies about market opportunities, and then assist in the follow-through by introducing the companies to likely commercial partners and customers and, if necessary, sources of financing. In a limited number of cases, venture managers have employed administrative devices to prevent key companies in developing sectors from falling under foreign control. For example, venture managers, in conjunction with the Treasury, prevented the takeover by American interests of a promising UK diving company which had a series of new products under development. The ban, which was accomplished through regulations drawn up by the Treasury to prevent the Arabs buying up UK companies of national interest after the OPEC oil price rises in 1973, maintained UK control of a company which could make a contribution to the establishment of an integrated diving capacity in the UK, and hence increase the UK diving industry's competitiveness both in the North Sea market and abroad.[70]

Some of the OSO venture managers' work has involved the provision of public money to firms under Section 8 of the 1972 Industry Act in order to assist in the establishment of new capability in the offshore supply industry. A total of four projects of this type have been supported since the OSO's creation. These have included an interest relief grant of £360,000 to a consortium attempting to establish a rig repair vessel, an additional interest relief grant of £784,000 to a group building a drillingship, a loan of £500,000 to a firm launching a new oil flow metering device, and, finally, a loan of £1,725,000 to a group building two specialised tug–supply vessels.[71] In addition, venture managers have played a part in obtaining financial assistance for Scott Lithgow, the shipbuilders, to build a dynamically positioned drillingship. The assistance for Scott Lithgow came from the Scottish Office and the Department of Industry.

The venture managers confront a number of problems in their work. Most of them have previous experience in merchant banking and engineering contracting, and have been recruited from outside the Civil Service. Their employment background and their rather unorthodox role as entrepreneurs actively seeking out commercial opportunities for companies have led to conflicts between venture managers and other civil servants. These conflicts have arisen because the venture management ethic does not conform with more traditional Civil Service collegial attitudes to such matters as individual decision-making, risk-taking and the type of relationships which are appropriate between government officials and independent firms. To be successful, venture management requires that risks be taken, sometimes involving public money, and often requiring rapid decisions. Needless to say, the emphasis on speed in decision-making, risk-taking and individual initiative is counter not just to the ethic of the Civil Service, but also to a decision-making mode in which policy decisions are committee decisions and are carefully and thoroughly checked and rechecked before being finalised.

This problem is most evident in the granting of financial assistance. Here, the administrative ethic of the Civil Service confronts the demands of effective venture management very openly. The average Section 8 assistance proposal takes anywhere from two to three months to process, providing there are no referrals, or particular problems with the application. Sometimes a decision can take six months or longer to finalise, and the process involves officials from several departments, the Industrial Development Advisory Board, and numerous committees. In all there are about fourteen decision-points in a Section 8 application involving OSO, departmental, inter-departmental and Cabinet committees.[72] The pace is slow, uncertain, and often frustrating both for venture managers and for the businessmen they assist, particularly because those involved in designing the system failed to recognise that certain applications require urgent attention because they are premised upon proposals for joint ventures or specific financing which can lapse very rapidly. In addition, within the OSO context Section 8 assistance is usually administered by the Department of Industry's Industrial Development Unit (IDU), and there were initial difficulties in co-ordinating activities, which further delayed the application process. These difficulties were the result of some early duplication of responsibility between the OSO and the IDU in connection with the preliminary negotiations following each application for Section 8 assistance. The IDU staff, consisting largely of traditionally trained civil servants, and the OSO venture managers, the majority of whom have financial backgrounds, had different approaches to the form negotiations should take, the conditions which client firms should fulfil and the time needed to complete these negotiations. These differences resulted in disputes and this, in turn, not only delayed decisions.

further, but also prompted IDU officials to adopt a less favourable attitude to OSO proposals for financial assistance generally.

The cumulative result of these difficulties has been that the number of Section 8 grants awarded is very low as a proportion of the applications received, and the actual sums of money dispersed have been relatively modest (see Table 5.2). Usually assistance is given either in the form of an interest relief grant or as a loan. Occasionally, the loan agreements will contain a provision whereby the Government takes an equity stake in the company in order to assist in raising the necessary funds for an investment project. In no case have the sums involved been substantial. Indeed, according to an official in charge of granting Section 8 assistance, the money is frequently sliced so thin by the Treasury that it usually has only a limited role to play in the assistance offered by venture managers to firms with investment proposals. While the venture managers themselves prefer to rely on the resources of the private sector to finance projects in which they have an interest, there are occasions when more generous allowances would enable them to structure their assistance more creatively.[73]

TABLE 5.2   Selective assistance applications and grants made under Section 8 of the 1972 Industry Act by venture managers

	1973–4	1974–5	1975–6	Total
Number of applications for assistance processed	3	21	n.a.	24[a]
Number of applications approved	0	3	1	4
Value of assistance[b] (£m.)	0	1.644	1.725	3.369

[a] According to officials the number of initial applications or inquiries was higher than this; these figures represent applications which were at least partially processed.

[b] Represents both grants and loans given under the Act.

Sources: Industry Act 1972, Annual Report for the following years: 1974 (HC 339, Session 1974), 1975 (HC 620, Session 1974–5), and 1976 (HC 619, Session 1975–6). Used with the permission of the Controller of Her Majesty's Stationery Office.

Finally, the venture managers also encounter difficulties in their relationships with industry because of the wariness with which industrial companies approach government. OSO officials note that companies are often reluctant to seek assistance from venture managers, or to follow up initial suggestions from them, for fear that a relationship with government may involve them in a loss of control over their own activities. This latent suspcion of the intention of government policy has often limited the effectiveness of venture management in individual cases. More generally, when it has been articulated (see Chapter 6), such suspicion has contributed to the wide-scale questioning of venture management, and OSO activities in general, within industry.

Despite the confidentiality which surrounds many of the activities of the venture managers, their work has attracted criticism. Industrial executives have noted that most of the projects which the venture managers assist have been concerned with the manufacture of subsidiary equipment or the supply of services rather than with the construction equipment side of the market (e.g. laybarges, crane ships, etc.). This imbalance stems in part from the restricted funds with which the venture managers must work, and in part from the emphasis which the Government has given to speed of development in choosing projects for assistance. Projects in the construction equipment field require higher levels of financing and longer lead times than other types of projects. Hence, venture managers have not been in a position to provide extensive assistance in these cases. The result has been, however, that the British Government has failed to give substantial encouragement to a section of the industry which could potentially have a large impact on the market by providing opportunities for a variety of specialist contractors in the service sector (e.g. the laying of pipelines). In short, then, government assistance has not promoted the development of the UK supply and service industry on lines similar to the US Gulf Coast example. Apart from platform building most large-scale offshore equipment manufacture remains located outside the UK, and, consequently, it has been very difficult to ensure that British firms obtain a good share of the sub-contract and service work resulting from such projects.

Apart from the above criticisms, criticisms, incidentally, which venture managers make of their own work, the other problem with venture management policy is that the projects which have received support and have come to the public's notice have not been conspicuous commerical successes. Of the four projects which have received Section 8 support, one project (Seaforth Marine) was effectively a rescue operation rather than assistance to a new venture, as the funds provided were intended to allow the company to complete the construction of ships it had already ordered. The three remaining projects were genuine new ventures, but of these only one could be considered a commercial success. Of the two remaining cases one was a company manufacturing oil flow meters, which encountered financial problems and went into receivership in November 1976. The other firm proposed the establishment of an oil rig maintenance facility (MOIRA) to the OSO, but it, too, has gone into receivership. The MOIRA venture was unfortunate, as the project seemed promising, and the market was obviously there. However, due to poor management and timing, the venture ran into cash-flow difficulties almost as soon as it started and without the necessary long-term financing it collapsed.[74] Undoubtedly, it is unfair to assess venture management solely on the basis of the record of those companies which have received Section 8 assistance, because to qualify for consideration under this section firms must be able to demonstrate that they have failed to obtain financing in the private sector. Venture managers have assisted many companies with various projects which did not require public finance and which are currently commercially successful. This is particularly true of firms involved in subsea and diving services. Yet the publicity associated with the Section 8 'failures' has certainly been detrimental to the image of venture management and the OSO.

The venture management function represents a departure in the conduct of industrial policy. As noted earlier, it requires the civil servant to adopt the stance of the merchant banker and, occasionally, the entrepreneur in his relations with industry. This is in contradiction to orthodox approaches to the conduct of industrial policy which, even if overtly interventionist in content, primarily stress *responses* to initiatives from industry. The closest comparison to venture management is probably the work of the Industrial Reorganisation Corporation (IRC), although the scale of venture management is obviously much smaller. Significantly, this is a comparison that venture managers themselves draw when describing their work. The difference is, of course, that the venture managers' activities are located within a government department and not within a quasi-independent non-departmental body such as the IRC. The implications of this for the level and quality of government contacts with industry are obvious. Under such circumstances it is possible for the Government's policy commitments to be interpreted directly into technical and financial negotiations at the level of the industry and the firm. Such direct translation of policy into commercial negotiations also permits officials to develop greater insight into the relationship between the Government's policy objectives and the structure of industry. They are, therefore, encouraged to discriminate between different types of firms in the pursuance of policy, although at present the basis on which they do so may not be much more refined than the criteria which apply in merchant banking.

CONCLUSIONS

A number of the policy instruments discussed in this chapter are unorthodox in that they represent significant departures from received means of implementing industrial policy. Others are orthodox in design, but have been transformed along unorthodox lines upon implementation. For example, the Offshore Interest Relief Grant Scheme is an orthodox financial assistance programme in the administrative sense. Yet, it is also unusual in fostering the development of a special relationship between a specific set of companies (the oil companies) and the Government. Thus, a programme, which in its inception was meant to treat firms impartially, in the end limited applicants to only one type of company, and thereby distinguished between various actors within the economy. Alternatively, unorthodox policy instruments like venture management and monitoring departed from established practices from the outset. These policy instruments are noteworthy both because they distinguish between industries and because they bring officials into very direct relations with firms.

Much of the impetus for the use of unorthodox policy instruments, and for the transformation of orthodox policy instruments along unorthodox lines, derives from the necessity for the Government to come to terms with the interests of both domestic industry and multinational industry simultaneously and within the same policy context. The result has been that novelty in the implementation of offshore policy is associated with increasing levels of discrimination between domestic and multinational industry, although this discrimination has not always been consistent. Unorthodox policy instruments like monitoring and venture management seem, on balance, to benefit domestic industry in its commercial relations with the oil companies. Similarly, the platform sites policy might also have favoured domestic industry over the oil companies had it not been for the difficulties which officials encountered in forecasting platform demand. However, while the more orthodox policy instruments (e.g. R and D, the IRGS, export credits) tend increasingly to distinguish between multinational and domestic industry, they are still rooted in non-discriminatory traditions, and, hence, their effects are much more ambiguous. For example, the IRGS, which was intended as a means of assisting domestic firms to overcome certain pricing difficulties, probably benefits the oil companies more than domestic industry. In Research and Development, the Department of Energy clearly distinguishes between the interests of domestic industry and the interests of the oil companies in choosing the membership of the OETB, but it is unclear which industry receives the weight of benefit from R and D policy. Nonetheless, the fact that an obvious attempt has been made by government to distinguish between the oil companies and domestic industry, even in implementing orthodox instruments, is significant in the light of reluctance in the past to favour the interests of domestic industry over those of multinational firms.[75]

The tendency to distinguish between multinational and domestic industry has been reinforced in the operation of some of the policy instruments by a further tendency to distinguish between firms in a particular industry. The Government has attempted to enhance the effectiveness of policies in support of the domestic offshore industry by selecting firms which are commercially strong and innovative for assistance. This type of selectivity is particularly apparent in the operation of certain unorthodox policy instruments like venture management. But it is also latent in the operation of certain nominally orthodox policy instruments, for example, R and D and export policy. In addition, unorthodox instruments, whether they discriminate between firms or not, bring officials into month-to-month and at times day-to-day contact with companies. This seems to have arisen in two ways: first, the civil servant is required to learn about and sometimes assist in firms' financial and commercial affairs. Second, the ethic associated with the use of unorthodox instruments often requires that the civil servant must actively seek out candidates for observation and assistance.

All of the policy instruments, but particularly those which involve officials in direct contact with firms, have had an effect upon civil service commitments and organisation. In the first place, most of the policy instruments discussed above have placed a heavy premium on the technical and commercial capabilities of the officials using them. It is not surprising, therefore, that most of the branches of the OSO are staffed by officials with technical or commercial training as opposed to traditional administrative skills. For example, the venture managers are drawn from the engineering contracting industry and banking; most of the staff involved in monitoring are engineers, many with private-industry backgrounds; the R and D branch is staffed by scientists, engineers, economists and statisticians; and the Platform Sites Directorate has a complement of local government planners and marine specialists. Second, the increased number of professional and technical staff in positions normally filled by administrators can and has led to conflicts within industrial policy areas of the Civil Service. These conflicts tend to centre upon the question of who should have policy responsibility for programmes, an administrator or a specialist. There is an important decision to be made here, because the choice of persons assigned to policy positions can influence not just the technical and commercial capabilities of policy-makers but also the types of policies which are likely to be emphasised and the perspectives which will be taken with regard to policy proposals.

Finally, as we have seen in venture management, and to a more limited extent in both monitoring and platform sites policy, the implementation of certain OSO policy instruments has involved risk-taking and more individual initiative and responsibility than is generally the case in the operation of government policies. The traditional attitudes and codes of conduct within the Civil Service which stress collective decision-making and the preference for 'no decision or action' to a potential failure, or wrong decision, can impede the effective implementation of unorthodox policies designed to assist commercial enterprises. This may mean that certain parts of the Civil Service will in the future employ 'business methods' more openly in their attempts to cater to the needs of specific industries and specific firms within the economy. Alternatively, collective norms of control within the Civil Service may be reasserted as policy concerns change or as those who implement unorthodox policies accummulate their 'failures'.

6 The Offshore Supply Industry and Government

Much of the preceding discussion has focused upon government and, in particular, the policy instruments which it has employed in the offshore sector. However, it should be emphasised once again that offshore intervention has been a response to economic change within the North Sea arena and is therefore conditioned, in part, by the circumstances associated with change. For example, when British firms failed to respond to the opportunities of the offshore market, and, later, when some suppliers faced difficulties in meeting development timetables, the intervention which followed was conditioned in part by the structure of the offshore supply industry to which it was addressed. The present chapter explores the influence of this structure upon offshore intervention, and then turns to a consideration of the impact of intervention upon the industry.

THE STRUCTURE OF THE INDUSTRY AND ITS CONSEQUENCES FOR INTERVENTION

As noted in Chapter 2, the offshore supply industry has a rather unusual structure. Unlike most industries, it is defined by its end-market, rather than by the nature of the industrial process involved, or its end-product, as is the case with most industries (e.g. steel, cars). The result is that the character of the firms involved in the industry varies considerably, and their interests are often far from identical. For example, there are firms which are primarily involved in providing services, and others which are primarily involved in supplying manufactured products; there are some firms which are heavily engaged in the market, and others which are only marginally engaged in it. Even among firms heavily involved – for example, in providing manufactured goods for the market – there may be substantial differences in size, organisation and the types of problems which arise (e.g. the differences between a firm building concrete platforms and one producing specialist control equipment to regulate oil production).

The structure of the offshore supply industry has had several implications for offshore intervention. For example, the heterogeneous nature of the industry has encouraged the development of a wide variety of policy instruments tailored to the specific circumstances of particular groups of firms. In addition, policy implementation has been highly selective owing to the differences which exist between firms in the industry. More importantly, the lack of cohesion within the industry has meant that government relations with offshore suppliers have been more direct than relations with other types of firms in other instances of industrial intervention.

The last point requires elaboration. Generally, government–industry relations are conducted through a single large trade association representing the majority of firms in the industry. The association acts as a bridge between government and the industry, assisting the passage of information back and forth between the two. For government an arrangement of this kind has several advantages. It simplifies the process of disseminating the particulars of government policies, and, in addition, allows government to 'sound out' the industry's reaction to policy proposals. In some cases, the Government accords the trade association 'consultative status', which means that the latter is consulted as a matter of course during the development of policies of interest to the industry. Under these circumstances, the association can act as a bargaining agent, offering the industry's compliance in one area for government concessions in another.

However, in the case of the offshore supply industry, no single trade association has emerged which could fulfil the above-mentioned functions. Trade associations tend to be organised on the basis of a shared product rather than a shared market. Thus, when a variety of firms expanded into the offshore field there was little incentive for establishing a unified association for the offshore supply industry. Instead, product-based trade associations in other industries expanded their activities to encompass the new offshore interests of their members. For example, the valve-makers' trade association caters to the offshore valve-makers, the process plant association to offshore suppliers involved in process plant, and so on. The result is that there are now about sixteen trade associations with a significant offshore constituency (including the British Marine

Equipment Council, the Electrical Contractors Association, the British Valve Manufacturers Association, and the Process Plant Association).[1] There are, in addition, a number of small informal groupings of companies, such as the Module Contractors Association, which attempt to co-ordinate the activities of highly specialised firms that do not readily fit into a traditional trade association. This situation contrasts markedly with that prevailing in the oil industry where a single association, the United Kingdom Offshore Operators Association (UKOOA), represents the interests of *all* the oil companies acting as operators in the North Sea.

Among the sixteen trade associations with members in the offshore supply industry a few have displayed a greater interest in the offshore market than the others. Perhaps the most notable of these are the Association of British Oceanic Industries (ABOI) and the Council of British Manufacturers of Petroleum and Process Equipment (CBMPE). However, the total number of firms with an interest in the offshore market in both of these associations is only a small percentage of the number of firms in the offshore supply industry as a whole (about 10 per cent if the industry is assumed to have 2000 firms; 1976 figures).[2]

Since 1973 there have been a number of attempts by both the industry and the OSO to establish a unified offshore trade association.[3] As of yet, none of these attempts has met with any success. This is partly due to the number of associations which would have to be merged in order to create such an organisation. An additional, and probably more important, consideration is that some of the industry's major trade associations have been reluctant to join in the venture. This is often because they would find it difficult to justify such a merger to the majority of their members who are not in the offshore market. Moreover, by participating in such a merger, they would be admitting their own inability to service the interests of those of their members in the offshore supply market.

One result of this situation has been that the Government has not been able or, it would seem, willing to establish close contacts with any of the trade associations in the industry. OSO officials attend the occasional trade association meeting to make a speech, and material about the Government's policies and programmes in the offshore field is distributed routinely to trade association officers. In addition, an OSO official is an *ex officio* member of the Offshore Committee of the CBMPE, and officials frequently attend meetings of the Module Contractors Association, but these two more or less formal arrangements represent the only regular contacts between the OSO and the trade associations.

In the absence of a traditional trade association structure within the offshore supply industry, government has been obliged to seek direct contacts with firms in order to implement its policies. Monitoring and the platform sites policy are examples of this. However, this approach has a number of risks associated with it. First and foremost, the firms which are the object of government policy frequently have few outlets for effectively expressing their grievances to ministers and officials. Compounded over several groups of firms this situation can result in a large amount of unfocussed animosity towards government. In addition, government may not be particularly effective in dispelling such animosity because it does not have the means of communicating with the industry as a whole. Nevertheless, these risks must be dealt with, for there is evidence to suggest that the Government may increasingly confront industries without developed trade association structures during the course of industrial intervention.

For example, in 1978 the British Government introduced plans to establish a British-controlled manufacturing facility for microprocessor 'chips' under the aegis of the National Enterprise Board in conjunction with a substantial programme of Department of Industry assistance to encourage firms to adopt microprocessor technology in their products.[4] This intervention was prompted by the failure of British firms to gain a significant stake in the semiconductor market in the face of competition within the UK market from highly aggressive American and Japanese electronics firms.[5] However, for present purposes, it is significant because the problems of persuading British firms to use microprocessors are similar to those of encouraging the development of the offshore supply industry. In both instances, the group of firms of interest to the Government is defined by a market rather than a product, although in the microprocessor case ministers and officials are concerned with customers rather than suppliers. Like offshore suppliers, microprocessor customers consist of a wide range of firms engaged both in manufacturing and the provision of services. Government has acted in this area because it regards microprocessor technology to be crucial to future British industrial competitiveness, but, once again, it confronts an assembly of diverse firms without a developed set of shared interests, and thus without an institutional structure through which ministers and officials can communicate with firms. Moreover, such situations are likely to become more common as successive industrial 'crises' emphasise the ways in which apparently divergent firms are interrelated.

THE IMPACT OF INTERVENTION UPON THE OFFSHORE SUPPLY INDUSTRY

Given the above outline of the influence which the structure of the offshore supply industry has had upon offshore intervention, we may now turn to consider how the industry has been affected by government actions. What follows is an assessment of the way in which suppliers have responded to government initiatives, based upon a survey of firms in the industry carried out in 1976.

The survey in question took the form of a postal questionnaire directed to the senior executives within firms who had responsibility for major policy decisions and who were likely to have had contact with government officials. In order to gain access to the names of firms in the industry and the appropriate executives the assistance was sought of a major trade association with a wide variety of members in most parts of the offshore supply industry. The questionnaire was circulated to these members under the auspices of the association. This arrangement had the advantage that the response rate was probably higher than it would have been using other methods of approach to firms. Also it allowed executives to be more frank in their comments than might otherwise have been the case. For the association's part, the exercise provided an opportunity to update and improve upon the information which it had gathered in a 1975 survey of its offshore members.

The questionnaire went out to 308 firms, of which 100 responded (a 32.5 per cent response rate). Before turning to the questionnaire results, it should be emphasised that the difficulties of conducting research in this area preclude any great claims for the survey. To begin with, no one, including government, has succeeded in determining the size of the industry in anything but the roughest terms. Even the definition of what falls within the offshore supply industry presents substantial problems because of the large number of firms which are only marginally involved in supplying offshore. Therefore, it is impossible to say with any great accuracy what proportion of the industry the questionnaire sample represents (estimates place it somewhere between 10 and 20 per cent). In addition, it is difficult to determine whether the respondents to the questionnaire are typical of the industry, for there are very few other studies of the industry's structure. The only major one to date has been that by the Department of Industry (DoI) and the Scottish Economic Planning Department (SEPD) undertaken in the mid 1970s, but it was confined to Scotland.[6] One 'can say that the offshore membership of the trade association which circulated the questionnaire is probably as representative of the industry as the offshore membership of any other association in the area, but there is not the information available to be more precise. The reader is, therefore, advised to take the results which follow as preliminary and subject to revision in the light of further work.

Of the 100 questionnaire respondents, most were small to medium-sized businesses both in terms of their annual turnovers and the number of people they employed (see Tables 6.1 and 6.2). About three-quarters of the respondents were subsidiaries of a relatively large parent firm. Only seven of the respondents indicated no involvement in the offshore market, although for most of the

TABLE 6.1   Annual turnover of respondents

Category	No. of firms	% reporting
Under £1m.	11	11.7
£1m.–£10m.	53	56.4
£11m.–£20m.	13	13.8
Over £20m.	17	18.1
Blank	6	
Total	100	100.0

TABLE 6.2   Number of employees of respondents

Category	No. of firms	% reporting
Fewer than 100	14	14.9
100–499	37	39.4
500–1000	20	21.3
Over 1000	23	24.5
Blank	6	
Total	100	100.0

remaining firms offshore work was not a substantial part of their overall business. Of those firms indicating involvement, about half estimated that offshore work accounted for a tenth or less of their annual turnover. However, about a further third of this group of respondents stated that offshore work accounted for between 10 and 50 per cent of their annual turnover, and another tenth of the group reported that over 90 per cent of their annual turnover consisted of offshore supplies.

The firms responding to the questionnaire were predominantly involved in manufacturing rather than services. Most of those involved in manufacturing had branched out from traditional areas of activity in the engineering industry, and were involved in various types of component manufacture, although there were also firms engaged in highly specialised offshore production (e.g. platform building, drilling equipment manufacture). The questionnaire respondents were apparently more involved in manufacturing than the respondents to the DoI and SEPD survey mentioned earlier. In addition, the respondents to the latter survey tended to be smaller in terms of number of employees than the respondents to the present questionnaire. Both differences may be due to the fact that the DoI–SEPD survey was confined to Scotland. It is generally accepted that Scotland has more service companies as a proportion of total firms in the offshore supply industry than the remainder of the UK. Moreover, service companies tend to be smaller than manufacturing firms. However, there is a possibility that the present survey overstates the manufacturing side and the size of firms in the industry.[7]

In summary, then, the survey respondents may be characterised as small to medium-sized firms, most of which are involved in manufacturing as opposed to services and have a moderate commitment to the offshore supply market.

One means of gauging the impact of government policy upon the offshore supply industry is to determine the type and frequency of contact which firms have had with government. The survey respondents were well aware of government policy initiatives with respect to the offshore supply industry and in many cases had been involved with them. Over four-fifths of the respondents had had some type of contact with the Government's primary agency for offshore supplies policy, the OSO, and the majority of these (about 60 per cent) had made contact with the OSO on their own initiative. Moreover, 64 per cent of the firms which had had contact with the OSO claimed to have had at least one personal meeting with OSO officials. There is apparently no association between size of firm or level of engagement in the offshore market and level of contact with the OSO. However, the larger the firm or the more heavily it is engaged in the market, the greater the tendency for it to have had personal meetings with OSO officials (see Tables 6.3 and 6.4).

TABLE 6.3   Personal meetings with the OSO by size of annual turnover (number in category)

Personal meetings with OSO	Annual turnover			
	Under £1m.	£1m.–10m.	£11m.–20m.	Over £20m.
Yes	4	31	11	14
No	7	21	2	3

Kendall's Tau $C = 0.30$.

TABLE 6.4   Personal meetings with the OSO by level of engagement in the offshore market (column percentages)

Personal meetings with OSO	% Turnover offshore		
	Zero–less than 1%	1%–20%	21%–100%
Yes	38.9	63.3	84.6
No	61.1	36.7	15.4
Total no.	18	49	26

Kendall's Tau $C = 0.32$.

The survey requested firms which had had personal meetings with OSO officials to indicate which government services had been discussed. It then requested the same group of firms to give their opinion of any services they had used. The assumption in this case was that the opinions of executives who had had personal contacts with the OSO and had used the services in question would be based on first-hand experience rather than hearsay.

The results for the question concerning the services which firms discussed with OSO officials are presented in Table 6.5. The most frequently discussed service was marketing advice, followed by advice about how to approach oil companies in connection with

TABLE 6.5   Frequency of discussion of OSO services by respondents (row percentages)

Services discussed	Never	Infre-quently	Quite in-frequently	Very in-frequently	Total (%)	Total (No.)
(a) Marketing opportunities	6.5	54.8	30.6	8.1	100	62
(b) Approaches to oil companies	28.6	42.9	28.6	–	100	56
(c) Discussions about joint ventures with other companies in the offshore market	60.0	32.0	8.0	–	100	50
(d) Assistance on matters relating to Industry Act grants	68.9	26.7	4.4	–	100	45
(e) Assistance on matters relating to research and development	73.5	16.3	8.2	2.0	100	49
(f) Assistance in contacting other government departments	51.0	36.7	12.2	–	100	49
(g) Other	(5)	(6)	(2)	–	–	13

( ) = Number in category.

supply contacts. The next two most frequent subjects of personal meetings between firms and OSO officials were assistance in contacting government departments and the possibility of joint ventures with other firms in the market. Few respondents had personal meetings with OSO officials about government financial assistance or research and development assistance (witness the large percentages in the 'Never' category).

Frequency of personal meetings with OSO officials is associated with size of firm, a tendency most evident in the case of assistance regarding marketing opportunities (see Table 6.6), but there appears to be no connection between frequency of personal meetings and market engagement.

TABLE 6.6   Size of annual turnover by frequency with which firm has discussed advice on marketing opportunities (number in category)

| Size of turnover | Never | Frequency advice sought on marketing opportunities | | | Total (No.) |
		Infrequently	Quite frequently	Very frequently	
Under £1m.	2	3	1	–	6
£1m.–£10m.	2	22	7	–	31
£11m.–£20m.	–	5	5	–	10
£20m. and over	–	3	6	4	13

Kendall's Tau $C = 0.40$

Table 6.7 presents the opinions which firms expressed concerning the government services they had used. Marketing assistance, assistance with Industry Act grants and assistance in contacting government departments were judged to be useful by a majority of those responding for each category. All other services were judged to be not useful by the majority of those responding for each category. Firms were also asked to comment about their contacts with OSO officials and/or the services which they used. Most of the written comments centred upon the usefulness of services which firms had employed, and the majority seemed to have reservations about OSO's capacity to undertake the varied and sometimes highly technical responsibilities which had been assigned to it.

The survey contained a further request for firms to indicate what additional services, if any, they felt OSO should be providing to the industry. Over half of the respondents wrote comments in connection with this subject. Of these, 40 per cent felt that the OSO did not need to extend its range of services. The remaining 60 per cent suggested increases in OSO services. Well over three-quarters of this latter group expressed a desire for improvement or expansion of

TABLE 6.7   Opinion of OSO services (row percentages)

Services	Very useful	Fairly useful	Not very useful	Not at all useful	Total (%)	Total (No.)
(a) Marketing opportunities	5.8	51.9	26.9	15.4	100	52
(b) Approaches to oil companies	10.5	28.9	23.7	36.8	100	38
(c) Discussion about joint ventures with other companies in the offshore market	5.6	33.3	38.9	22.2	100	18
(d) Assistance on matters relating to Industry Act Grants	(2)	(5)	(2)	(1)	–	10
(e) Assistance in matters relating to research and development	(1)	(4)	(5)	(3)	–	13
(f) Assistance in contacting other government departments	4.5	63.6	22.7	9.1	100	22
(g) Other	(2)	(2)	–	(2)	–	6

( ) = Number in category

existing services, most notably marketing advice and efforts by the OSO to persuade oil companies to purchase British goods and services (including auditing). The other suggestions for further OSO services mostly centred upon export promotion, a function which has recently received new emphasis within the OSO.

The survey also had a question which elicited firms' opinions of the effectiveness of auditing procedures. Firms were approximately evenly divided between those which felt that auditing had been an effective policy instrument and those which felt it had not (see Table 6.8).

TABLE 6.8   Respondents' opinions of OSO's ability to influence oil company
purchasing patterns

Category	No. of firms	% of respondents
Very effective	4	4.4
Fairly effective	26	28.6
Not very effective	20	22.0
Not at all effective	12	13.2
No opinion	29	31.9
Blank	9	–
Total	100	100.0

Finally, firms were asked if they had had regular contacts with any government agencies aside from the OSO. Just over half of the respondents indicated that they had had such contacts; the agencies most frequently mentioned were the British Overseas Trade Board, the ECGD and various divisions of the DoI. However, for many of the respondents their contacts with the OSO represented their only connection with a government agency. A specific question about contacts firms had had with government research establishments was included in the survey. Few firms (only eighteen) indicated that they had been in touch with such establishments in connection with offshore supply work.

CONCLUSIONS

It is clear from the above description that a large number of the firms which responded to the postal questionnaire had had some contact with the OSO, and in many cases these contacts were extensive. If the respondents are at all typical of the offshore industry as a whole, the evidence suggests that the OSO has been in contact with a large proportion of the firms in the industry and, by implication, that it has made the industry aware of at least some of the ways in which government policy can be of assistance to firms. Also, the fact that a large proportion of the firms which had had dealings with OSO initiated the contact seems to indicate a willingness on the part of the firms in the industry to seek assistance from government. This, combined with the high level of contact generally between firms and the OSO, bring into question the traditional assumption that industry is hostile to government initiatives in the field of industrial policy. While firms may resent certain types of policy instruments, there appears to be no great reluctance to make use of government services in general.

In addition, the survey respondents seem to have had a clear view of the role which they expected the Government to play in its relationship with the industry. As indicated by the types of services firms used, and the comments they made about existing services and the scope for new services, there is a tendency for respondents to look upon the Government's role as primarily a supervisory one concerned with correcting imbalances in the market by providing market intelligence and introductions to oil companies and by preventing the oil companies from discriminating against British industy. This view corresponds fairly well with the original general principle under which the OSO operated, that is to say, the 'full and fair opportunity' principle. Alternatively, from the type of contacts they had had with the OSO and from their opinions of OSO services most firms were not especially enthusiastic about the 'activist' programmes which OSO has developed, such as those for R and D support, financial aid and assistance with joint ventures, although the latter service proved to be more popular than the first two. Part of this lack of enthusiasm may, of course, be explained by the fact that these last-mentioned services have a limited appeal in any case.

The relative conservatism of the survey respondents with regard to government services is also indicated by the fact that few firms expressed a desire for 'activist' services when asked to comment on the OSO's role with respect to the industry. Indeed, in these comments, respondents stressed the need for improvements in supervisory services such as marketing intelligence and auditing, whereas demands for the extension of R and D assistance or venture management were virtually non-existent. This is not to say the OSO is misguided in pursuing these types of policies, merely that the recognition of the need for them is likely to be limited within the industry. This is an area in which there is likely to be a divergence between the Government's and the industry's views of what are the appropriate policies for government to be pursuing. There seems to be, however, a clear identity of interest between domestic firms and the OSO over the more standard types of assistance and, significantly, over the question of the control of oil company purchasing decisions by government. This may indicate a growing awareness amongst some domestic firms of differences of interest between themselves and the multinational oil companies.

None of the above should be taken as meaning that the firms in this survey were entirely pleased with the quality of the services they experienced. While the more traditional services were well used (e.g. market intelligence, assistance in getting introductions to oil companies), and were the most popular, it would be fair to say that criticism was often harsh with respect to the full range of OSO services. Even the most popular service (marketing intelligence) received favourable comment from only slightly over half of the respondents expressing an opinion on it. In general, from the written comments which firms provided it would appear that the criticisms of OSO services were not that they were inappropriate, but that they were ineffective, either because of lack of experience of OSO staff in dealing with the industry, or because the OSO did not have the necessary technical expertise. However, the task of making OSO services more effective in the eyes of the industry may centre upon considerations other than the technical expertise or experience of OSO officials.

Part of the OSO's difficulty in making an impact with offshore services stems from the nature of its relations with firms in the offshore sector. For example, because the OSO does not have close commercial ties with the oil companies it cannot exchange commercial favours with them in return for the oil companies' serious consideration of those British contractors which the OSO recommends to them. Consequently, the OSO is limited in its ability to influence the oil companies and their engineering consultants on behalf of the domestic firms which request the OSO's assistance. The same problem applies to the OSO's attempts at encouraging joint ventures between domestic firms. While OSO venture managers are able to provide advice, moral suasion and limited access to funds, they are still not merchant bankers in the full sense of the term, as they have neither the high level of commercial discretion nor the *ready* access to substantial lines of credit typical of their counterparts in the City (see Chapter 5).

7 Government and the Multinational Oil Companies

INTRODUCTION

Little of the British Government's offshore supplies policy can be understood without reference to the relationship which has evolved between the oil companies working in the North Sea and the Government. As the principal purchasers of the offshore supply industry's goods and services, the oil companies play a crucial part in determining the nature and pace of the industry's development. In consequence, both the Conservatives and Labour have attempted to influence the pattern of oil company purchasing operations through the use of an administrative device called 'auditing'. The implementation and significance of the auditing procedure are discussed in full in the next chapter, but that discussion presupposes some understanding of the characteristics of the oil companies working in the North Sea. In particular, this chapter focuses upon the multinational status of these companies and the special problems which this has created for the Government in implementing its offshore supplies policy.

THE IMPLICATIONS OF THE MULTINATIONAL NATURE OF THE OIL COMPANIES FOR THEIR RELATIONS WITH GOVERNMENT

As Hodges and many other authors have noted, there is no authoritative definition of a multinational corporation (MNC).[1] However, for present purposes it is defined as a parent company and a collection of subsidiary companies located in several countries in which the former controls the commercial objectives and activities of the latter. Such a corporation is capable of mobilising capital, resources and manpower within and between a number of national economies. Hence, for many purposes the management of a multinational corporation is not overtly constrained by national boundaries in planning and executing the corporation's activities.

Most of the oil companies dealt with in this chapter are multinational corporations by the standards of the above definition. The first task, then, is to identify which characteristics of MNCs are significant in determining the course of government–oil company relations in the field of offshore policy. In some respects, of course, government–oil company relations in this policy area resemble government relations with other commercial entities within the UK economy. Yet, as the following pages illustrate, the execution of offshore supplies policy has hinged upon the manner in which the multinational oil companies in the North Sea *differ* from other types of companies in Britain, and particularly from companies that are UK-based and non-multinational.

Unfortunately, there are difficulties in defining the peculiar impact of multinational corporations upon the development of national industrial policies, in this case the promotion of a domestic offshore supply capability in Britain. For example, much of the literature on MNCs has been addressed to issues which are not of direct relevance here, such as the problems which developing countries confront in controlling the activities of MNCs, especially in the field of natural resource exploitation.[2] Where the literature has dealt with the role of MNCs in advanced industrial economies, most of the attention has been focussed on the economic impact of MNCs on government policy in areas such as taxation, regional development, industrial location, exchange and foreign investment controls and the like. Recently, however, there has been more interest in the general impact of MNCs on a country's ability to determine its industrial structure. First expressed in France in Servan-Schreiber's *Le Défi américain*,[3] and later in Britain in Macmillan and Harris's book, *The American Take-over of Britain*,[4] the dominant concern in this new field of interest has been with the control which large, foreign (and, more specifically, American) MNCs have come to exercise within leading sectors of European national economies. Authors writing in this field have argued that the presence of MNCs in certain key sectors can lead the host country to become technologically and industrially dependent relative to the economy (usually American) which serves as the home base for the powerful

MNCs operating in Europe.[5] Moreover, a number of these commentators have stressed that if foreign MNCs are allowed to expand their sphere of commercial influence within Europe, a number of nations, including the UK, would be permanently relegated to secondary positions within the world industrial hierarchy. The assumption has been that in such circumstances the most rewarding and strategic economic activities (for example, research and development) would be located outside Europe and beyond the influence of European governments.[6] Furthermore, managerial control over many of the leading industrial sectors within Europe would then reside in, for example, America, and would be exercised by executives with no commitment to European priorities.

It is in this context that I propose to examine the British Government's relations with the multinational oil companies involved in the North Sea. However, in this particular instance the issues differ somewhat from those involved when the effect of MNCs on a sector, or industry, in an advanced, industrial economy is analysed in the tradition of Servan-Schreiber *et al*. These authors have been primarily concerned with sectors or industries in which an MNC retains a key place because it controls access to advanced technology or resources required in production. Such a corporation is often able to determine the nature, pace and direction of developments within its particular market. An excellent example of this type of control – and one which has concerned many national governments – is the ability of IBM through its initial dominant position in the field of computer technology, and its consequent control of the strategic American market, to occupy and maintain a position of control within the world computer market. In turn, IBM's hegemony in the world computer market enables it to dominate virtually any national market it chooses to enter in a substantial way.

In discussing MNCs such as IBM most commentators have confined themselves to an examination of the industrial sector within which the MNC functions and has an ownership stake. Yet many MNCs have substantial 'indirect' effects upon national economies. For example, in the case of the offshore supply industry, analysis must be extended to consider the impact of a *group* of MNCs (the oil companies) upon an industry in which they are not productively involved and in which they have no ownership stake. In this instance, the MNCs in question exercise a 'patron/client' control over the offshore supply industry which arises from their position as *exclusive purchasers* of the industry's output. This type of control assures the multinational oil companies in the North Sea a dominant influence in determining the technical and commercial evolution of their 'client' industry. It also implies that government is obliged to deal with the oil companies in any policy designed to assist the offshore supply industry because of the dominant influence which they retain over the offshore sector. In doing so, government has had to come to terms with the multinational character of the 'patron' companies in the sector. As is demonstrated in the following pages, the multinational character of these companies allows them a degree of leverage in their relations with government which significantly exceeds even that which would be characteristic of a group of large, but nationally based, companies acting as commercial 'patrons' for an industry of policy interest to government.

Not all of the oil companies currently involved in the North Sea are of interest here. In this analysis I propose to confine the discussion to those companies which in 1976 were engaged in actively developing commercial oil deposits on the UK Continental Shelf. Of the sixty-three oil companies designated as operators in the North Sea,[7] only ten were officially credited with having made discoveries which were both commercially viable and actively under development.[8] Discussion has been limited to these ten companies because they were the largest purchasers of goods and services for operations in the North Sea, and were, therefore, most deeply involved in issues surrounding the emergence of a viable domestic offshore supply industry. Their larger stake in the offshore market arises from the fact that the development of a commercial oil field requires purchases of goods and services on a larger scale and of a much greater variety than those associated with exploration work only.

An examination of Table 7.1 immediately reveals several of the most important features of the companies under consideration. In the first place, they are all, with the exception of Hamilton Brothers, very large companies. Their 1975 assets ranged from a low of $2481.9 million to a high of $28,348.7 million and their net incomes for that year are almost all in the hundreds of millions of dollars. Secondly, ownership is predominantly American. Of the ten firms listed, seven are US-based and only three could be said to be British (this total drops to two if we note that Shell is 60 per cent owned by Dutch nationals).[9] Finally, again with the exception of Hamilton

TABLE 7.1   Operators in the North Sea with commercial discoveries (at end of 1975)

Company	No. of fields	Nationality	Current assets[a] ($m.)	Net income[a] ($m.)
Shell	4	UK/Dutch	28,348.7[b]	2,110.9[b]
Burmah	1	UK	2,481.9	−23.2
Mobil	1	US	15,050.3	809.9
Conoco	1	US	5,184.6	330.8
BP	1	UK	14,615.0	369.2
Unionoil Company of Great Britain	1	US	3,776.1	232.7
Occidental	2	US	3,503.4	171.9
Hamilton Bros	1	US	n.a.[c]	n.a.[c]
Chevron	1	US	12,898.1	772.5
Amoco	1	US	9,854.1	787.0

[a] All figures are for the 1975 financial year, and rounded to the nearest $100,000. Assets and income figures are in US dollars, and are for the *parent* firm.
[b] Figures for the Royal Dutch/Shell Group.
[c] Not available.

Sources: The following publications were used to compile the information contained in this chart: Department of Energy, *Development of Oil and Gas Resources of the United Kingdom, 1976* (London: HMSO, 1976) pp. 30–2; and *Fortune*, May and Aug 1976.

Brothers, we are dealing with a group of companies all of which can reasonably be termed multinationals, as they each have substantial overseas investments and commitments.[10] Indeed, in this list of ten companies are four of the famous 'Seven Sisters', four of the seven largest and most international of the world's oil companies.[11]

As indicated in the previous paragraph, virtually all of the ten oil companies under discussion possess financial resources which place them amongst the largest corporate entities in the world.[12] This is highly significant given the tremendous resources which are required to develop the offshore oil fields in the North Sea on a commercial basis. For example, in March 1975 BP estimated that the cost of bringing the Forties Field into commercial production would be well over £600 million.[13] Given the magnitude of offshore developments of this type, only a few companies in the world retain the extensive capital resources necessary in order to negotiate the substantial financing needed to exploit the North Sea oil fields.[14] As a result of this, British governments have been in a weak bargaining position *vis à vis* the oil companies operating in the North Sea in so

far as there are virtually no alternative ways of financing the North
Sea developments, with the possible exception of direct government
engagement. Moreover, a number of considerations prevented
extensive consideration of the latter option in the first years of oil
exploration and exploitation. During the period when many of the
major, initial investment decisions were being taken by the oil
companies (i.e. 1970–4), the Conservative administration then in
power was committed to ensuring that private enterprise (which
more often than not, given the structure of the industry internationally, meant American firms) retained the major role in the
development of North Sea resources. In addition, both Labour and
Conservative governments in the 1970s have been influenced by
another strategic consideration. Ministers feared that early commitments by government to participation and direct state investment in
the North Sea might lead oil company managements to develop
serious doubts about their future role and profitability rates in any
further undertakings in the North Sea. Such doubts might have led
to sizeable slowdowns in the pace of oil field development, and this
was something which both types of governments wanted to avoid at
all costs.[15]

Government reliance upon the extensive capital resources and
financial credibility of the multinational oil companies in the
exploitation of the oil fields meant that it could not assume a direct
role in the process of field development. Hence, it could not exercise
a direct influence over the way in which the oil companies dealt
with their client industry, the offshore supply industry. However,
another characteristic of the oil companies as multinationals had a
much greater impact on the Government's ability to influence oil
company action. This was the oil companies' virtual monopoly of
the technical and managerial skills necessary to develop the offshore
oil fields.

Marine petroleum engineering is a small and highly specialised
field, and despite the huge amounts of money spent in the area,
shortages of skilled managers and engineers have always been a
problem, even for the oil companies, which, along with a very few
large engineering consulting firms, employ almost all the specialists
in the field.[16] As is the case with many other types of multinationals,
this monopoly of expertise places the oil companies in a very strong
position *vis à vis* the Government. First, because they possess a
monopoly of expertise in both field development and offshore
supplies, the oil companies have become operationally indispens-

able to the Government. In short, government is forced to leave the primary initiatives concerning the manner in which the oil fields are developed to the oil companies. Thus, the conditions laid down for British offshore supply industry operations are determined almost entirely by executives within the oil companies and their engineering contracting firms. Consequently, the Government is obliged to deal directly with the oil companies if it wishes to have a specific impact upon the way in which British firms are encouraged to enter the market and upon how those firms are treated once they are in the market. Yet owing to its reliance upon the oil companies in other areas government is limited in the pressure it can bring to bear in its attempts to ensure that the oil companies utilise British technical and commercial capabilities. However, there is also a second reason why the oil companies' control over technical expertise poses problems for the Government in implementing its policy objectives for the offshore supply industry. As the oil companies have a virtual monopoly of the skilled manpower necessary to organise the exploitation of offshore oil fields, it becomes very difficult for the Government to recruit sufficient trained manpower even *to supervise* the equipment purchases of the oil companies.

Referring back to Table 7.1 for a moment, it is possible to detect a further characteristic of the oil companies as multinationals which has presented difficulties for the Government within the policy context we are studying. As has already been noted, seven out of the ten oil companies under discussion are foreign (i.e. American-owned and based). In Chapter 2 I emphasised that the dominance of US oil companies in the North Sea is to a large extent a function of the technological lead which American engineering firms acquired in offshore supply work during the 1940s and 1950s in the Gulf of Mexico. These specialised firms were closely linked with their sponsoring oil companies, and, hence, it is hardly surprising that when the US oil multinationals established operations in Britain they turned to their traditional sources of supply in the United States. Thus, US contractors gained the vast majority of supply contracts in the first stages of North Sea development.

This tendency to favour American suppliers has been reinforced by a number of further considerations. To begin with, most of the foreign oil companies have been present in the UK for only a short period of time. This has meant that they have had only a limited ability to recruit UK engineering staff and to become aware of UK engineering capacities, commercial practices and bidding pro-

TABLE 7.2   Oil companies acting as operators in the North Sea, 1975

Company	Nationality	Date established in UK	Date exploration activity started in UK[a]	Date first oil discovery declared commercial
Shell	Dutch/UK	1897	1964	1970[b]
Burmah	UK	1902	1964	1973
Mobil	US	1964	1964	1972
Conoco	US	1964	1964	1974[c]
BP	UK	1909	1964	1971
Unionoil Company of Great Britain	US	1972	1972	1973
Occidental	US	1971	1972	1973
Hamilton Bros	US	1964	1966	1971
Chevron[d]	US	1964	1964[e]	1974
Amoco	US	1959	1964	1969[b]

[a] Date stated is date from which exploration licence was granted; actual exploration activity may have occurred much later.

[b] Shell and Amoco had discovered commercial gas fields in the southern North Sea in the late 1960s.

[c] Conoco was also involved in commercial natural gas discoveries in the southern North Sea in the late 1960s.

[d] Chevron took over an exploration licence which had been awarded to Burmah Oil Developments. The licence covered the development of a field (Ninian Field) which Burmah controlled as the operator. Due to Burmah's financial problems it had to relinquish its operator's status for the Ninian Field to Chevron Petroleum Ltd.

[e] In joint partnership with Texaco under the name Amoseas.

Sources: W. G. Nightingale (ed.), Oil and Gas International Yearbook, 1974 (London: Financial Times, 1975); The North Sea: The Search for Oil and Gas; Development of the Oil and Gas Resources of the United Kingdom, 1976

cedures. If we examine the companies listed in Table 7.2, it is clear that not only are most of the operators engaged in developing commercial discoveries foreign-based, but most of them have also been established in the UK only within the last decade. Indeed, many of these oil companies did not recruit management and engineering staffs of substantial size until their oil discoveries were declared commercial, and for many of them this did not take place until the early 1970s. This late start in recruitment meant that many of the foreign oil companies were obliged to meet the need for a rapid increase in skilled staff by importing personnel directly from their parent companies in America and/or reliance on the services of the large international engineering consultancy firms specialising in the management of offshore oil development projects. (As will be demonstrated later in this chapter, most of these engineering consultancy companies are themselves foreign-based and owned.) Thus, in the foreign oil companies many of the staff handling the design work and procurement operations have acquired most of their engineering and management experience in the US, and are, therefore, naturally predisposed to look first to American firms for industrial capacity and contracts.

Also, of those oil companies working in the North Sea, only Shell, Burmah and BP maintain substantial 'in-house' engineering and purchasing divisions within the UK.[17] It is difficult to generalise about the purchasing and engineering sections of the remaining foreign-based oil companies as they differ so greatly one from another, and their structures frequently change.[18] However, in general, most of the foreign firms have temporary engineering and purchasing divisions located in the UK to manage immediate needs, but most of the planning and specifications work and many of the large purchasing decisions are sent back to the American head office for final approval.[19] In the case of the all-important work connected with drawing up development plans and working out designs (a process which involves the laying-down of specifications and the selection of the primary contractors), many firms use the services of the parent company's engineering division. For example, Mobil North Sea, which is developing the Beryl Field, used the services of Mobil Research and Development Corporation, a wholly owned Mobil subsidiary, based in Princeton, New Jersey, to carry out the basic design proposals and supervise the initial procurement work.[20] For project management (i.e. the management of the construction and installation of equipment, and the selection and supervision of the great number of sub-contractors who are engaged in any large-scale development programme) most of the oil companies have tended to use the services of the engineering consulting firms with experience in offshore oil development work.

Many of these consulting companies are very large and highly specialised, and frequently based in the US. Table 7.3 sets out the connections between operators and project management firms. The majority of the firms listed in the table are US-based (e.g. Brown and Root, Bechtel, Earl and Wright), although most also have branch offices throughout the world. Interestingly, the British-based oil companies acting as operators (Burmah, Shell and BP)

TABLE 7.3   Oil companies and their principal design and management contractors, 1975

Operator	Nationality	Project management	Jacket design
BP	UK	BP, Brown and Root	BP, Brown and Root
Hamilton Bros	US	Hamilton Bros and Bechtel (US and London)	Bechtel (US)[a]
Mobil	US	Mobil Research and Development Inc., and Mobil North Sea	A/S Høyer-Ellefsen (Norway)
Occidental	US	Occidental	J. Ray MacDermott
Shell	UK/Dutch	Shell Expro	Shell Expro[b]
Burmah[c]	UK	Taywood–Santa Fé	CJB/Earl and Wright
Amoco	US	Earl and Wright (Houston, San Francisco, and London)	Amoco, Earl and Wright (Houston)
Unionoil Company of Great Britain	US	Unocal, J. Ray MacDermott	J. Ray MacDermott

[a] Bechtel designed the special features needed to convert the drilling rig into a platform, and set the design criteria. The special riser involved was designed and built by another US company.
[b] General contracting and engineering work on the jackets was supervised by Shell Expro assisted by London Bridge, Foster Wheeler, and Protec Ltd. Design work for the concrete platforms was handled to a large extent by the firms constructing the platforms.
[c] Burmah handled the assignment of the original contracts for Chevron's platforms in the Ninian Field.
Sources: oil-company interviews, and Offshore Engineer, Jan 1975.

have tended to concentrate their design and project management work either within the company (as in the case of Shell), or in a partnership between their engineering division and a foreign-based firm (e.g. BP and Brown and Root). In the case of Burmah, very little of the project management work has been done 'in house', but the firm which received the management contract was a joint partnership between an American company (Santa Fé) and a British engineering consultancy firm (Taylor Woodrow). In contrast, the US-based oil companies listed in Table 7.3 have employed very little British engineering talent in this area. Thus, the predisposition to favour US manufacturers that already exists within the engineering departments of American oil firms (for reasons that have already been discussed) is reinforced by the tendency for US oil companies to hand the major role in organising and selecting contractors for work in the North Sea oil fields to US-based engineering consulting firms.[21]

Moreover, it is not only the US supply industry that benefits from this arrangement; the contracting process is also 'internationalised' as a result of the commitments of those making crucial decisions about the destination of equipment orders. While staff in engineering consulting firms are likely, in conjunction with oil company executives, to favour traditional US suppliers and contractors in highly specialised areas of the offshore supply industry, the international complexion of the major engineering organisations based in the US is also likely to encourage executives to look to the *whole* of Western Europe for contracting capacity and supply rather than simply to the UK, even in making decisions about the less highly specialised aspects of offshore supply work. This in itself has had a major impact on the level of competition which British industry has had to face.

Little concrete evidence is available concerning the performance of individual oil companies in purchasing British goods and services, although it is clear that until the mid 1970s British industry did not obtain a significant share of the North Sea market.[22] While the OSO annually publishes an analysis of the overall penetration of British industry in the North Sea market, it does not provide information on the purchasing performance of individual oil companies. Thus, it is difficult to know exactly to what extent foreign oil companies favour US over UK suppliers.[23] One can, however, analyse the purchasing patterns of the oil companies for production platforms. Here the identity of the oil company and the contracting yard are public knowledge, and it is possible to compare the relative performance of the oil companies under discussion. The results of this analysis are presented in Table 7.4.

The information contained in Table 7.4 has certain limitations. While the data include all platform and some module purchases made in the UK sector by North Sea operators, platforms and modules constitute only a fraction of the total North Sea equipment market, although they do cost substantial sums of money in each case. For example, the average production platform costs about £100 million, including the value of deck and production equipment.[24] However, platforms are large single items and the lumpiness of this type of expenditure makes the numbers dealt with necessarily small, and therefore subject to problems of comparison. In addition, because of the nature of steel platform construction work, many of the components are sub-contracted to firms other than the main contractor, which in this case usually acts more as an

TABLE 7.4 Ordering patterns for oil company production platforms in the UK sector by oil companies operating in the North Sea (till end of 1976)

Operator	Nationality	UK-built platforms ordered	Foreign-built platforms ordered
Hamilton Bros[a]	US	1	0
Shell	UK/Dutch	4	3[b]
BP	UK	4	0
Mobil	US	0	1[c]
Amoco	US	0	1[d]
Occidental	US	1	1[e]
Unocal	US	1	0
Burmah	UK	1	0
Chevron[f]	US	2	0
Totals		14	6
Totals in Concrete		2	4

[a] The UK-built platform for Hamilton Brothers was, in fact, a US-built semi-submersible drilling rig which was converted at a British shipyard into a floating production platform; as a result, the cost was considerably less than that for a fixed steel or concrete production platform.

[b] Two placed in Norway, one in Holland.

[c] One placed in Norway.

[d] One placed in France.

[e] One placed in France.

[f] The two platforms for the Ninian Field were ordered in 1974 by Burmah before it was replaced in early 1975 by Chevron as operator for the field.

Source: Offshore Engineer, issues of Jan 1975, Aug 1975, Jan 1976 and Aug 1976.

assembler than as a fabricator of platform components. As many of the firms doing sub-contract work are located in different countries, one has to be careful not to assume that all the work on a steel platform has been done in the country in which it is assembled. On the other hand, because of the nature of the method of constructing concrete production platforms, almost all of the work associated with the building of the structure of concrete platform is usually done within the yard of the contractor, and is therefore less subject to problems of assessment.

If we examine the figures in Table 7.4, some interesting comparisons can be made. While most platforms ordered for the UK sector of the North Sea were built in Britain, the performance of UK and foreign-based companies differs substantially with regard to the origins of their platform purchases. As Table 7.5 demonstrates, for every foreign platform purchased by a British-based

TABLE 7.5   Ratio of foreign to domestic orders placed by oil companies, 1976

Company group	UK-built platforms	Foreign-built platforms	Ratio
UK-based companies	9	3	3 : 1
Foreign-based companies	5	3	1.7 : 1

Note: Shell counted as a UK company.

oil company, three UK-built platforms were purchased. However, if we look at the record of foreign-based companies, we find that for every foreign platform purchased, just under two platforms were purchased in the UK.

These figures indicate that foreign-based oil companies are less disposed to purchase UK-built platforms than UK-based oil companies. If, however, we adjust these figures to take into account the fact that the two British-built platforms listed as being purchased by a US company (Chevron) were in fact ordered by the British Burmah company before it had to relinquish its operator status to Chevron, a slightly different picture emerges (see Table 7.6).

TABLE 7.6   Ratio of foreign to domestic orders placed by oil companies, 1976 (Chevron orders counted as British)

Company group	UK-built platforms	Foreign-built platforms	Ratio
UK-based companies	11	3	3.7 : 1
Foreign-based companies	3	3	1 : 1

Note: Shell counted as a UK company.

We find now that the propensity for British firms to place orders in the UK is increased from 3:1 to 3.7:1, and the propensity of foreign-based companies to purchase British-built platforms decreases from 1.7:1 to 1:1. Thus, there would seem to be some evidence to indicate that foreign-based oil companies are more likely to take an international approach in their purchasing requirements for platforms than are British oil companies, and are less likely to concentrate their orders in the UK.

Another interesting fact that emerges from this analysis is that fewer concrete platforms are ordered in the UK than from abroad (two as opposed to four). This is significant because the steel platforms, as has been pointed out, are built such that a substantial part of their value goes out in sub-contract work, often to yards outside the country where the platform is being assembled. Concrete platforms, on the other hand, tend to be built (apart from the deck and modules) almost entirely on site, thus adding a larger proportion of value to the local economy than the steel platforms. Overall, therefore, British industry has done less well proportionately than the situation outlined in Table 7.4 would indicate. Although more platforms, over all, were ordered from the UK than from abroad for the North Sea, a higher proportion of the foreign orders were for concrete platforms (one out of every seven platforms ordered from the UK is in concrete, whereas one out of every two platforms ordered from abroad is in concrete).

The above tables indicate that British industry has confronted a number of barriers or obstacles in its efforts to enter the offshore supply market. Undoubtedly, a number of the difficulties which British industry has experienced (sce Chapter 2) have been of its own making, but there is also reason to believe that British firms have lagged in the offshore market because some of the oil companies in a position to influence the degree of engagement of British firms in North Sea work are committed to traditional foreign suppliers. This is partly due to the fact that many of the oil companies under discussion are foreign-based and have only tenuous links with the UK for exploration and development work. It is also partly because, as multinationals working in a global commercial milieu, oil companies (and this includes the British oil companies) have grown accustomed to seeking their suppliers within an international context. The 'international' outlook characteristic of multinational management tends to discourage an oil company from seeking out British suppliers. Moreover, given the initial competitive position of British industry in the offshore market, it is unlikely that oil company practice would have changed markedly without some form of government encouragement.

SUMMARY

In developing an industrial encouragement policy for the offshore supply industry British governments have been obliged to recognise that the industry they wished to assist was and is dependent upon a predominantly foreign-based group of multinational oil companies. Furthermore, these foreign multinationals retained links with the offshore supply industry in their own country – links which they wished to strengthen for operational and commercial reasons (see Chapter 2). Finally, these multinationals exercised a monopoly in the technical skills and large-scale financial resources necessary for oil field exploitation. Thus, they had no competitors to whom the Government could turn for alternative services or advice, and the state was not in a position either to undertake the work itself, or even to supervise the work effectively. For these reasons government retained only a limited ability to exercise any sanctions against the oil companies which would have benefited the domestic offshore supply industry.

In the next chapter, I turn to an examination of the manner in which British governments have come to terms with these industrial 'realities' and of the policy instruments which they have employed in their efforts to achieve offshore objectives given their tactically weak position in the field of North Sea operations generally.

Appendix: Industrial Rank of Oil Companies under Examination within their own Industrial Communities, 1975

Company	Rank	
	US [a]	UK [b]
Mobil	4	
Chevron	7	
Amoco	13	
Conoco	18	
Occidental	24	
Unocal	35	
Hamilton Bros	n.a.	
BP		1
Shell		2
Burmah		16

[a] Rank of US corporations according to sales.
[b] Rank of UK corporations according to assets.

Source: The Times 1000, 1975–76 (London: Times Books, 1975).

8 The Attempt to Influence Oil Company Purchasing

INTRODUCTION

When most people in Britain today think of the Government and its relationship with the oil companies working in the North Sea, their minds immediately turn to the confrontations after 1974 between the Labour Government and the oil companies over taxation and the creation of the British National Oil Corporation. However, a significant, although less well known, development in the oil-company–government relationship has been the attempt by both Conservatives and Labour to influence the purchasing activities of the North Sea oil companies. This attempt to control the oil companies' purchasing activities has resulted in a significant extension of government intervention in the daily commercial operations of the oil industry through the use of an innovative administrative procedure which has come to be known as 'auditing'.

In the previous chapter I reviewed a number of the problems which government has confronted in its dealings with oil multinationals. This chapter discusses how the Government has attempted to overcome some of these problems through the use of auditing. It describes the implementation of auditing and presents an assessment of the instrument's impact. In addition, attention is devoted to the way in which auditing highlights some of the limits of the Government's position *vis à vis* the oil companies operating in the North Sea and of administrative approaches to policy-making generally. Finally, the chapter presents an evaluation of the significance of auditing for government relations with both the oil multinationals and the UK offshore supply industry.

AUDITING AND THE OIL COMPANIES

The first public suggestion that some type of government supervision of the purchasing activities of the oil companies was needed
emerged, as has been outlined before, in the IMEG Report. The
IMEG consultants recommended a system of quarterly confidential
returns in which each operator would report its offshore purchases
to government.[1] They believed that such a procedure would

> on the one hand . . . counteract the tendency [on the part of the
> oil companies] to stick to traditional patterns of supply and on
> the other . . . provide possible UK suppliers, through the
> Government, with information on the types of equipment and
> services required.[2]

The Government adopted this recommendation, and developed a
procedure which became known as 'auditing'.[3]

By requiring the oil companies to reveal the exact nature of their
offshore purchases of goods and services the Government intended
to ensure that oil company purchasing executives were continuously
aware of its concern with the offshore supply issue.[4] Yet, as is
demonstrated in the course of this chapter, officials found that the
reporting procedure suggested by the IMEG consultants did not
fulfil all the Government's aspirations in this area. In particular, it
did not seem to have a significant impact upon the level of British
participation in the offshore market. Consequently, auditing was
later expanded to include other procedures designed to further the
Government's ability to change traditional oil company purchasing
patterns.

The first task was still, however, to gain access to information
about purchasing patterns by convincing the oil companies that the
submission of quarterly returns was in their best interests.
Fortunately, as noted in Chapter 3, the political climate in 1972 was
such that the oil companies were anxious to confirm their standing
as 'good corporate citizens'. The reader will recall that the oil
industry encountered a large amount of adverse publicity in late
1972 owing to growing media and public disquiet about the state of
the British offshore supply industry and the generous tax advantages
which the oil companies were to receive in connection with their
operations in the North Sea. Thus, while oil executives did not
relish the emergence of 'yet another' form of government involve-

ment in their affairs, they felt they could compromise on the purchasing issue and thereby demonstrate their good faith both to the public and to the Government. Hence, when DTI officials eventually approached the oil companies about an auditing procedure, they did not meet much resistance.

The initial approach to the oil companies was made in October 1972, about a month after Ministers had been given confidential versions of the IMEG Report. Senior officials from the DTI first made overtures to the oil companies' representative body, the Offshore Operators Committee (OOC), concerning the possibility of introducing a reporting procedure. Later, the issue was discussed formally at a Council meeting of the OOC on 8 November 1972, when Leonard Williams, a senior DTI official, and four other civil servants presented a potential reporting procedure to oil company representatives. The Government originally proposed a quarterly reporting system for an experimental period of a year. The system incorporated a common reporting format, but officials emphasised that this could be modified to suit the needs of the individual oil companies. Under the system oil companies were to report all purchases over £25,000, and the Government, in turn, would treat the information in a confidential manner. The oil companies agreed to this proposal and promised to submit their returns for the past year (1972) and for the coming year on a quarterly basis.[5] This arrangement was renewed by the Government and the oil companies at the end of 1973 for an indefinite period of time and the reporting format was standardised for all companies so that comparative records could be kept on an annual basis.[6]

The current reporting procedure (1977), that was confirmed at the end of 1973, requires the company acting as operator to submit a summary of purchases including 'orders placed for goods and services needed for exploration, development, production and transport of oil and gas on the U.K. Continental Shelf'.[7] Returns are filed by all operators, whether they are engaged in exploration or development work (in 1975 this totalled sixty-one oil companies). The companies list the type of product or service ordered, the name of the manufacturer or supplier, the nationality of the manufacturer or supplier, and the approximate UK and foreign content of the order. If an order is placed with a foreign company, the operators are requested to explain the reasons for this. They are also asked to list the UK firms which were approached to supply the equipment or service, but failed to obtain the contract. Finally, operators are requested to file their major equipment purchase forecasts for the coming year by equipment and service categories, as well as their general plans for field development. This final section of the report is a type of rolling forecast of purchasing requirements, and it is a highly important part of the return for it allows the OSO's auditing staff to forecast the demand within the oil industry for offshore equipment and services and to predict which sectors of the offshore industry are likely to benefit from future orders placed by the oil companies.[8]

The quarterly returns procedure forms the basis of the OSO's and the Government's formal relationship with the oil companies, but officials involved in establishing this 'auditing procedure' were very early aware that a simple reporting mechanism is a potentially weak device if there is no follow-up. Therefore, to complement the formal reporting procedure, the OSO established a team of audit engineers whose task it is to keep a close watch on the purchasing decisions of the oil companies. Audit engineers are organised into teams of two men each, and each team is responsible for analysing the quarterly return data for a set of oil companies in order to determine the degree to which these oil companies are using British contractors. In addition, however, they regularly visit the project management offices of the oil companies or their engineering contractors. At these meetings audit engineers discuss the details of oil company purchasing plans with oil company executives. More importantly, they question oil executives concerning their reasons for choosing foreign over British contractors in instances in which contracts have gone or are going abroad. This procedure is designed to remind oil company executives at all times of the need to consider British capability in the field.[9]

Naturally, the audit engineer's special knowledge of both the needs and the plans of an oil company is very important in enabling him to assess whether specific companies can make use of British firms in their development plans. Often, for example, given the purchasing plans of an oil company and its past record in making use of British contractors an audit engineer can predict which contracts are likely to be placed abroad, and act accordingly. To further strengthen their ability to pre-empt purchases going abroad, audit engineers are also each responsible for familiarising themselves with certain categories of oil field purchases. Every audit engineer is thus a specialist in a particular type of offshore good or service, and this allows them to use each other as 'resource-persons' when trying to determine what British capability may be of use to an oil company planning a set of major contracts. This 'division of labour' is also useful when audit engineers are trying to ascertain if the reasons given by an oil company for not purchasing British equipment (e.g. because British firms are not in the area or they are not producing goods or services of the correct type) are justified.[10]

If in reviewing the purchasing pattern of an oil company an audit engineer suspects British capability is being ignored, he will raise the matter with the appropriate oil company executives, and attempt to ensure that British firms are asked to bid in future contracts. In cases in which British firms are consistently losing out to foreign suppliers, the audit engineers will make detailed inquiries about the conditions under which the oil company in question accepted bids, in order to determine if British contractors were given a fair opportunity to compete. If British firms were given fair opportunity, the engineer will try to discover why British firms lost the contract. In certain cases, if the audit engineer considers it worthwhile, the causes of bidding 'failure' may be relayed back to British firms so that they can correct any weaknesses in their bid submissions to the oil companies, and thereby perhaps win future contracts.[11]

During the first months the main emphasis of the OSO's auditing work was, not surprisingly, upon gathering information rather than upon explicit attempts to influence the purchasing decisions of the oil companies. This was a direct result of the fact that few people within government, or for that matter outside, had any idea of the extent to which British industry was engaged in the offshore sector. Therefore, in the initial period officials connected with auditing concentrated upon building up a comprehensive bank of information concerning the nature of British engagement in the offshore supply industry. They also attempted to determine the exact status of British firms within the offshore market, in particular whether or not the oil companies were permitting British firms to compete on an equal basis with traditional foreign suppliers.

The results of the first comprehensive survey of the annual pattern of orders for offshore supplies indicated that the level of British engagement in the offshore supply industry in 1974 was substantially higher than the level estimated by the IMEG Report for 1972. According to the new figures, British firms had gained approximately 40 per cent by value of the total offshore market in 1974 (as compared with the IMEG Report's estimate of 25–30 per cent for 1972). However, although British engagement seemed to have improved, British firms were not performing equally well in all sectors of the offshore market.

Table 8.1 gives the results of the 1974 returns. As is evident from the table, there are a number of sectors within the industry as a whole in which British firms were performing very poorly in 1974. Moreover, even in those sectors in which British industry had a substantial share of the market officials suspected that levels of performance should have been much better.[12] Indeed, in examining the first sets of comprehensive annual returns civil servants began to have serious reservations about the pattern of offshore engagement which seemed to be emerging. In the first place, given that the engineering industry is highly developed in Britain, it was surprising that many parts of the industry were not more fully engaged in the North Sea, as many of the products which the oil companies require in this area are not highly specialised. While there are many high-technology sectors within the offshore market

TABLE 8.1   Analysis of orders placed by offshore operating companies in 1974

Item	Total value of orders placed (£m.)	UK share (%)
CAPITAL GOODS		
Fabrications		
1. Production platforms – concrete	161	37
2. Production platforms – steel	87	64
3. Modules and other fabrications	187	50
Production plant		
4. Power generation equipment	22.4	83
5. Pumps	5.8	88
6. Compressors	8.5	41
7. Process plant and equipment	11.9	80
Pipe and fittings		
8. Pipe	85	7
9. Pipe coatings	25.8	90
10. Pipe fittings	18.5	49
11. Casing	26.7	44
Miscellaneous		
12. Communications equipment	8.0	85
13. Wellhead and completion equipment	8.7	61
14. Safety equipment	3.8	95
15. Total for capital goods	*600*	*47*

Table 8.1 (Contd.)

Item	Total value of orders placed (£m.)	UK share (%)
SERVICES		
Exploration and drilling		
16. Rig hire	146	25
17. Surveys	14	79
18. Drilling tools and equipment	13.3	47
19. Pipe laying	127	18
20. Installation operations	123	6
21. Diving	7.4	42
22. Helicopter and air services	13.4	60
23. Marine transport	21.2	55
24. Mud-logging and well-testing	9.7	62
25. Barytes and mud chemicals	6.6	64
26. Cementing services	3.2	59
27. Inspection testing and maintenance	6.7	69
28. Other services	42.3	68
29. Total for services	*534*	*29*
ENGINEERING		
30. Design and consultancy	*85*	*60*
31. Grand total	*1279*	*40*

Source: Department of Energy, *Offshore Oil and Gas: A Summary of Orders Placed by Operators of Oil and Gas Fields on the UK Continental Shelf During 1974* (London: HMSO, 1975) pp. 6–7. Used with the permission of the Controller of Her Majesty's Stationery Office.

in which it would be difficult for British firms to compete, and while some British firms had gained bad commercial reputations *vis-à-vis* late delivery and the like, the degree of British engagement in 1974 did not seem to reflect Britain's standing as a major industrial nation. Hence, officials speculated that there might be reasons for the poor performance of British industry other than its initial lack of technical and commercial competitiveness. This was confirmed as audit engineers' experience with the nature of the offshore supply (and especially engineering) industry increased.

To begin with, according to an official responsible for the auditing procedure, it had become common practice for the oil companies to discourage direct contacts between OSO audit staff and the consulting engineering firms handling procurement and supply contracts for the oil companies. Thus, the audit engineers were denied access to the executives who made purchasing decisions at the project definition stage, the stage at which it is most desirable to bring influence to bear on the purchasers (i.e. before plans become so advanced that a development project is 'locked' into a set group of suppliers).[13] The audit engineers also learned that some oil companies were engaged in a number of practices which were designed to ensure that British firms were not able to compete with foreign suppliers in bidding for contracts. One of the most common forms of exclusion, sometimes used deliberately, sometimes arising from the importation of a foreign practice into the UK, was the tendency for oil companies to write specifications for their contracts using industrial standards (e.g. API or UL)[14] which are not in use in Britain. This practice meant that British firms' products were often rejected only because the specifications outlined in the British bids were based upon BSI standards or other standards approved or tested by British standards authorities which are not recognised in the US, and hence are not used in US oil company engineering departments. Other practices employed by the oil companies which effectively excluded serious British competition were the imposition of unrealistic delivery times on orders and the provision of advance notices to overseas suppliers of contract specifications so that foreign firms had an additional time advantage when contract tenders were made public.[15] In addition, some oil companies attempted to overstate their purchases of British goods and services by acquiring foreign-made equipment through UK-based supply houses, or through US subsidiaries based in Britain, and then counting such purchases as British in their returns.[16]

The reasons for these attempts to favour foreign equipment suppliers have been examined in Chapter 2 (e.g. experience of trusted suppliers, better performance of foreign manufacturers in terms of delivery times, etc.). However, in addition to these 'structural' or 'economic' reasons for the oil companies to favour foreign suppliers, there were a number of personal considerations which induced oil executives to favour foreign-made equipment. Peter Gibson, Director-General of the OSO, commented in evidence given before the House of Common Select Committee on Science and Technology that a certain 'old-boy' network existed in the offshore engineering industry which tended to favour foreign

firms. In answer to a question directed to him concerning the degree
to which the OSO was able to learn about oil companies' future
plans for purchases and the degree to which oil companies were
deliberately trying to hide their purchasing plans to give themselves
greater freedom to favour foreign suppliers, Gibson replied:

> I think it varies from company to company, obviously. It varies
> also according to the strength of the resources we can deploy in
> discussing the companies' future plans. . . . Certainly some of
> them in the early days were extremely cagey and we had one or
> two rows about it. Their performance in this respect is better than
> it has been . . . but there will always be the situation where the
> operator appears to be evasive and if you dig and delve [you will
> find] he has an old chum waiting around the corner for his
> contract . . . . [17]

The social foundations of this type of 'old-boy' network are not
difficult to discern. Executives of foreign oil companies do not
always stay with the same company; they often return home and
seek a new career with the domestic offshore engineering industry.
Obviously, a record of assisting the industry could serve to improve
an executive's employment prospects when he wishes to seek new
employment. In addition, if an executive can do a home-based
equipment supplier a favour by giving him a contract, the firm
concerned may be able to help the oil executive out on another
project later when he needs specific equipment supplied at very
short notice or at a lower than normal price to meet stringent budget
limits.[18]

Regardless of the specific reasons, it became clear to OSO's staff
and the Department of Energy that the OSO required other devices
than simple auditing if it was to exert substantial influence in the
critical area of contract tendering. Officials feared that unless new
initiatives were taken OSO staff would not be in a position to
evaluate whether or not British firms were truly being given a fair
opportunity to compete by the oil companies. The Department
decided, therefore, to expand the auditing system so that it
encompassed the process whereby the oil industry tenders for
offshore products and services.

Early in 1975, the then Secretary of State for Energy, Eric
Varley, wrote to the oil companies expressing his conern with the
equipment purchase issue and stating that the Department was

under pressure to assist British suppliers and producers of offshore equipment to obtain a better share of the offshore market. Varley mentioned in his letter that the Government was considering bringing in legislation concerning offshore supplies as part of a series of regulatory measures to be included in the forthcoming Pipelines Bill.[19] The oil companies, through their representatives on their new joint organisation, the UKOOA,[20] objected to the proposals as unnecessary. They argued that the industry was already committed to supporting British firms in the offshore field and that this had been demonstrated by the oil industry's increased use of British suppliers. The oil companies further reiterated their 'belief' that it was in their own best interests to encourage the development of a viable offshore supply industry in the UK which would service the oil companies' long-term equipment needs.[21]

The Department seemed to accept these reasons, and temporarily dropped the issue. However, within a few months the Department again approached the oil companies stating that it was under further pressure from the trade unions and some trade associations to do *something* about the offshore supplies question.[22] On this occasion the Department did not threaten legislation, but instead proposed that the Government and the oil companies should agree upon a 'code of practice' governing the purchasing of offshore supplies.[23] In August 1975 officials sent a draft code of practice to the oil companies, and UKOOA formed a working party to consider it. The oil companies examined the Department's draft code, and objected to the draft's wording in three specific areas: (a) the question of which party should have the final say upon where a contract was to be placed; (b) the question of whether a British firm should be able to receive information from the OSO concerning the status of their bids relative to the competition during the bidding process; and (c) the question of the degree to which the OSO, through its auditing procedures, should be able to delay equipment ordering for field development. The oil companies were concerned that if they signed an accord regarding their purchasing activities, the question of where the ultimate responsibility for equipment purchases lay might be 'fudged'. They, therefore, requested a clear statement in the code to the effect that, as the purchasers of equipment and as the parties paying for the equipment, the oil companies should have the final responsibility for the award of contracts.[24] The oil companies were also opposed to the OSO giving British firms any indication of how their bids compared with their rivals' bids, as they claimed this was against established commercial practice. Finally, they wanted guarantees from the Government that the OSO would not delay oil field development by reviewing every purchasing decision in detail.[25]

The Department of Energy accepted these reservations and drew up a revised code of practice which it submitted to the oil companies. This code, which was incorporated in a Memorandum of Understanding, was signed by the various members of UKOOA in November 1975 with no further alterations. From the perspective of the Government the memorandum[26] was intended to ensure 'the maximum possible involvement of UK manufacturers, consultants, contractors and service companies in the provision of supplies and services to the offshore hydrocarbon industry'.[27] For their part, the oil companies agreed 'fully [to] support this policy'[28] in their treatment of UK suppliers. The code of practice formed, in effect, a set of rules which would govern the commercial procedures involved in placing tenders for offshore supply projects. Specifically, it was designed to prevent the use of commercial practices, such as those mentioned previously, which placed British suppliers at a disadvantage in comparison with their foreign competitors. Thus, guidelines were laid down to ensure that all those bidding for a contract would have an equal period of time in which to prepare and submit a bid. The memorandum also included clauses to ensure that oil companies would phrase their tenders in such a way as to take account of British industrial specification standards. Other conditions in the memorandum related to the details of bidding and tendering practice. In order that it might have a way of verifying that these procedures were followed, the OSO was given authority to examine tender documents and the lists of bidders asked to tender for contracts. The OSO can also suggest the names of potential UK suppliers for inclusion in the bidding lists mentioned in Chapter 2.[29]

In practice, the Memorandum of Understanding obliges an oil company to inform the OSO of its intention to place contracts over the value of £500,000, in the case of construction and service work, and over £100,000 in the case of materials and manufactures. The OSO is also able to examine the contracting procedure in the case of contracts of a value of £5000 or more in certain special product or service areas in which the OSO has expressed a specific interest. The oil company not only informs the OSO about the details of prospective contracts, but also provides a list of the firms which will be asked to tender for the contract. The OSO then has the right to suggest that additional British firms be added to the tender list if any foreign firms are on the company's original list of potential contractors. Only after the OSO has approved a tender list (which contains the names of all potential foreign contractors) will the tender be sent out to the firms concerned. In this way it is possible for the OSO to ensure that British firms are asked to compete for all contracts on an equal basis with foreign firms.[30]

Both the oil companies and the OSO seem to have gained something from the implementation of the Memorandum of Understanding. No doubt this is the reason why the form of the memorandum and code of practice was settled so quickly. For their part the oil companies have avoided legislative complications while maintaining their position as the final authority on where and how contracts should be placed. At the same time, they have prevented the OSO from interfering in their commercial relationships with supply contractors by stopping the OSO from giving information concerning the status of contracts to British firms while bids are being called. Finally, the code of practice constituted excellent public relations for the oil companies in that it was a demonstration that they were living up to their responsibilities as 'good corporate citizens' by supporting British industry.[31]

The OSO and the Government, on the other hand, preferred the code of practice to the former lack of any oil company commitment concerning the purchase of British offshore supplies. OSO staff acknowledge that they are now less able than previously to give direct assistance to British firm bidding for contracts. Under the new arrangement they cannot give British firms information on the relative standing of their bids until after a contract has been let. However, they are convinced that the OSO's present access to the bidding procedure has considerably increased their ability to ensure that British firms receive equal treatment because they are now able to monitor the selection of potential contractors. According to official opinion, this will yield longer-term benefits to the industry than any *ad hoc* government advice given to individual firms on their contract bids.[32]

The development of the auditing procedure from the simple reporting procedure of the early months through to the emergence of the code of practice is significant in that it considerably deepened the involvement of Government in the commercial affairs of both the oil companies and British offshore contractors. Officials have had to become intimately acquainted with the details of producing equipment and services for the North Sea, whether they relate to design, engineering, production, marketing or finance. In addition, they have been obliged to familiarise themselves with the manner in which offshore purchasing is integrated into the total operations of the various oil companies, both from a technical and a commercial standpoint. Undoubtedly government is at a disadvantage with respect to the oil industry in the first stages of the application of procedures such as auditing, although this becomes less true as the Civil Service gains experience of the offshore sector. It is appropriate at this point to explore how the procedures mentioned above have altered both government–oil-company relations and the commercial dealings between the oil companies and the British offshore supply industry.

THE IMPACT OF GOVERNMENT POLICY ON THE OIL COMPANIES

The evolution of the auditing procedure within the OSO has given the Government both a greater knowledge of the relations between the oil industry and the British offshore supply industry and a greater ability to influence these relations. However, a number of difficult problems remain. In the first place, while the OSO is thorough in recording and examining oil company offshore purchases, it has only a limited staff to deal with the large number of oil companies involved in the *full range* of North Sea activities – oil companies that are collectively spending well over £1,000 million annually on equipment and service contracts.[33] Not surprisingly, although all contracts are reported, OSO staff have not had the resources or time to follow up or examine in detail the nature of every contract placed. Second, there has been a long 'learning curve' associated with the OSO's work in equipment purchase auditing, and it was only after three years experience of the auditing procedure that a sufficient body of knowledge and enough trained staff had been gathered to conduct an effective auditing operation. The commercial and technical details of offshore engineering work are highly complex, and it takes a long time to train staff who are proficient enough to know not just the mechanics of the business, but also whether purchasing decisions made by experienced oil company executives are conducted with sufficient regard to UK engineering and contracting capabilities. Adequate training is especially important because OSO auditing staff are always in an adversary position *vis-à-vis* oil executives and others; they must be credible as experts in the field. This has been a particular problem for the OSO, as it has had difficulty in recruiting staff with previous experience in the oil industry. For example, of the fifteen audit engineers on OSO staff in early 1976, only two had previous experience in oil-related industry. Of the remaining thirteen, eleven had previous industrial experience, but not in firms associated with the oil industry, and two were recruited from other technical branches of the Civil Service.[34] Given an initial lack of experienced staff, it has taken the OSO some time to assemble the expertise necessary to implement policy commitments effectively.

There is another constraint upon the OSO in its dealings with the oil companies, and this relates to the specific nature of the code of practice. The code is an agreement between the Government and the oil companies, but it has no legal force. The Department and the OSO have no recourse if the oil companies choose to ignore it. Hence, the implementation of the code is, in essence, an exercise in moral suasion, modified to some degree by the knowledge on the part of the oil companies that if the system breaks down legislation would in all likelihood follow to compel them to open their purchasing operations to government supervision, as indeed was threatened originally. Therefore, under the present procedures, civil servants rely to a great extent on the willingness of oil companies to observe their undertakings with the Government.

When there is a dispute between OSO officials and oil company executives over the placing of a contract, the audit engineer will normally refer it to the director of engineering who will, in turn, take the matter up with senior oil company executives. If the dispute is not resolved at that level, the matter will be referred to the Director-General and then to the Minister of State responsible for the OSO. Obviously, at each stage the OSO brings pressure to bear on the oil company concerned, but in the ultimate case the only real powers at the disposal of the Government are the threat of legislation, or the threat that uncooperative attitudes could damage the company's chances in future licensing rounds.[35]

Despite the lack of legal sanction in the offshore supply area, the Government has had some success in using the auditing procedure to influence oil company purchasing decisions. Most of the major oil companies try not to antagonise the Government over issues such as offshore supplies where they do not stand to lose substantially from a compliance with government wishes, particularly when other issues of greater importance to them are pending (e.g. taxation or participation). Indeed, one former minister stated in an interview with the author that there have been several occasions when ministerial intervention prevented a large contract for the North Sea from being place abroad. In each case the oil company concerned changed the contract in the final award to ensure that a UK supplier received it. The minister claimed that oil companies had been quite receptive to such pressure.[36]

Traditional supply relationships have inhibited the growth of a British offshore supply industry as outlined in earlier chapters. Nevertheless, the oil companies do have a certain interest in promoting the development of a domestic offshore supply industry. A viable offshore supply industry located close to the sites of exploration and development has the operational advantages of low transport costs and ready access to the sites (allowing rapid and specific modifications of equipment if necessary). However, in the British case the objective of developing an offshore supply capacity in the country (which is really a long-term objective to be achieved over a decade or more given the high-technology features of parts of the industry) conflicts with the short-term commercial objective of rapid oil field development. This latter objective is usually upper-most in the minds of oil company executives. It is also likely to lead to a preference within the oil companies for established suppliers of equipment and services with proven commercial reputations. These considerations are usually only outweighed when the sheer physical size of the equipment (e.g. production platforms) makes it un-economic and impracticable to rely on overseas suppliers, especially those located in the south-east of the United States.[37]

Since 1973 the level of engagement of British industry has improved, and British firms are now receiving a rising proportion of offshore equipment and service contracts. The DTI started to collect figures on oil company purchases in late 1972, but it was not until 1974 that a standardised reporting procedure emerged, and, as a result, detailed examinations of equipment purchase returns submitted by the oil companies are not possible for the period prior to 1974. In the latter year the definition of a 'British purchase' was also uniformly interpreted by the oil companies for the first time.[38] Since the start of the standardised reporting procedures five reviews of the level of equipment purchases have been published by the Government covering the years 1974 to 1978 inclusive.[39] The results of these reports are set out in Figures 8.1 and 8.2, and a detailed breakdown of the performance of British industry by product and service category is given in Appendix II (see p. 221).

Figures 8.1 and 8.2 show that since the IMEG Report was published in 1973 the level of British involvement in the market has increased from an estimated 25–30 per cent to 66 per cent at the end of 1978. Moreover, these percentages relate to a rapidly expanding market. The 66 per cent figure for 1978 refers to £1037 million worth of UK orders, while the 1973 figures are based upon a UK share estimated at about £90 million. Thus, even taking into account the high levels of inflation which have prevailed in the British economy during the 1970s and the fact that the IMEG consultants were only in a position to supply estimates of total market and market share in 1973, it is apparent that the *value* of goods and services which UK companies produced for the North Sea increased by several hundred per cent between 1973 and 1978. By any standard this is a substantial improvement in the competitive position of British offshore suppliers.

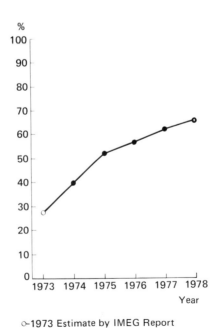

○–1973 Estimate by IMEG Report

FIGURE 8.1   Growth of UK share of offshore supply market, 1973–8

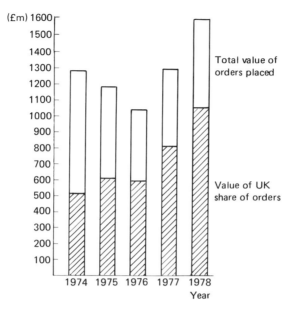

FIGURE 8.2   Size and UK share of offshore supply market, 1974–8

Sources: Department of Energy, *Offshore Oil and Gas: A Summary of Orders Placed . . . during 1974* (London: HMSO, 1975); *Offshore 1976: An Analysis of Orders Placed* (London: HMSO, 1977); *Offshore 1977: UK Goods and Services for Developments Offshore* (London: HMSO, 1978); *Development of the Oil and Gas Resources of the United Kingdom 1979* (London: HMSO, 1979) p. 24. Used with the permission of the Controller of Her Majesty's Stationery Office.

How much of this improvement in the industry's position is due to government policy is, of course, a very difficult question to answer. There are two possible dimensions: first, internal improvement in the competitive position of the offshore supply industry resulting from greater familiarity with the needs of the market, and second, a greater receptivity on the part of the oil companies to the existing or potential products and services of British industry, due, in part, to the effect of government policy. In addition, however, there is a possible third dimension to this improvement, which is that British industry responded to the market on the basis of encouragement from government. In the light of the evidence presented in Chapter 6 concerning the impact of government assistance policies on the domestic offshore supply industry, it is doubtful if this latter possibility contributed greatly to the rapid increase in British industry's involvement in the offshore supply market, especially given that direct government industrial assistance policies (e.g. R and D assistance, financial aid) were either too 'long-term' (R and D) or too 'limited' (financial assistance) to have a substantial impact. The efforts of the Government to interest firms in the market, by making them aware of its potential may, however, have had some impact on the industry's rapid involvement in the market. But, on balance, it would seem that the first two dimensions, internal improvement in the competitive capacity of the offshore supply industry and the auditing policy, are probably the principal causes for the industry's expansion. The question to ask now is: what role did these two factors play in increasing the UK industry's share of the North Sea market?

The evidence supporting the contention that an internally generated expansion of UK capacity contributed substantially to the improvement of British industry's share of the offshore market is fairly strong. In late 1973 the number of firms engaged in North Sea work in Britain was estimated to be about 2000, many of which were new to the market.[40] Naturally, as both experience and investment have increased, these firms have become much better at meeting competition, and have also become financially and technically capable of replacing foreign suppliers in many sectors of the market. This internal improvement in the competitive capability of British industry, something attested to by most of the oil company executives interviewed for this study, does not, as discussed previously, seem to owe much to government assistance. Yet what is apparent is that British suppliers *did* face initial difficulties in obtaining contracts from the oil companies, and the Government *did* have a role to play in broadening the receptivity of the oil companies to British goods and services. The improvement in performance on the part of British firms could not have taken place without internally generated improvements in technical and commercial capability; but it is also evident that, given the nature of the purchasing organisations of most of the oil companies, it is unlikely that oil company willingness to purchase British goods and services would have emerged without some sort of government pressure. Alternatively, the improvement in oil company attitudes to British suppliers cannot be entirely attributed to government intervention. Hence, we must now ask how great an effect government policies have had on decision-making processes within the oil companies?

In the first place, although auditing has a number of weaknesses, it has been successful in making the oil companies aware that offshore supplies is an issue of some importance to the Government and it obliges the oil companies to justify their pattern of choices in the offshore market. Few of the oil company executives interviewed for this study were in favour of the auditing procedure, and most saw it as a rather cumbersome and time-wasting addition to their work load. Some were frankly bemused by the sight of civil servants attempting to familiarise themselves with the technical details of equipment purchase procedures, and a few had doubts whether OSO officials had sufficient technical expertise to 'understand' the factors which dictated the direction of oil company purchases.[41] Despite these reservations, all the oil company executives interviewed took the audit procedure seriously, and were very sensitive about their role in providing British firms with a competitive opportunity in the offshore market. If nothing else, it would seem that the auditing procedure has obliged purchasing executives within the oil companies to consider British capacity seriously at all times. While auditing may not be all that significant in those companies which have large numbers of engineering staff trained in the UK (e.g. Burmah, Shell and BP), who are aware of British industrial capacity and who are likely at least to consider it in the first instance, it has had an impact on those oil companies who have not had the opportunity to recruit local engineering staff in large numbers.

A second aspect of the effectiveness of auditing relates to the strategic position of the oil companies within the economy as a whole. As mentioned earlier, during the period when the OSO audit procedures were being established North Sea operators were under mounting political pressure on a number of fronts. During 1973 the 'tax bonanza' that the oil companies had been enjoying, and were to continue to enjoy under North Sea taxation rules, became the object of public debate through the publication of the House of Commons Public Accounts Committee Report on the North Sea,[42] and later as a result of a barrage of newspaper reports on taxation.[43] Then, early in 1974, North Sea oil development, and its management by the Conservative Government, became an election issue with the result that after the election the oil companies confronted a Labour Government which had pledged in its election manifesto to seek a more effective tax regime for the North Sea and a direct equity holding (participation) in the oil fields through the establishment of a British National Oil Corporation (BNOC).

These rapid changes in the political climate forced the oil companies on to the defensive. They were far more concerned about the possible effects of the new Petroleum Revenue Tax, the administrative controls on oil production and depletion contained in the Pipelines Bill, and the possibility of participation, than they were about the introduction of procedures concerned with offshore supplies. Given their desire for concessions in other areas during the first three years of the auditing procedure (i.e. 1973–6), the oil companies were anxious not to appear uncooperative in the supplies area. Indeed, there was some incentive to be cooperative so that future bargaining positions regarding taxation and participation might be improved. In addition to the foregoing, the oil companies were made aware that their purchasing record would be taken into account in the awarding of future production and. exploration licences in the North Sea, and under the new conditions published for the fifth round of exploration licences in the summer of 1976 the contribution of the applicant to the development of the offshore supply industry and its purchasing record are listed as specific criteria to be applied in the final evaluation of licence applicants.[44] For any company planning to remain in the North Sea and anxious to expand its exploration effort this condition was one of some importance.

The above considerations applied to all contract awards, but one can also isolate a number of specific instances in which OSO pressure on the oil companies resulted in the reversal of company contract decisions in order to illustrate some of the particular conditions which applied in these cases. For example, in one instance an oil company initially decided to place a major order for a large single-point mooring buoy system abroad (i.e. with a Dutch firm).[45] The OSO requested that the company consider a British design, but it objected, stating that the British design was not technically suitable for the kind of operational characteristics required in its field development. However, after consultations with the OSO, the oil company concerned agreed to have the Dutch-designed system built in the UK on a sub-contract basis, thus ensuring that a UK firm gained the work and employment from the project, if not the design leadership.[46]

Another instance of this form of administrative pressure occurred in 1973 when the US company, Phillips, in its plans for the development of its North Sea oil fields intended to let a large multi-million pound contract for the shore facilities to store and process its oil at Teeside. Phillips originally planned to give the contract to an American firm, an action that would have been very damaging to the UK industry given that it had proven capability in the area. After extensive discussions with the OSO, Phillips changed its mind and decided to award the contract to the British firm of SimChem. While OSO officials deny that any direct political pressure was brought to bear on the company, it is clear that the OSO played a substantial role in encouraging the oil company to change its intended contract location to the UK and to give the contract to a UK firm.[47]

The above examples are typical of the kind of influence OSO can bring to bear on the decision-making process within the oil companies. However, there are also examples in which oil companies have chosen to ignore OSO pressure, and have proceeded with the purchase of services or equipment from abroad regardless of British government policy. For example, only two months after the signing of the Memorandum of Understanding one oil company, Occidental, decided to purchase eight expensive production modules from US suppliers despite the existence of several British firms with experience in the area and surplus capacity in that sector of the UK offshore supply industry. The oil company claimed that the decision to purchase abroad was made on the basis that the UK products were 15 per cent more expensive than their American counterparts. Ironically, the US modules were built with steel specially stockpiled for British module work by the British Steel Corporation.[48]

The above incident illustrates one of the weaknesses of the auditing procedure. The Government's auditing mechanisms do provide it with some leverage in the award of the oil companies' supply contracts, but this leverage is only exercisable at the margin. When British products are closely comparable on commercial and technical grounds with those of foreign competitors British firms are able to benefit from OSO pressure on the oil companies. Otherwise, OSO pressure may have little or no effect. Indeed, according to officials, the OSO generally only brings pressure to bear on the oil companies when the competitive margin is small for both price and delivery. Wide variations in price (figures quoted to the author indicate the limit is a price differential of about 10–15 per cent) between British and foreign firms' quotations will result in the OSO simply allowing the British firm to lose the order. However, in instances in which the price margin is close, OSO officials are inclined to put pressure on the oil companies to accept the British bid.

The limits of the OSO's ability to influence the decision-making process within the oil companies also became apparent in the unsuccessful attempts by the Department of Energy and the OSO to bring pressure to bear on the oil companies concerning the award of contracts for North Sea production platforms. On purchases such as production platforms oil companies have large investment risks to consider. The oil companies are, therefore, likely to be highly resistant to government pressure which attempts to encourage them to make a large investment against their commercial judgement. For example, in the middle of 1973, the OSO attempted to persuade Shell and Mobil to place some prospective orders for concrete platforms in the UK rather than in Norway. The OSO held meetings with the various UK companies which were capable of building the concrete platforms, and encouraged them to submit bids to the two oil companies. The bids submitted by the UK companies were, in OSO's opinion, in all respects as commercially competitive as the Norwegian offers. Despite this initiative, both Shell and Mobil decided that their original choices were best and placed their orders with the Norwegian firms, thus effectively resisting OSO pressure.[49]

More recently, in the latter part of 1975 and the first half of 1976, the Department of Energy tried to persuade the oil companies to bring forward orders for oil production platforms in order to prevent a major recession within the platform-building yards. During this period a noticeable slackening occurred in the pace of platform orders, and it became evident that, unless some measures were taken, several of the eight UK platform-building yards would be without work by the end of 1976.[50] Fearing the employment implications of this fall-off in orders, and a loss of capacity in the industry if the skilled labour force and engineering talent which had been built up by the industry during the early 1970s were dissipated by redundancies resulting from yard closures, John Smith, the junior Energy Minister, held talks with the oil companies over the summer and autumn of 1975 in an attempt to see if development schedules could be moved ahead so that orders for platforms could be placed with British firms.[51] In particular, pressure was brought to bear on the American Chevron Company to place an order for a third platform for the Ninian Field.[52] Despite intensive negotiations with the oil companies no firm commitments were forthcoming, and in November of 1975 the new Energy Secretary, Anthony Wedgwood Benn, was forced to tell union leaders that he could not 'hold out much hope of overcoming the problem'.[53] Indeed, by the spring of the following year the Government had still not been able to influence the oil companies' order schedules, and it was contemplating granting companies with marginal fields an exemption from the $12\frac{1}{2}$ per cent royalty payments due on oil produced in the North Sea in the hope that this exemption would make the economics of those fields more attractive for development and, hence, encourage orders for more platforms.[54] The fact that the Government did not proceed with this initiative strongly indicates that the oil companies were not convinced that such an exemption would be sufficiently beneficial to them to offset the financial costs of proceeding with field development.

The oil companies had been reluctant to place orders for platforms for a number of reasons, most of which related to the cost impact of changes in offshore technology. The constant flow of new ideas on construction methods and alternative designs for production platforms (e.g. the development of 'tension leg platforms') led oil company executives to expect lower costs in this area. In addition, improvements in drilling techniques reduced the number of platforms required to develop a particular field, and this also has had a cost-reduction potential. A number of oil companies still had extensive exploration commitments, and new discoveries were being made as a result of these commitments. Hence, the companies were reluctant to commit themselves until all exploration results were in and a choice between discoveries could be made. In addition, as a result of increased experience with the hazardous conditions in the North Sea, oil companies were planning their developments more carefully, especially with regard to correct design criteria for projects. Naturally, all of these changed circumstances lengthened the time that oil companies took over their decisions about the choice of field development timetables and strategies, and this resulted in delays in the ordering of platforms.[55]

Apart from the above technical considerations, many oil companies, particularly the larger ones, were so fully committed to existing project work in the North Sea by 1975 that it was difficult for them to take on any additional development work which would involve new platform orders. This problem of over-commitment was also compounded by the fact that many of the larger companies already had substantial financial investments in the North Sea totalling hundreds of millions of pounds, and it was difficult for them to raise further development capital without first showing some return from existing commitments in the North Sea.

Thus, in the 'uncertain' environment of the 1975–6 period, government found it difficult to encourage the oil companies to invest substantial sums in capital equipment. However, by 1977 several oil companies had decided, on their own initiative, that they were ready to place orders for steel production platforms, and it appears that government was successful in ensuring that the resulting orders were placed in Britain. Despite spare capacity in all European yards at the time, two of the three oil companies which ordered platforms in 1977 (Chevron and Conoco) placed their construction contracts with UK yards. The remaining company (Texaco) is known to have resisted government pressure to place its platform order in Britain. Texaco wished to give its contract to a French platform construction company, but after the British Government brought considerable pressure to bear upon Texaco, the order was split between a British and a French yard.[56]

Given that technical and commercial considerations are ultimately paramount in determining *when* an oil company will make substantial capital investments, government has not been able to influence investment phasing to any great degree. It has, however, been able to influence the placement of orders once an oil company has decided to invest. Clearly if the Government were a full commercial partner in groups making decisions about development timetables, it might have been in a position to influence order scheduling. However, because government has been removed from decision-making within the oil companies, auditing can at best be an instrument to encourage companies to consider British industrial capacity when this will not materially harm their commercial operations. In other words, auditing in many respects is no more than a means for some competitive British suppliers to enter a market which would normally be closed to them for other than strictly commercial reasons.

CONCLUSIONS

The Government's auditing procedure reflects some of the fundamental restrictions in the present scope of government policy. The OSO's task is officially to ensure a 'full and fair opportunity' for

British firms to compete with foreign firms for offshore orders.[57] Although this has probably been partly achieved through the activities of the OSO in the auditing field, it is clear that the Government has accepted that the final authority in making purchasing decisions lies with the oil companies themselves. The Government is only in a position to challenge this authority when the oil companies violate the canons of free-market practice (i.e. by choosing foreign suppliers when British firms are competitive). In addition, government only attempts to transcend 'free-market practice' when it occasionally tries to ensure that preference is given to British firms as competitive, or slightly less competitive, than foreign suppliers. However, these attempts are severely limited both by the OSO's physical inability to supervise all purchases and contracts tendered and by the conditions which are contained within the Memorandum of Understanding. For example, a section of the memorandum states that the Government shall not implement policies which violate EEC rules concerning free competition.[58] This provision weakens the Government's position *vis à vis* the oil companies, for it must cope with the fact that many of its attempts to persuade the oil companies to purchase British goods are, strictly speaking, illegal, as often the foreign suppliers who are excluded by such administrative pressure come from EEC member countries.[59] Thus, the Government's acceptance of the 'full and fair opportunity' guidelines and the provisions of the Memorandum of Understanding have meant that its ability to promote the interests of British industry is highly constrained. This is especially the case when British firms are competing against suppliers, for example from the US, with a commanding industrial lead and established relationships with the foreign-based oil companies operating in the North Sea.

This is not to say that the Government has not had some success in reducing the impact of a number of the non-market elements in the relationship between the oil companies and the foreign-based offshore supply industry which have prevented British firms from gaining access to the offshore market. However, it is one thing to give British industry an *entrée* to a market and quite another to make up for the competitive disadvantage that British firms may suffer in comparison with the offshore supply industry in the United States which is already well established in world markets. It seems that the auditing procedure has brought British firms to the attention of oil company executives, but there is nothing in the policy to overcome or compensate for the commercial weaknesses of British industry, especially in the more specialised sectors where foreign competition is strong. At present civil servants only go as far as pressing oil company executives to accept UK contractors at slightly more than 'competitive' price levels. Intervention of a type that would 'correct' the commercial weaknesses in the offshore supply industry would require government commitment to industrial promotion far beyond the simple adherence to 'full and fair opportunity' which underpins auditing. Concomitantly, such a commitment could only be implemented through a far more elaborate set of policy instruments than exists at present.

The impact of government policy apart, it is important as well to examine the implications of the Government's activities in the auditing field for the relationship between the Government and the oil companies. Regardless of the degree to which government policy has changed the nature of the oil companies' commercial activities, the policy instruments described in this chapter are important because they give an indication of current trends regarding a number of issues which have been mentioned previously: first, the state of the art in the development of policy instruments in the realm of industrial policy; second, the Government's role *vis-à-vis* multinational industry; and, third, the general character of government–industry relations.

What emerges from the evidence presented in this chapter is that government involvement with the oil companies now extends beyond matters of normal regulatory concern (e.g. the safety of offshore platforms, or reservoir management) or matters which relate only to strategic economic concerns (control of oil company activities for balance of payments considerations or the disposition and export of refinery products, etc.). Government intervention has come to encompass specific regulation of the commercial activities of companies with the express intention of achieving broad industrial policy goals. The use of the specific attributes of multinationals (in this case their position as large-scale purchasers) as a foundation for government policy initiatives is not entirely new (it has been proposed in other countries[60]), but it does represent a departure in British experience from the normal range of policy options at the disposal of the Government. The auditing procedure is an exceptional policy instrument by previous British standards in that it combines a type of administrative exhortation with a very technical and specific kind of supervision which borders on regulation. Auditing seems to exist in a vague area between informal government–oil-company cooperation and direct, legal, government supervision of the workings of the oil companies. This new form of government involvement in industry demonstrates the difficulties in evolving policy instruments which can deal effectively with complex and technical policy issues, while at the same time recognising the realities of the political and economic power of the industrial units which the Government wishes to influence. Not surprisingly perhaps, the policy *mélange* which emerges does not readily fall into one of the categories which have been used in the past to describe the role of the state and its involvement in industrial affairs.[61] Thus, certain features of auditing are *dirigiste* in character; others very clearly display the limits of the Government's present ability to monitor and influence the commercial operations of the oil companies. These limits derive from a number of official commitments, varying from respect amongst civil servants and ministers for the traditional mechanisms of the market system,[62] to a genuine belief that, given the extensive powers of the multinational companies, the Government is very constrained in its ability to affect the commercial practices of these companies. These some-what contradictory elements have combined in a policy instru-ment which may best be described as a type of administrative supervision of wholly commercial activities of companies. In other words, it is an attempt to influence the detailed commercial activities of firms through administrative means for ends connected with national industrial strategies.

In a sense, one might argue that the auditing procedure is not very different from the type of administrative supervision of commercial behaviour which characterises the work of such state bodies as the Monopolies and Mergers Commission (MMC). However, there is a difference of degree. In the case of auditing, the supervision is both continuous and free from any form of statutory limitation. In the case of the work of bodies such as the MMC commercial direction usually constitutes only a single action (or set of actions) arising from an investigation of a complaint. In addition, the activities of bodies such as the MMC are specifically constrained by legislation. It might also be argued that the auditing process is similar to other common types of policy instruments, such as various forms of regulatory control with regard to safety, exchange control and the like, except that in these instances government intervention has arisen because the activities of an industry impinge upon areas which are normally considered within the public domain (e.g. national economic policy, environmental control, etc.). In the case of auditing, on the other hand, the Government is seeking to influence commercial practices through administrative means in order to obtain changes in the normal commercial relationships between one sector of industry and another – changes in commercial relationships which benefit but *one* section of the private sector.

This last-mentioned characteristic of the auditing process not only sets it apart from other types of policy instruments, it also demonstrates to some degree a change in the way the Government interprets its relationship with the oil companies and with industry in general. As has been shown in Chapters 4 and 5, the evolution of the offshore policy area led to the gradual realisation on the part of the Civil Service and ministers that there are fundamental conflicts of interest between various sectors of national industry and the multinational oil companies. To a great extent auditing represents a recognition in policy terms that in these conflicts government should align itself with national industry. In interviews conducted with civil servants responsible for implementing the auditing policy I found a very explicit and conscious awareness that this alignment implied what one senior official described as a 'quiet state of war' between the oil companies and the Department of Energy.[63] Thus, perhaps for the first time, the Government has deliberately sided with a set of domestically based firms against a set of multinationals to the degree that it has seen fit to become involved in the multinational industry's commercial operations with the intention of promoting the interests of the national industry.[64]

However, government activity in this area has been tempered by two other considerations. The single-minded pursuit of a policy seeking maximum benefit for UK industry has been constrained by wider policy objectives relating to the speed of development of the North Sea oil fields for balance of payments and tax revenue considerations. Thus, the limits of policy in this area are dictated by the degree to which the Government is willing to undertake the risks involved in using new or untried suppliers in the offshore field when this may cause a slow-down in the development timetable of the oil fields, and hence create severe difficulties for government planners banking on the balance of payments and revenue boost to the economy of the production of North Sea oil in sufficiently large quantities. If speed of development were not essential, then delays in timetables to allow adequate time for the orderly development of British offshore capability would be a viable policy option for the Government, whatever the intentions of the oil companies. However, because of the larger issues at stake, speed of development has always taken precedence, both during the Conservative Government's period in office, and also under the Labour Government after 1974. Constraints of this kind are important to the oil companies in their attempts to persuade the Government to acquiesce in purchasing decisions which favour foreign suppliers. The Government may find it difficult to resist such oil company pressure, particularly when field development work may be behind schedule due to engineering problems, poor weather conditions, or the poor delivery-time performance of some new British contractors.

The Government is also limited in the pursuit of an 'anti-multinational' stance because of the general framework of government industrial policy which requires it at least to appear to be supporting market mechanisms and to avoid favouring one industry unduly over another. This can clearly be seen in the fact that the auditing system is based on the assumption that British industry is to be given a 'full and fair opportunity to compete', and no more. In many respects the policy is simply an attempt to strengthen the market ethic in the offshore area by removing some of the 'non-market' inducements for the oil companies to favour foreign contractors. This interpretation of the role of government in the market place acts as a constraint on any initiatives of a more overtly *dirigiste* nature in policy implementation. A positivist and entrepreneurial role for the Government, something which has emerged in other countries faced with similar problems (e.g. Norway and France), does not seem likely to develop in Britain for the present.

Finally, it is important to remember that the auditing process is not *necessarily* symptomatic of a long-term 'anti-multinational' stance. Any success for government policy in the offshore supply industry will be of long-term benefit to the oil companies (as indeed, they themselves recognise).[65] Such success would create additional sources of innovation and additional sources of supply for the oil companies in the long term. Thus, it is perhaps not accurate to speak of industrial interests which are of necessity in conflict, although certainly in the short term the oil companies' desire for rapid development and their predilection for established suppliers of equipment clashes with the aspirations of government and national industry.

In the case examined in this chapter government has subordinated the short-term interests of the oil companies to the long-term interests of domestic industrial capital, and indeed, the oil companies themselves. However, this policy of seeking benefit from multinational firms for nationally based industry has been constrained both by other government policy objectives (i.e. rapid exploitation of North Sea reserves) and by a reluctance and inability on the part of the Government to thwart the commercial objectives of the oil companies entirely.

9 Intervention in the 1970s: The Offshore Case

Government intervened in support of the offshore supply industry in response to a variety of economic challenges centring upon the failure of British industry to rise to the opportunities presented by North Sea oil development. In the process the commitments of ministers and civil servants were altered and new areas of government endeavour emerged. The present chapter focusses upon these latter aspects of offshore intervention, and, in particular, attempts to specify what the offshore episode indicates about why and how government capabilities in the field of industrial policy have expanded since the late 1960s and early 1970s. Of course, this expansion has not been without limits, and these too are examined, as is the impact of intervention upon industry. Thus, what follows is an analysis of the dynamics, the constraints and the impact of offshore intervention and of the significance of these for other instances of industrial policy-making in the 1970s and 1980s.

INDUSTRIAL POLICY INITIATION IN THE 1970s

Government intervention in the affairs of the offshore supplies industry and the multinational oil companies is a single episode in the recent history of British industrial policy. Yet in comparison with previous episodes it serves to illustrate that the nature and scope of government–industry relations have altered between the late 1960s and the latter half of the 1970s. Some of the more significant changes centre upon the manner in which industrial intervention is initiated.

Writing in the mid 1970s Stephen Young observed that in the years from 1964 to 1972 industrial policies were frequently constrained by lack of knowledge of the structure of British industry.[1] Often officials and ministers had little or no information concerning the specific operations of firms falling within their brief, much less of the relations between firms in an industry or across industrial boundaries. Furthermore, such information as was collected about industry, either within government or by outside consultants, rapidly became dated. Under these circumstances there was little opportunity for analytical work to proceed, the limitations of theory in disciplines such as economics aside. Thus, government relied extensively upon a number of assumptions about industry and industrial development stemming from 'conventional wisdom' within the business and financial community. Young has documented the influence of the private-sector-inspired 'bigger is better' assumption upon mergers policy, especially in the case of the IRC. Similarly, the science and technology policies of MinTech were founded upon the conventional belief that innovation, and therefore improved industrial performance, follows naturally from increased research and development. Yet, as Young notes, this belief had little theoretical, much less empirical, basis at the time it was being applied.[2] In both cases, as in others, intervention was premised upon linear cause–effect models, but little attention was devoted either to the general validity of these models or to the nature of the specific contexts in which they were being used.

In contrast, the process whereby intervention was initiated in the offshore sector was characterised by substantial efforts to accumulate information which could be used in defining both the structure of the offshore supplies industry and its relations with other industries. The early history of the development of policies in the fields of marine technology and ocean engineering is replete with instances in which ministers and officials apparently did not have adequate intelligence, and therefore could not proceed much further than listing, and at times categorising, the prominent issues in specific areas of policy interest. By 1972–3, however, circumstances had altered significantly. Officials in the CPRS and the DTI recognised from the first that government action in the offshore sector, if it was to be effective, had to be founded upon detailed analyses of market opportunities, of the structure of the industries operating in the sector and of the relationship between the two. The result was the IMEG Report. Moreover, particularly in the development of the auditing procedure, officials and consultants emphasised the use of information-gathering and analysis as levers to change offshore purchasing patterns. Later in the evolution of offshore strategy this emphasis was repeated during the formulation of the monitoring function. In all of these cases it was envisaged that information-gathering and analysis should be continuous functions feeding into each stage of policy development so that the problem of dated intelligence could be avoided as much as possible.

The stress upon information-gathering and analysis in the preparation of policy initiatives is but one of a complex of interrelated changes which often distinguish intervention in the 1964–72 period from intervention several years later. For example, the analytical work undertaken in connection with the development of an offshore strategy reflected an increasing tendency for officials and ministers to view industry and government–industry relations in a structured way. There are several facets to this. In the first place, the concept of the 'strategic industry' had acquired new meaning. During the 1960s a variety of industries were identified as in some sense crucial to national objectives and, therefore, eligible for government support. Certain industries (e.g. computers) were singled out because they appeared to have the potential to expand, especially in export markets, and thereby lessen balance of payments shortfalls. Others were identified as strategic in the face of impending collapse. In other words, they were regarded as too important to be allowed to fail, either because they were sufficiently large for collapse to lead to severe economic dislocation or because they closely affected other industries. In this latter case the threat of collapse highlighted backward and forward linkages between industries and firms with the result that, after mediating in the myriad industrial failures of the late 1960s and early 1970s, officials and ministers were more acutely aware of the importance of industrial interdependencies in defining what is and is not strategic. By 1972, therefore, they were focussing upon the relationships between industries and firms within the economy, and interpreting these in the light of national objectives. Often, as in the case of the offshore sector, this involved co-ordinating the development of several areas of industrial activity over time against a background of fluctuating economic conditions. For example, in offshore strategy it was regarded as essential to strike the right balance between promoting oil company investment, including rapid development of the oil fields, and pressing the oil multinationals to buy British goods and services. During the early 1970s priority was given to encouraging oil company exploration and development because no other benefits, among which were orders and revenue for British industry, could be obtained without the initial fixed investment. In

1972 the balance moved significantly in favour of giving British industry a greater share of the market by attempting to change the purchasing patterns of the oil companies. Yet, a year later, in the wake of the twin fuel crises, field development had once again taken priority, although by that time the problem had been complicated by the need to ensure that British suppliers met their contractual obligations and, therefore, did not subvert development time-tables.[3] Thus, offshore policy involved constant efforts to define the state of play in the relationship between the oil companies and their suppliers so that various national objectives of differing priority (e.g. security of oil supply, balance of payments benefits from oil, Exchequer revenue and contracts for British industry) could be fulfilled most effectively.

A second facet in the development of a structured view of industry in official circles centred upon the multinational–national distinction. As outlined in Chapter 3, even in the early 1970s both Conservative and Labour ministers, Conservative MPs and senior civil servants failed to differentiate to any great degree between multinational and national companies in the discussion of policy. Moreover, according to Hodges, when the question of the influence of multinationals within the British economy was forced upon government, as in the cases of ICL and Rootes, it was reluctant to control multinationals, and focussed instead upon creating 'a vital British element wherever possible'.[4] In contrast, the evidence presented in preceding chapters clearly indicates that the multinational–national distinction was at the centre of policy formulation for the offshore sector. Many of the policy instruments employed in this field, both orthodox and unorthodox, distinguished between the interests of multinational and national firms. Auditing, in particular, was based upon an official assumption that the multinational North Sea operators, because of their international corporate stature, were likely to frustrate the development of a viable British offshore supplies industry by allocating supply contracts on other than strictly commercial grounds. The result was an unprecedented level of government influence upon basic allocation functions within private-sector corporations.

The focus on multinationals characteristic of offshore policy is undoubtedly a product of several specific features of the offshore sector, for example, the concentration of multinational corporations in the oil industry and the magnitude of the implications for the British balance of payments if most of the goods and services for the

North Sea had been imported. Yet it yielded a variety of precedents with many ramifications for the future quality of government industrial intervention. For instance, coupled with the emphasis on backward and forward linkages discussed previously, the focus on multinationals as major corporate actors led to the innovative use of policy instruments directed towards the activities of one industry in order to aid the fortunes of another.

More importantly, the focus on multinationals served to modify long-standing commitments in official circles concerning the integrity and independence of the firm. Young has observed that government intervention in the 1964–72 period was constrained in many cases because firms refused to respond to government measures. Moreover, government had no answer to this dilemma, for many ministers and senior officials remained convinced that the independence of the firm had to be preserved in order to ensure its financial and commercial viability. Indeed, it was for this, among other, reasons that the multinational issue did not become salient until the mid 1970s. In government circles multinationals operating in Britain were firms like any other, and in the interests of competitiveness and efficiency the preservation of their independence was desirable. However, by 1972 ministers and officials had identified a number of adverse effects upon British suppliers arising from the multinational character of the oil industry. Under such circumstances, the 'national' interest appeared to be clear, and there was relatively little concern about violating the integrity and independence of the oil companies during the formulation of the auditing procedure. Yet, what is even more significant is that auditing served as a precedent for a type of intervention – monitoring – which could be viewed as a violation of the integrity and independence of *British-owned* firms. Having employed highly interventionist tactics in extracting information about purchasing patterns from the multinational oil companies, officials and ministers were apparently not reluctant to intervene extensively in the affairs of certain British suppliers to ensure that the benefits achieved through auditing were not lost. Thus, auditing and monitoring are complementary both in their purpose and in the manner in which they extend the Government's capacity to oblige firms to act in specific ways.

Finally, and very crucially, the focus on multinationals characteristic of offshore policy led government to align itself fairly clearly with one set of firms as against another, with domestic as opposed to multinational industry. This indicates not only that government is ceasing to view industry as a homogeneous entity, but also that it is prepared to act in a partisan manner on the basis of the analytical distinctions it has at hand.

In connection with the last point, it is important to note that the development of a more structured view of industry has been accompanied by changes in the attitudes and expertise of those closely involved in intervention, especially members of the Civil Service. For example, in 1972–3 officials evidently believed that on the basis of the analysis contained in the IMEG Report and other internal documents they were capable of modifying commercial relationships in the private sector to the benefit of both government and industry. Any reluctance to 'interfere' in the affairs of individual firms seems to have largely evaporated. Furthermore, officials were convinced that the Civil Service either contained, or had access to, the technical, managerial and administrative expertise necessary for the gradual meshing of government and industrial operations. Indeed, under this interpretation of intervention, government had a role to play in overcoming what officials regarded as barriers to competition in the oil industry and a lack of entrepreneurial initiative among British offshore suppliers. To this end they were prepared to mobilise a wide variety of government services and, when necessary, to enlarge the capabilities of the Civil Service, either by importing skills or by recasting the roles of those already involved in industrial policy. Clearly, the emergence of a more structured view of industry, together with the emphasis upon information and analysis which has characterised this instance of industrial intervention, have accelerated the diversification of tasks and skills within the Civil Service. This process has proceeded to the point that on certain fronts (e.g. venture management) the activities of officials have come to resemble those of industrial personnel very closely.

The process described in the previous paragraph also appears to have had implications for the distribution of influence concerning industrial intervention within government. Specifically, it is significant that the decision by CPRS and DTI officials to launch a major review of the offshore supplies industry and the offshore market was taken without resort to ministers and in the absence of any pressure from industrial interest groups (either management or labour) or from the media. Moreover, in this instance civil servants were able to initiate an intervention strategy directed at a *new* rather than an established industry on the basis of a preliminary analysis which highlighted *potential* rather than actual industrial problems. These observations are certainly not meant to imply that officials are fully autonomous in the field of government–industry relations. There were a number of pressing considerations which induced offshore intervention, among them the media's belated recognition of the size of the offshore market in 1971, the balance of payments reverses which would have resulted if British industry had remained lax about North Sea opportunities, and the depressed state of much of the engineering industry, especially in Scotland and the North of England. In addition, ultimately officials remained responsible to ministers during the process of developing offshore policy proposals. However, the relative autonomy of officials in this sphere has been substantial. This is in keeping with the analysis contained in previous pages. In particular, it is the Civil Service which assembles information about industry and performs any analytical work felt to be necessary for the development of policy. Hence, as a structured view of industry and, consequently, analysis become more important to the framing of industrial policy, officials are likely to be increasingly thrust into the centre of debates about industrial strategy, providing data, interpreting recent developments and giving advice to ministers. Under these circumstances, it can be argued, officials have the capacity to act with a greater degree of discretion than previously, especially given that the pace of change in the economy has served to reduce the importance of traditional party differences in the field of industrial intervention (see Chapter 4). This explanation of the enhanced autonomy of officials in the offshore sphere is given further weight by the fact that much of their increased discretion centres upon the *anticipatory* nature of their initiatives, and anticipatory policy formulation is not possible without a well-developed view of industry and analytical work to support it. There is every reason to expect, furthermore, that as officials gain increased confidence in their ability to anticipate future industrial developments their autonomy will increase concomitantly. Already there is evidence that anticipatory policy-making is becoming more common. One prominent recent instance was the 1977 nationalisation of the British aircraft industry in preparation for the rationalisation of the European aircraft industry which government believed would accompany the major civil aircraft projects of the last quarter of this century.[5]

NEW FORMS OF INTERVENTION

Having examined the process whereby offshore intervention was initiated, we may now turn to a consideration of the character which intervention assumed upon implementation. As noted in Chapters 4 and 5, offshore policy has been marked by a high degree of innovation. Even orthodox policy instruments acquired an unorthodox stamp upon implementation. It is worthwhile pausing for a moment to consider why this was so.

In late 1972, when officials and their consultants became convinced of the need to assist the offshore supply industry, there were several considerations which prompted unorthodox policy responses from government. Officials had concluded that without government action the multinational oil companies would tend to rely upon traditional linkages with experienced, foreign suppliers. Moreover, there was a question of timing. If government did not act quickly foreign competition would become entrenched and increasing the British market share that much more difficult. Under these circumstances, officials and ministers had little choice but to attempt to influence the purchasing patterns of the oil companies in the quickest and most direct way possible. The result was auditing, an innovative policy instrument which involved officials in screening the commercial transactions of the oil companies.

In the case of policy directed towards the offshore suppliers, there were other considerations which prompted innovation. As outlined in Chapter 6, in the early and mid 1970s the offshore supply industry lacked cohesiveness. In particular, there was no network of trade associations to liaise between government and individual suppliers. This meant that if government were to assist suppliers effectively it had no option but to establish direct contacts with firms. Furthermore, after the 1973 fuel crises officials and ministers concluded that intervention in the affairs of suppliers was not optional, but vitally necessary if the all-important development timetables were to be met. These two considerations compounded led to an unprecedented level of government influence in the day-to-day activities of specific groups of firms, in the form of monitoring and the platform sites policy.

How, then, did the policy instruments which emerged in the offshore field differ from those characteristic of earlier episodes in industrial intervention? Stephen Young in his book, *Intervention in the Mixed Economy*, has formulated a typology of policy instruments in

	(i)	(ii)	(iii)	(iv)	(v)
	Economic and Legal Framework		Non-Regulatory Measures		
	Economic & Fiscal Controls	Legal Regulation	Encouragement & Exhortation	Provision of Advice & Services	Financial Inducements
A Policies that are neutral between primary manufacturing & service industries					
B Policies that discriminate between industries					
C Policies that discriminate between firms within industries					

FIGURE 9.1   Range of government policies towards the private sector, 1964–70

Source: S. Young with A. V. Lowe, *Intervention in the Mixed Economy* (London: Croom Helm, 1974) p. 18.

use up to 1972 in the industrial field.[6] A diagrammatic outline of this typology is given in Figure 9.1. In it, Young distinguishes between the 'economic and legal framework' and the range of 'non-regulatory' industrial measures which government has developed since the war. The 'economic and legal framework' is essentially the summation of the Government's regulatory legal structure and its macro-economic policy instruments. Young states that instruments which fall within the 'economic and legal framework' tend to be neutral in their effect on industries and firms, although he notes that there are cases in which discrimination occurs. Non-regulatory measures include exhortation and the provision of advice and financial assistance. In contrast to instruments within the economic and legal framework, these are more likely to be directed at specific industries, or firms, and hence tend to be discriminatory. However, as Young notes towards the end of his book, it is generally acknowledged that many of the non-regulatory policies which government has pursued have failed. This has been due to the reluctance of firms to take advantage of the government services or financial inducements which have been offered to them. Young explains this phenomenon by pointing to the frequent lack of congruence between government objectives and the objectives of firms. In the past government has often seen its aims and the aims of firms as similar, whereas in practice they may be widely divergent.

In Young's words: 'persuasion and cajolery will not always achieve the government's end, because the independence and autonomy of the firm enables it to resist government's attempts to influence its decision-making'.[7]

The above categorisation of government policy and Young's statements about the failure of non-regulatory devices are of interest in any attempt to characterise the policy instruments developed by the Government to deal with the offshore supplies industry. While some of the policy instruments discussed in preceding chapters fit into Young's typology (e.g. market assessment, exhortation), others, such as auditing, monitoring and venture management, do not. These latter *unorthodox* policy instruments fall neither into the economic and legal framework nor the range of non-regulatory instruments. Instead, they are hybrids involving aspects of both the non-regulatory and regulatory approaches. For example, as out-lined in Chapter 8, auditing represents an attempt to combine exhortation with a type of administrative supervision of the oil companies' commercial affairs which is akin to a regulatory control procedure. Similarly, although it is less regulatory in character than auditing, monitoring is a very advanced, very specific form of exhortation given a regulatory aspect by the implicit threat of government sanctions if British suppliers fail to meet their contractual commitments in the North Sea. Venture management, too, is more than a non-regulatory device. In this case, the reluctance of firms to act on government information and to respond to exhortation and the provision of financial assistance has been tackled through venture managers actively seeking out 'clients' for government assistance and providing them with the financial, commercial and, where necessary, entrepreneurial ex-pertise necessary to support industrial initiatives. Thus, the charac-teristics of all three policy instruments constitute evidence that Government has moved substantially beyond 'persuasion and cajolery' in its efforts to prevent firms from evading its policies. By drawing firms into semi-contractual 'understandings' of some benefit both to the firms and government (i.e. auditing) or, at the other end of the scale, by catering to the highly specific needs of individual firms with advice about financing and joint ventures (i.e. venture management) the Government has limited the ability of firms to act independently and, thereby, strengthened its influence over the development of the offshore supply industry.

The three unorthodox policy instruments discussed in the

previous paragraph do not fit into Young's typology, primarily because he established a relatively rigid divide between regulatory and non-regulatory policy instruments, and, indeed, given the state of industrial policy-making in the 1964–72 period, this separation appears to be perfectly justified. However, with the emergence of policy instruments which combine 'regulatory' and 'non-regulatory' aspects, it is appropriate to modify Young's presentation to take this change into account. I have recast Young's scheme so that the characteristics of the unorthodox instruments discussed above can be accommodated. The new presentation allows one to locate the unorthodox instruments in the space defined by two axes as in Figure 9.2. In this figure, an ordinal scale for compulsion (a synonym for 'degree of regulation') is ranged along the 'A' axis. Compulsion refers here to the severity of the sanctions which government is prepared to invoke in implementing a policy instrument. Thus, compulsion is high when legal sanctions are invoked, less when sanctions involve the withholding of, for

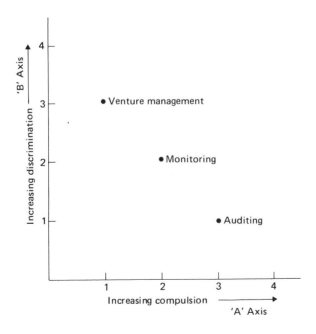

FIGURE 9.2   Unorthodox policy instruments

example, financial assistance or tax advantages, and low when sanctions are synonymous with 'government disapproval'. An ordinal scale for the degree to which policy instruments discriminate between sub-divisions within the economy (i.e. between sectors, between industries, between firms) is ranged along the 'B' axis. By definition, greater or smaller numbers along these scales can be interpreted as 'more than' or 'less than' for the variables in question. Of course, these numbers have no meaning with relation to the questions 'how much greater' or 'how much smaller'.

The three unorthodox policy instruments have been mapped on to this space, and it is worthwhile reviewing the reasons for their specific locations. Auditing is located furthest to the right because it is the most compulsory of the policy instruments under consideration, resting as it does upon a written agreement between the Government and the oil companies, supported by the implicit threat of legal sanctions if the agreement fails. Auditing is also the least discriminatory of these instruments because it is potentially applicable to all firms in an industry, namely the oil industry. Monitoring involves a lesser degree of compulsion than auditing in that it does not rely upon a written agreement. Nevertheless, monitoring engineers have employed fairly strong forms of exhortation; rapid field development has been an obvious national priority and the Government has to some degree attempted to 'shame' companies jeopardising this objective into better performance. In extreme cases, monitoring has involved ministers 'threatening' firms with unspecified government sanctions. On the other hand, monitoring is more discriminatory than auditing because it is applied only to that group of firms within the offshore supplies industry which are failing to meet their contractual obligations in the North Sea. Finally, venture management is located furthest to the left in Figure 9.2 because it involves the least degree of compulsion of the three unorthodox instruments. Firms have complete discretion in accepting or not accepting the services of venture managers. Yet government does attempt to make its wishes felt in a very explicit way in venture management by singling firms out for assistance. Moreover, once a firm has accepted assistance from venture managers it becomes involved in moral and at times financial obligations vis-à-vis government, particularly as assistance is so closely tied to individual projects within firms. Turning now to the 'B' axis, it should be noted that venture management is the most discriminatory of the three policy instruments; venture management, unlike monitoring, has no meaning beyond the context of the individual firm and its particular commercial problems.

One final point should be made in concluding the discussion of Figure 9.2. The platform sites policy, another unorthodox policy instrument, has not been mentioned so far because it very much resembles venture management for the purposes of the present analysis. It, too, is highly discriminatory, but with few elements of compulsion. The major difference between the two instruments is that the platform sites policy has involved the Government in long-term, speculative investments on behalf of the offshore supply industry. However, with reference to 'compulsion' and 'discrimination' the two may be regarded as virtually identical; what applies to one, applies to the other.

The above presentation demonstrates that there have been noticeable changes since 1972 in the range of policy instruments employed by government in its relations with industry. Whereas in the past, policy instruments tended to be *either* compulsory and applied to all firms *or* non-compulsory and applied selectively to a few firms, many of the newer policy instruments are to some degree both selective and compulsory. The fusion of 'regulatory' and 'non-regulatory' features in the development of policy instruments has meant an expansion in the Government's capacity to influence corporate decision-making. Moreover, this expanded capacity may be used to greater effect, because with the introduction of the unorthodox instruments discussed above the relations between government and industry are also more directed than in the past.

As Young documented, during the 1960s and early 1970s, government increasingly emphasised industry-specific and firm-specific policies in the wake of the 'failure' of monetary and fiscal policy and indicative planning to stem the decline in growth rates. However, this pursuit of influence at more and more micro levels within the economy tended to lack definition and purpose. For example, government failed to evolve a clear conception of how its many specific interventions were to be integrated and aligned with national objectives. In addition, as noted earlier, firms were frequently able to evade government policies because the more specific policy instruments were non-regulatory out of respect for the independence of the firm.

Offshore intervention has a different pattern. Just as the development of a structured view of industry affected policy initiation, so too it had an impact upon policy implementation. In contrast to earlier intervention episodes, policy implementation in the offshore area hinged upon translating a number of analytical distinctions regarding the structure of the offshore sector into action of a relatively partisan variety. Compulsion was not a significant aspect of earlier 'specific' policies because government had generally not had a developed view of industry upon which to found compulsory instruments. Yet, for example, after the multinational–national distinction became current a certain degree of compulsion applied to the oil companies was acceptable 'in the national interest', and the result was auditing. Similarly, the auditing precedent combined with an increasing tendency for officials to distinguish between British suppliers on the basis of their contribution to the fulfilment of development timetables provided justification for monitoring, a relatively compulsory instrument directed at British-owned firms. Significantly, this type of compulsion is targeted in the sense that it is directed only at those firms which are manifestly 'threatening' the Government's interpretation of the national interest. In addition, the compulsion is scaled according to the degree of the threat. This analysis suggests that the simple pursuit of influence at more and more micro levels within the economy is no longer as central to policy implementation as it was in the past. In the offshore area intervention was a product of government estimates concerning which structural component of the offshore sector was crucial for national interests – an industry, a group of firms, or a single company. It is in this sense that government–industry relations tend to be more directed than previously.

One further point deserves to be made before turning to other subjects. As explained above, all of the unorthodox instruments have regulatory features and this has meant that even in the case of a relatively non-discriminatory instrument such as auditing government contacts with firms are more immediate and more detailed than was the case with any of the firm-specific, non-regulatory instruments of the past. In many respects 'firm specificity' has not been an issue in offshore intervention because a certain degree of compulsion guarantees direct government influence upon in-dividual firms. If Figure 9.2 is any indication, there may still be a tendency for new policy instruments which are more compulsory in nature to be applied to larger groups of firms. Yet in all cases government influence over decision-making at the level of the firm has been expanded, and under certain circumstances even highly discriminatory, highly compulsory policy instruments might emerge, although these are probably as yet politically unacceptable.

THE LIMITS OF OFFSHORE INTERVENTION IN THE BRITISH CONTEXT

As indicated above, the unorthodox policy instruments characteristic of the offshore area constitute departures in the history of industrial intervention. However, they are also rooted in certain fundamental traditions of industrial policy-making in Britain to date. Specifically, all of these instruments centre upon an administrative approach to the implementation of policy in which government intervenes in industry equipped only with massive files and survey forms. The administrative tradition of intervention constrains the Government's role to that of a 'third party' attempting to correct abuses and inadequacies in the relations between offshore suppliers and the oil companies. We may now inquire after the nature of the limits which this type of tradition imposes and the possibilities for alternative intervention strategies.

The administrative tradition of intervention is limited in a variety of ways. First and foremost, officials responsible for the implementation policy are not participants in the industrial decision-making processes which fall under their scrutiny. At best they are informed observers who attempt to employ their knowledge of corporate structure and activities to influence executive decisions in certain directions. As such, they are often not privy to the full range of considerations which bear upon executive choices. More importantly, officials are limited in the degree of compulsion which they can exercise if firms refuse to comply with government policies. For example, even though the auditing procedure was supported by the implicit threat of legal sanctions, oil company executives were fully aware that drafting legislation and bringing it into force is a lengthy and time-consuming process which government would be reluctant to launch unless auditing violations were numerous and/or sufficiently important. Thus, the oil companies retained some freedom of manoeuvre under auditing because the sanctions which underpinned the policy instrument were neither direct nor immediate.

Other limitations of the administrative tradition centre upon the process of gathering and maintaining such information as is necessary to the implementation of policy. For example, the use of devices like quarterly return forms can be cumbersome, especially if the nature of the device itself becomes an issue between government and firms. The Government may become 'locked' into a certain format for collecting information despite changing requirements. In addition, once the forms in question are assembled, officials must engage in the often lengthy procedure of isolating significant developments within their sphere of interest. Finally, in the ensuing negotiations with firms they must continually compensate for the fact that the information at their disposal is to one degree or another dated.

The administrative tradition also to some extent constrains the use of non-administrative expertise in policy-making. As in the case of the unorthodox instruments discussed above, the deployment of commercial and professional expertise can be vital to the implementation of policy instruments in the industrial field. However, meshing these latter specialisms with administrative expertise has not always been easy. In the first place, the work patterns associated with the administrative tradition of intervention are seldom congruent with those of the financial establishment or the professions, and this has led to a variety of demarcation disputes between different types of officials. Moreover, the criteria which non-administrative officials have been trained to apply in judging the merits of certain developments within industry are frequently very different from those applied by their administrative counterparts, and, as a result, there have been conflicts over which type of criteria should command ultimate authority.

Having reviewed a number of the limitations of the administrative approach to policy implementation, we may now ask whether the Government had other options, with fewer constraints, which it might have employed in the offshore field. Superficially, the answer to this question is yes. In particular, government might have adopted the Norwegian approach to offshore intervention. Contrary to the British, who have focused upon promoting the development of a native offshore supplies industry by administrative means, the Norwegians have encouraged the creation of a viable native offshore supplies capacity by taking an equity stake in the oil industry.[8]

Briefly stated, the Norwegian Government has vested the responsibility for ensuring Norwegian commercial participation in the development of the Norwegian oil fields in the state oil company, Statoil. Statoil fulfils this responsibility in its commercial capacity as a partner in oil field development for most of the fields in the Norwegian sector of the North Sea. This arrangement gives Statoil officials the right to sit on the various committees of each consortium developing an oil field in which the state has a commercial interest. Some of these committees, usually referred to as the development or operating committees, are responsible for equipment purchases for the oil fields and, hence, approve the major equipment contracts placed by the operator in charge of developing the field. As a full commercial member of these committees, Statoil is able to participate in decisions about the placing of equipment contracts and other important issues connected with field development. Under a general government directive Statoil makes every effort to increase the offshore participation of Norwegian industry through its membership of several operating committees. This is more than the moral suasion which the OSO exercises. Statoil's efforts are supported by the force of commercial law in that, as a full partner in an oil consortium, it has the right to be consulted about equipment purchases and is entitled to vote on the operating committee in accordance with its ownership share. Furthermore, these are not inconsequential powers, for in all recent licence awards and in the largest oil field currently under development in Norway, Statfjord, the state oil company has a 51 per cent controlling interest, which allows it, in effect, to control decision-making concerning equipment purchases and other issues within the consortia of which it is a member.

To date, the evidence suggests that Statoil is using its power to considerable effect. For example, in the Statfjord Field, where Statoil has a controlling interest, 1977 estimates indicate that Norwegian industry had gained contracts for about 60 per cent of the value of goods and services in use,[10] a remarkable figure given the size of the Norwegian economy. Undoubtedly, Statoil has many advantages in comparison with the OSO in pursuing its policies. The company's equity stake in the oil industry allows its officials immediate access to information about purchasing and frequently guarantees direct leverage in decisions regarding the allocation of supply contracts. However, the Norwegian offshore intervention strategy is also based upon a number of particular features of the Norwegian economy which are not characteristic of the British economy. Most importantly, Norway has not been in desperate need of North Sea oil revenues. Indeed, the Norwegian Government has been much more preoccupied with limiting the effects of North Sea development upon Norway's fragile resource-based economy than with the process of oil extraction. Hence, Norway has an oil policy which is not centred upon rapid depletion, and the Government has, therefore, been able to pursue field development in a relatively restrained fashion. In these circumstances government can afford to focus its attention upon the offshore supplies issue without fear of delaying field development. It can also take an equity stake in the industry and use its position to promote domestic industry without fear of curtailing investment on the part of the oil multinationals.

The importance of these latter observations in determining whether the Norwegian policy option was viable in a British context is perhaps best illustrated by examining the record of a number of British nationalised industries in the North Sea arena. Superficially, the Norwegian policy option has been available in Britain for a number of years, even before the creation of the British National Oil Corporation (BNOC), as a result of the participation of the National Coal Board (NCB) and the British Gas Corporation (BGC) in consortia working the North Sea. These nationalised industries have, in fact, claimed to be instrumental in assisting UK industry to obtain contracts from the consortia to which they belong. Moreover, the NCB has such a condition relating to offshore supplies written into its agreement with its partner.[11] However, a study by the House of Commons Select Committee on Nationalised Industries has shown that the performance of these state industries in assisting British industry has been less than impressive (see Table 9.1).

TABLE 9.1   Orders placed by consortia in which the National Coal Board and British Gas Corporation were involved, compared with those placed by other consortia in the North Sea

	UK content (%)	
	1973	*1974*
Orders placed by operators of groups in which the NCB or BGC were involved	29	44
Orders placed by other consortia	37	45 (est.)

Source: First Report of the Select Committee on Nationalised Industries, *Nationalised Industries and the Exploitation of North Sea Oil and Gas*, HC 345, Session 1974–5, para. 152.

The table demonstrates that, on average, the consortia in which NCB or BGC had participated purchased fewer British goods and services than did other groups. The Select Committee was anxious not to draw too many conclusions from these data, owing to the limited period of time over which figures had been collected, but they did state that 'it is fair to say that the claim that the presence of NCB or BGC in a consortium materially increases the proportion of UK purchases is, at the least, unproven.'[12]

The Norwegian case has demonstrated that in appropriate circumstances state industries are capable of playing an effective role in persuading oil consortia to purchase domestic goods and services. The apparent failure of BGC and NCB to make efforts in this direction (despite their claims to the contrary) indicates that there were major considerations in the British case which prevented the implementation of an offshore strategy along Norwegian lines. The most obvious explanation is that executives within the two nationalised industries were reluctant to promote British suppliers in the face of the 'maximum speed of development' objective. Had government been able to tolerate a slower pace of development, nationalised industry executives might have been persuaded to take a stronger stand on the purchasing issue. In the event, the focus on speed of development probably meant that the latter course of action had little to recommend it over and above the administrative means which the Government eventually employed. In short, then, there is little indication that the British Government was in a position to benefit substantially from employing some type of equity-based intervention strategy in the offshore field. Indeed, as a result of the priority assigned to field development, government policy could never be consistently devoted to the promotion of domestic industry. This, in turn, has meant that even now, with between 60 and 70 per cent of the market, British industry is probably still 'under-performing' in the North Sea.

Recent events, however, indicate that government policy may be about to change direction. Now that the first phase of North Sea development is over and the Government is assured that North Sea oil will be coming ashore in sufficient quantities by the end of the 1970s to obviate the need for crude oil imports, the pressure on it to give priority to speed of development is less pronounced. Moreover, the 1976–8 recession in the offshore market has encouraged government to devote more resources towards ensuring that the offshore supply industry is as fully engaged as possible.

The result has been a new emphasis within the OSO on industrial promotion, exports and assistance with the development of new technology. The redirection in policy is most evident in the character of the reorganisation of the OSO which took place in 1977. In it the Platform Sites Directorate was dissolved and an Exports Branch created. In addition, all policy concerns were relocated directly under the Director-General. Other changes were that the Engineering Branch (Branch 4) and the R and D Branch (Branch 3) have been reorganised, with the result that the auditing function has been de-emphasised and the industrial promotion aspect of OSO's work given renewed attention. The Engineering Branch, for example, has a reduced number of audit engineers concerned with reviewing the oil companies' quarterly returns, with the result that much of the audit engineers' work in bringing pressure to bear on the oil companies is now undertaken by the Director-General and his staff or, in unusual cases, by ministers. Furthermore, a new section has been created within the Engineering Branch concerned with analysing the capability of UK industry to serve the offshore market. It is intended to provide information to other sections of the OSO, including the venture managers and audit engineers, concerning both the availability of UK suppliers with particular capabilities and the commercial reputations of UK firms with respect to meeting delivery schedules and other issues. The reorganisation also resulted in the expansion of the R and D branch to four sections. Apart from the administration and co-ordination of the OSO's R and D policy, this branch is now responsible for the technical and economic assessment of future technology in the industry and for providing economic, statistical and forecasting advice to the OSO as a whole. Finally, the position of Deputy Director has been changed to that of Industrial Director in keeping with the new emphasis on industrial development. The structure of the OSO in mid 1977 is given in Figure 9.3.

A typical example of the new tasks which have emerged as a result of the above changes is the OSO's work in organising consortia in the UK to participate in the newly negotiated bilateral agreements between Britain and Norway, Brazil, Venezuela and the Soviet Union for exchange of oil-field technology and management expertise.[13] Many of these agreements hold out the prospect of substantial export contracts for British firms. If such arrangements become more common, and there seems every likelihood that this will occur because of the emergence of state oil companies in most

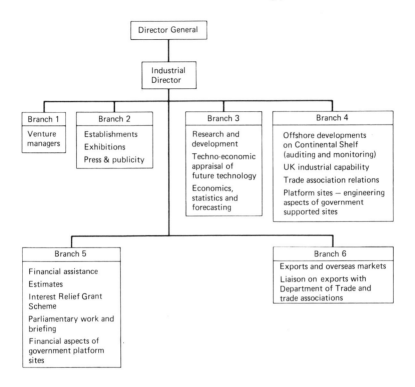

FIGURE 9.3   OSO organisation in mid 1977

Source: 'Offshore Supplies Office Organisation Chart', July 1977 (mimeo.). Used with the permission of the Controller of Her Majesty's Stationery Office.

countries with oil fields to develop, then the OSO will become increasingly concerned with co-ordinating the relations between British industry and foreign state oil companies.

The outlook, therefore, in general terms, seems to be that in the next few years there will be a shift in emphasis away from the auditing function, although it will probably remain an important aspect of the OSO's work. More attention will be directed to services designed to assist British firms in adapting to the new markets opening up in the North Sea and in offshore operations elsewhere in the world. There seems little likelihood of a decline in the role of government in the offshore area, although it will clearly change. Indeed, given the precedents set during the first few years of North Sea developments, the interaction between government and domestic industry will probably be extended. Whether the Government's relations with the oil companies will become less salient (at least with respect to the purchasing question) remains to be seen. Auditing will probably remain as a policing mechanism to discourage oil companies from reverting to their former purchasing practices, but now that British suppliers dominate the offshore market in most sectors its importance in tHe range of OSO policy instruments will probably diminish gradually. It is possible that closer relations between government and the oil companies may emerge in the offshore field as a result of the presence of the British National Oil Corporation (BNOC) as a major partner in oil-field development. Certainly the BNOC would appear to be the obvious instrument to employ in championing domestic industry both in the North Sea and elsewhere in the world, especially in cases in which other state oil companies are involved.

THE IMPACT OF OFFSHORE INTERVENTION

Limited as it may have been in comparison with strategies, such as the Norwegian one based upon equity holdings, British offshore intervention has had a substantial impact upon government–industry relations. In particular, the plight of the domestic offshore supply industry in the early 1970s obliged government to support the interests of a nationally based industry against those of a multinationally based industry. In so doing it promoted the development of new industrial capacity, with the result that the offshore supply industry is at least to some degree a product of government policy initiatives. What, then, have been the consequences of these parallel undertakings?

    As mentioned earlier, the decision to promote the domestic offshore supply industry by auditing the purchasing activities of the oil multinationals is a departure within the framework of British industrial policy-making. In this instance, the British Government, apparently for the first time, sought to modify the commercial operations of foreign firms for the explicit benefit of a domestic industry. In short, government became an ally of domestic firms in their attempts to wrest supply contracts from oil companies favouring foreign suppliers. Frequent alliances of this kind would mark the end of the past tendency for British governments to identify their interests closely with what may be designated as modern 'liberal' capitalism summarised by the phrases 'free trade' and 'free movement of capital', and by a welcoming attitude to multinational companies and foreign investment. Whether the offshore instance of government intervention in the affairs of multi-nationals will prove to be an isolated one (prompted only by the crucial importance of oil to the British economy) remains to be seen. However, there is every likelihood that policies of this kind will become more common as Britain's relative position within the world economy declines and as its national interests become more distant from those of the economic 'leaders' such as the United States, Japan and West Germany. This is not to underestimate the continued importance of commitments to liberal capitalism within British society and government (particularly given the influence of the City of London and a select group of large British-owned multinationals upon policy-making). Yet increasingly government may not be able to afford to allow domestic industry to fail in the face of foreign competition and the dominance of certain economic sectors by multinationals. Naturally, Britain's membership in the EEC will impose restraints on the country's ability to pursue nationally based industrial policies, owing to Community rules concerning trade and investment between member countries. However, if Britain's competitive position within the EEC continues to deteriorate, government may have little option but to press for changes in the way EEC rules apply to Britain or, if that fails, to reassess its position within the Community.

Offshore intervention has also had more specific types of impact upon the relations between government and industry. For example, through auditing government for the first time broke the oil companies' monopoly of detailed information on oil field development, thus improving its ability to control the manner in which oil field exploitation occurs. The participation of BNOC as a commercial partner in oil field development will expand this capacity, and will result in a significant dilution of the autonomy which the oil companies previously enjoyed in conducting their commercial operations. While it is difficult to foretell future relations between government and the oil industry in this area without more information concerning the manner in which offshore intervention has altered expectations within the oil companies[14] it would certainly appear that a major shift in the boundary of authority between the Government and the oil companies has occurred to the detriment of the latter. On another front, government has become the defender and protector of an entire industry. Specifically, its decision to promote an offshore supply capacity in Britain has involved it in a wide variety of obligations ranging from organising the bidding for export contracts to maintaining unused platform construction yards. Domestic firms are not always enthusiastic recipients of this type of sponsorship. They have voiced criticisms of the usefulness of many of the Government's policy instruments and, at times, of the competence of those operating them. However, domestic offshore suppliers also now tend to regard government as a guardian for their commercial interests. They often remain suspicious of the intent of government's policy prescriptions in the offshore field, but continuous contacts with government officials have also convinced them that they can depend upon government to argue their case with the oil companies. Some of these firms, furthermore, are even willing to accept government advice and financial assistance in pursuing offshore contracts. There is every likelihood, as well, that as offshore opportunities increase abroad, domestic offshore firms will look more and more to government for assistance in furthering their export interests, especially if negotiations with foreign governments and foreign state oil companies are involved.

Appendices

APPENDIX   I
*Memorandum of Understanding between Department of Energy and UK
Offshore Operators Association Ltd*

1 It is the declared intention of the Government that the UK
offshore industry should provide, on a competitive basis, a major
and progressively increasing share of the goods and services
required for the development of our continental shelf, and should
establish a growing export market. For this purpose, the
Government has made it clear that UK industry should be given full
and fair opportunity to compete and Members of the United
Kingdom Offshore Operators Association Limited (UKOOA) fully
support this policy.

2 The Offshore Supplies Office (OSO) of the Department of
Energy is responsible to the Secretary of State for ensuring the
maximum possible involvement of UK manufacturers, consultants,
contractors and service companies in the provision of supplies and
services to the offshore hydrocarbon industry. This includes the
creation of new industrial capacity to meet existing and emerging
needs and measures to ensure that such new capacity is as fully and
continuously utilised as possible. For this purpose, the Government
stands ready, in selected cases, to make use of the resources of the
Industry Act 1972, the new powers to be granted by the Industry
Bill now before Parliament and the proposed Scottish and Welsh
Development Agencies.

3 Members of UKOOA have undertaken to give UK industry a
full and fair opportunity to manufacture and supply the goods and
provide the services necessary for the programme of exploration,
field delineation and the development of a field and associated
facilities to full production and beyond. Further, individual
Members recognise the potential benefits of encouraging, through
appropriate technical and contractual support, the creation of UK

capacity to meet the mutually agreed needs, both existing and emerging, of their respective offshore activities. The Members shall use goods and services of British origin in these activities whenever they are competitive in regard to specification, service, delivery and price.

4 To satisfy the Secretary of State for Energy that the procedures and practices adopted by all Members are such as to support the Government's policy described above, the Members of UKOOA (detailed in Appendix A of this Memorandum) have individually agreed to comply with the Code of Practice set out in the attached annex and to make available to officers of the OSO such information as those officers may reasonably require to satisfy themselves that the Government's objectives are being met.

5 HMG and OSO recognise that Members remain fully responsible for the safety and commercial success or failure of their operations and will take all reasonable steps not to delay the Members' decision-making processes and commercial practices (consistent with the other obligations in this document). Further, the strictest confidentiality will be maintained by the Department in respect of competitive commercial information submitted to OSO under the terms of the Code of Practice.

6 This Memorandum shall be interpreted and applied in a manner consistent with the provisions of the Treaty establishing the European Economic Community.

3 November 1975

Annex (1) to Memorandum of Understanding: Code of Practice for Purchasers of Goods and Services for Oil Related Activities on the UK Continental Shelf

INTRODUCTION

This Code of Practice defines the procedure which Members of UKOOA have undertaken to apply in the procurement of materials and services required to support oil related activities on the UK Continental Shelf. While this Code of Practice applies to all purchases, the principle of prior information of intent to make a purchase or place a contract outside the UK will not normally apply to orders for materials and manufactures below £100,000 and to construction and services contracts below £500,000, except in those cases in which OSO has a special interest as agreed in discussion with the operators.

In accordance with the associated Memorandum of Understanding between the Department of Energy and UKOOA dated 3 November 1975 the Department undertakes to observe the strictest confidentiality on all aspects relating to the commercially competitive data submitted to them under the terms of this Code of Practice, and operators undertake to maintain strict confidentiality on such discussions with OSO.

CODE OF PRACTICE

1 To ensure that UK organisations are given a full and fair opportunity on each and every contract, the operator will ensure that:

(a) all potential suppliers selected to bid receive a fully definitive enquiry specification in the English language for the goods and/or services required;

(b) the specification is in accordance with the accepted oil industry standards or British standards; it indicates a willingness to accept equivalents and states the equivalent whenever possible;

(c) the specification is drawn in a manner which does not deliberately preclude UK suppliers from tendering or diminish their prospects of submitting a successful tender;

(d) any amendments to the specification that emerge during the course of the tender preparation are notified to all bidders so that there is full equality of information;

(e) all potential suppliers selected to bid are given an equal and adequate period in which to tender, such period to take into account the need to meet demonstrably unavoidable critical construction or production schedules of the operator;

(d) any special conditions attached to the materials, the source of supply of components and materials, and the inspection of goods are stated in the specification or enquiry documents;

(g) stated delivery requirements are not more stringent than is necessary to meet the construction and/or production schedules of the operator;

(h) where the requirement includes the need to develop equipment or proposals in conjunction with the operator, all bidders are given equal information at the same time;

(i) when the operator is unable to identify a reasonable number of suitably qualified UK suppliers for his invitation to tender, he will consult the OSO before issuing enquiries;

(j) the enquiry documents require the potential bidders to estimate the value of the UK content of the goods and/or services to be supplied.

2 At the tender evaluation stage, the operator will ensure that:

(a) anomalies or inequalities between the submissions and the enquiry documents are fully resolved relative to the short-listed bidders;

(b) delivery promises of all bidders are assessed for their reality in the light of past performance and an assessment of current performance;

(c) when costs are compared, account is taken of financial assistance available to buyers;

(d) the foreseeable impact of currency fluctuations and the effects of escalation clauses are taken into account.

3 When the operator has determined his decision for the award of contract, in the case of non-UK award, he will inform OSO prior to notifying selected suppliers and will give OSO a reasonable time, in the circumstances applying, for representation and clarification. This procedure will be followed in the case of sub-contracts referred by main or sub-contractors to the operator for approval. Where the operator does not intend to call for prior approval of sub-contracts the procedure for adherence to the Memorandum of Understanding and this Code of Practice will be agreed between the operator and OSO. Where this gives OSO access to the operator's contractors and sub-contractors this procedure will not diminish the direct and normal contractual relationship between the operator and his suppliers. The principle shall be adopted that following disclosure of prior information to OSO on intended awards no subsequent representation to the operator by a potential supplier, other than at the express request of the operator, shall be entertained.

4 To satisfy the OSO that full and fair opportunity is being given to

UK suppliers operators will, on request, make available to officers of the OSO such information as they may reasonably require about:

(a) the programme of intended enquiries to industry necessary to implement the anticipated overall programme of exploration and/or development to the extent that this information has not already been made available to the Department of Energy. (The operators may supply this information in any format convenient to themselves provided it is sufficiently comprehensive to enable OSO to assess the potential opportunity for UK industry);

(b) the specifications and tender documents at the earliest possible time and, prior to the issue of the documents to the suppliers, the list of suppliers to whom it is intended to issue invitations to tender;

(c) the bid summaries so that when necessary and reasonable OSO may request sight of bid summaries and all relevant documents for examination;

(d) the names of appropriate representatives within the operators' organisation with whom OSO can make contact should further discussions be required.

3 November 1975

Appendix A of Memorandum of Understanding: UK Offshore Operators Association Ltd, List of Member Companies (as at 31 October 1978)

Amoco (UK) Exploration Co.
Arco Oil Producing Inc.
BNOC (Development) Ltd
BP Petroleum Development Ltd
Chevron Petroleum Co Ltd
Cluff Oil Ltd
Conoco North Sea Inc.
Elf Oil Exploration and Production (UK) Ltd
Esso Exploration and Production (UK) Ltd
General Crude Oil (UK) Ltd
Gulf Oil Corp. – United Kingdom and Ireland Exploration & Production Division
Hamilton Bros Oil and Gas Ltd
Hunt International Petroleum (GB) Ltd
Hydrocarbons Gt Britain Ltd
Kerr-McGee Oil (UK) Ltd
Mesa (UK) Limited
Mobil North Sea Ltd
Monsanto Oil Company of the UK Inc.
North Sea Sun Oil Company Ltd
Occidental of Britain Inc.

Pan Ocean Oil Corp. (North Sea)
Phillips Petroleum Co.
Placid Oil Co. (UK)
Premier Consolidated Oilfields Ltd
Ranger Oil (UK) Ltd
Shell UK Exploration and Production Ltd
Siebens Oil and Gas (UK) Ltd
Tenneco (UK) Ltd
Texaco Production Services Ltd
Texas Gas Exploration (UK) Corp.
Total Oil Marine Ltd
Trans Ocean Oil (UK) Inc.
Unionoil Company of Great Britain
Zapata International Corp.

APPENDIX II: Orders placed by Oil Companies in the North Sea (UK Sector), 1974–7

Supply category		1977[a] Value (£m.)	1977[a] UK Share (%)	1976 Value (£m.)	1976 UK Share (%)	1975 Value (£m.)	1975 UK Share (%)	1974 Value (£m.)	1974 UK Share (%)
Capital goods									
Fabrications	Production platforms – concrete	—	—	25	88	59	50	161	37
	Production platforms – steel	—	—	57	70	75	95	87	64
	Modules and other fabrications	—	—	116	53	171	60	187	50
Production plant	Power generation equipment	—	—	10	85	27	71	22.4	83
	Pumps	—	—	5	100	10.8	80	5.8	88
	Compressors	—	—	5	60	3.6	42	8.5	41
	Process plant and equipment	—	—	18	89	31.7	91	11.9	80
Pipe and fittings	Pipe	—	—	15	33	58	5	85	7
	Pipe coating	—	—	17	100	1.4	100	25.8	90
	Pipe fittings	—	—	10	70	15.4	61	18.5	49
	Casing	—	—	54	85	45	69	26.7	44
Miscellaneous	Communications equipment	—	—	12	83	13.4	83	8	61
	Wellhead and completion equipment	—	—	9	56	9.5	88	8.7	61
	Safety equipment	—	—	6	92	8.2	98	2.8	95
Total for capital goods		—	—	*359*	*70*	*529*	*63*	*660*	*47*

Appendix II (Contd.)

Supply category		1977ᵃ Value (£m.)	1977ᵃ UK Share (%)	1976 Value (£m.)	1976 UK Share (%)	1975 Value (£m.)	1975 UK Share (%)	1974 Value (£m.)	1974 UK Share (%)
Services									
Exploration and drilling	Rig hire	—	—	105	26	159	33	146	25
	Surveys	—	—	14	64	19.7	62	14	79
	Drilling tools and equipment	—	—	13	54	13	52	13.3	47
General services	Pipe laying	—	—	100	27	76	11	127	18
	Installation operations	—	—	131	34	92	19	123	6
	Diving	—	—	22	61	15.6	69	7.4	42
	Helicopter and air services	—	—	20	60	23.3	59	13.4	60
	Marine transport	—	—	56	40	81	42	21.2	55
	Mud logging and well testing	—	—	8.5	41	12.6	31	9.7	62
	Barytes and mud chemicals	—	—	13.5	70	9.6	68	6.6	64
	Cementing services	—	—	8	50	6.7	85	3.2	59
	Inspection testing and maintenance	—	—	12	67	14.4	69	6.7	69
	Other services	—	—	92	87	62	89	42.3	68
Total for services		—	—	595	45	585	41	534	29
Engineering	Design and consultancy	—	—	87	82	71	60	85	60
Grand total		1295	62	1041	57	1185	52	1279	40

ᵃ As the Department of Energy substantially changed the manner in which it presented the results of its surveys of oil company purchasing behaviour in 1977, it is difficult to compare the results from 1977 and later years with those from 1974 to 1976, except for the grand total of all orders placed.

Sources: Department of Energy, *Offshore Oil and Gas: A Summary of Orders Placed . . . during 1974,* pp. 6–7; Department of Energy, *Offshore 1975: An Analysis of Orders Placed* (London: HMSO, 1976) pp. 6–7; Department of Energy, *Offshore 1976,* pp. 4–5; Department of Energy, *Offshore 1977, Developments Offshore* (London: HMSO, 1978) p. 7. Used with the permission of the Controller of Her Majesty's Stationery Office.

Notes

CHAPTER I

1. See, for example, F. Broadway, *State Intervention in British Industry, 1964–1968* (London: Kaye & Ward, 1969); A. Knight, *Private Enterprise and Public Intervention* (London: Allen and Unwin, 1974); S. Young with A. V. Lowe, *Intervention in the Mixed Economy: The Evolution of British Industrial Policy, 1964–72* (London: Croom Helm, 1974); S. Holland, *The Socialist Challenge* (London: Quartet Books, 1975).

2. This theme is at the centre of a number of writings concerning intervention. See, for example, Broadway, *State Intervention*; and I. Papps, *Government and Enterprise: An Analysis of Government Regulation or Control of Industry* (London: Institute of Economic Affairs, 1975). Much of this literature derives from the impetus provided by M. Friedman, *Capitalism and Freedom* (Chicago: University of Chicago Press, 1956).

3. The degree to which the state is an organ of the capitalist classes or alternatively has developed a measure of autonomy with respect to other formations in society is a matter of some debate among Marxist writers. See, for example, N. Poulantzas, *Political Power and Social Classes* (London: New Left Books, 1975); R. Milliband, *The State in Capitalist Society* (London: Weidenfeld and Nicolson, 1969); J. Holloway and S. Piccioto (eds), *The State and Capital: A Marxist Debate* (London: Edward Arnold, 1977), esp. the Introduction.

4. J. K. Galbraith, *The New Industrial State* (Boston, Mass.: Houghton Mifflin, 1967).

5. Ibid., pp. 307–10.

6. Ibid., pp. 309–13.

7. R. Heilbroner, 'Rhetoric and Reality in the Struggle between Business and the State', in *From Capitalism to Socialism* (New York: Vintage Books, 1970). Heilbroner, however, also had reservations about Galbraith's work, and these are reviewed on pp. 225–35 of the above.

8. Andrew Shonfield, *Modern Capitalism: The Changing Balance of Public and Private Power* (London: Oxford University Press, 1969).

9. Ibid., pp. 93–4.

10. Ibid., pp. 164–5.

11. Holland, *The Socialist Challenge*, p. 49. Holland cites works by S. J. Prais and by G. Newbould and A. Jackson as the sources for these figures.

12. M. Hodges, *Multinational Corporations and National Government: A Case Study of the United Kingdom's Experience, 1964–70* (Farnborough, Hants: Saxon House, 1974) pp. 21–2. For another work concerned with the impact of multi-nationals on Britain, see J. Macmillan and B. Harris, *The American Take-over of Britain* (London: L. Frewin, 1968).

13. Hodges, *Multinational Corporations*, p. 28.
14. Young with Lowe, *Intervention*, pp. 34–119.
15. Ibid., chs 4 and 7.
16. Hodges, *Multinational Corporations*, pp. 204–9.
17. Ibid., ch. 6.
18. As in the case of Upper Clyde Shipbuilders and Rolls Royce. The crises of the late 1960s and early 1970s prompted a number of works which focussed upon issues such as public accountability and 'management', and 'institutional co-ordination', in the relations between government and industry. They included E. Dell, *Political Responsibility and Industry* (London: Allen and Unwin, 1973); N. Abraham, *Big Business and Government: The New Disorder* (London: Macmillan, 1974); A. Knight, *Private Enterprise and Public Intervention: The Courtaulds Experience* (London: Allen and Unwin, 1974).
19. Young with Lowe, *Intervention*, Conclusions. See also D. Winch, *Economics and Policy: A Historical Survey* (London: Fontana, 1972), esp. chs 12–14; J. C. R. Dow, *The Management of the British Economy, 1945–60* (Cambridge: Cambridge University Press, 1968); R. Opie, 'Economic Planning and Growth', in W. Beckerman (ed.), *The Labour Government's Economic Record, 1964–70* (London: Duckworth, 1972); J. Hayward and M. Watson (eds), *Planning, Politics and Public Policy: The British, French and Italian Experience* (Cambridge: Cambridge University Press, 1975).
20. Young with Lowe, *Intervention*, Conclusions.
21. Department of Energy, *Development of the Oil and Gas Resources of the United Kingdom 1978* (London: HMSO, 1978) p. 27.

CHAPTER 2

1. Department of Energy, *Development of the Oil and Gas Resources of the United Kingdom 1979* (London: HMSO, 1979) p. 24.
2. See 'North Sea Oil Hunt to Cost £40 Billion', *Financial Times*, 2 Dec 1977.
3. 'Implementation of the IMEG Proposals', memorandum by Department of Energy, Select Committee on Science and Technology, *Appendices to the Minutes of Evidence Taken by the Sub-Committee on Sea Bed Engineering*, HC 266, Session 1974, p. 473. (Hereafter referred to as HC 266, Session 1974.)
4. Petroleum Times and Department of Energy, *British Offshore Suppliers Guide* (London: Petroleum Times, 1974).
5. See Department of Industry, 'Oil Related Developments in Scotland', *Scottish Economic Bulletin*, no. 7 (Feb 1975) and 'The Impact of North Sea Oil-Related Activity on Employment in Scotland', *Scottish Economic Bulletin*, no. 11 (Winter 1977). Further results were published in R. Pounce, R. Upson and C. Walker, 'Scottish Industry and North Sea Oil', *Trade and Industry*, 14 May 1976. The Department of Industry administered the first study in 1974.
6. 'The Impact of North Sea Oil-Related Activity on Employment in Scotland', *Scottish Economic Bulletin* no. 11 (Winter 1977) p. 11. See also 'The Output of North Sea Oil-Related Industry', *Scottish Economic Bulletin* no. 12 (Summer 1977). For a broader overview of the impact of North Sea oil on Scotland, see M. Gaskin *et al.*, *The Economic Impact of North Sea Oil on Scotland* (Edinburgh: HMSO, 1978).

7. *Scottish Economic Bulletin*, no. 11 (Winter 1977) p. 11.
8. *Trade and Industry*, 14 May 1976, p. 419, Table 4.
9. Ibid., p. 417.
10. Ibid., p. 417.
11. For a fuller description of the regional distribution of the offshore supply industry, see K. Chapman, *North Sea Oil and Gas: A Geographical Perspective* (Newton Abbot: David and Charles, 1976) ch. 5.
12. Shell UK Exploration and Production Ltd, *The Pattern of Capital Purchases for a Typical Northern North Sea Offshore Oil Production Platform* (London: Shell Expro, 1973).
13. North of England Development Council/Department of Trade and Industry (NEDC/DTI), *Oilfield: The Market Place for Northern Firms* (Newcastle: NEDC/DTI, 1972) p. 12.
14. See latter part of this chapter and ch. 7.
15. See ch. 7.
16. J. E. Brantley, *History of Oil Well Drilling* (Houston, Texas: Gulf Publishing Co., 1971) p. 1364.
17. Ibid., p. 1372.
18. Ibid., p. 1384.
19. American Petroleum Institute (API), *History of Petroleum Engineering* (Dallas: API, 1961) p. 965. For a general description of the impact of technology during this period, see National Petroleum Council (NPC), *Impact of New Technology on the U.S. Petroleum Industry 1946–65* (Washington: NPC, 1967) esp. ch. 5.
20. API, *History of Petroleum Engineering*, p. 965.
21. Brantley, *History of Oil Well Drilling*, pp. 1392–7.
22. Cazenove & Co., *The North Sea: The Search for Oil and Gas and the Implications for Investment* (London: Cazenove & Co., 1972) p. 10.
23. First Report from the Committee of Public Accounts, *North Sea Oil and Gas*, HC 122, Session 1972–3, p. 23. (Hereafter referred to as HC 122, Session 1972–3.)
24. *The Exploration for and Exploitation of Crude Oil and Natural Gas in the OECD European Area including the Continental Shelf: Mining and Fiscal Legislation* (Paris: OECD, 1973) pp. 32–3.
25. HC 122, Session 1972–3, p. 23.
26. For three descriptions of the early exploration and development work in the North Sea during this period, see B. Cooper and T. F. Gaskell, *North Sea Oil— The Great Gamble* (London: Heinemann, 1966); C. Callow, *Power from the Sea: The Search for North Sea Oil and Gas* (London: Gollancz, 1973); and P. Hinde, *Fortune in the North Sea* (London: Foulis, 1966).
27. HC 122, Session 1972–3, pp. 23–34.
28. International Management and Engineering Group of Britain Ltd, *Study of Potential Benefits to British Industry from Offshore Oil and Gas Developments* (London: HMSO for DTI, 1972) p. 88. (Hereafter referred to as IMEG Report.)
29. HC 122, Session 1972–3, Annex 11, p. 53.
30. IMEG Report, p. 88.
31. There were, in fact, six gas fields found in the North Sea during the 1965–8 exploration phase; three came into production during 1967–9, and three in the

early 1970s. See Department of Energy, *Development of Oil and Gas Resources of the United Kingdom 1976* (London: HMSO, 1976) pp. 34–5.

32. Interview with former senior oil company executive, London, 5 Dec 1975. See also Scottish Council (Development and Industry), *Oil and Scotland's Future* (Edinburgh: Scottish Council, 1972) pp. 159–60.

33. NEDC/DTI, *Oilfield*, p. 10.

34. *Petroleum Times*, 29 Mar 1968, p. 482; *Petroleum Times*, 2 Nov 1966, p. 1158.

35. This figure is the author's estimate based on the fact that the cost for developing one of the larger gas fields over a four-year period was £40 million, and, as five of the six fields were being developed during the 1960s, this would make a total development cost of £200 million. The additional £50 million is an estimate of the costs of laying pipe-lines to connect the main fields with the terminal at Bacton.

36. IMEG Report, p. 89.

37. Department of Energy, *Development of Oil and Gas Resources 1976*, pp. 30–1.

38. Ibid.

39. British Petroleum Briefing Note, 'B. P.'s Forties Field Development' (London: BP Public Affairs Department, Mar 1975) pp. 1–2; 'North Sea Background Notes' (London: BP Public Affairs Department, Mar 1975) pp. 35–6.

40. See, for example, 'North Sea Oil Development Bill put at £1,000 Million', *The Times*, 18 Nov 1971; 'Exciting North Sea Oil Prospects for Britain', *Trade and Industry*, 9 Dec 1971.

41. The other problem here was, of course, that US firms effectively dominated the market.

42. IMEG Report, pp. 85–91.

43. Ibid., pp. 40–53.

44. See ch. 7.

45. IMEG Report, p. 40.

46. See ch. 7.

47. D. I. MacKay and G. A. Mackay, *The Political Economy of North Sea Oil* (London: Martin Robertson, 1975) pp. 79–80.

48. For some early success stories, see 'North Sea Hardware: Britain Makes a Late Start', *Financial Times*, 19 Dec 1972. See also Report of the Select Committee on Science and Technology, *Offshore Engineering*, HC 313, Session 1974, para. 35. (Hereafter referred to as HC 313, Session 1974.)

49. Scottish Council (Development and Industry), *Oil and Scotland's Future*, p. 160; interviews with senior British oil company executives, 1975.

50. NEDC/DTI, *Oilfield*, p. 10. BP reported that of its British suppliers of heat exchangers 43 per cent of deliveries were late, of its British suppliers of pressure vessels 62 per cent of deliveries were late, and of its British suppliers of pumps 49 per cent of deliveries were late.

51. HC 313, Session 1974, para. 39.

52. This has been especially true of platform construction.

53. Interviews with senior oil company executives, 1975.

54. IMEG Report, p. 24.

CHAPTER 3

1. The *Research Index*, which lists the serious daily press and the important industrial trade magazines, was checked on a subject basis for the years 1965–

74 to ensure general coverage, and the following journals were reviewed individually for the period 1971–5: *Petroleum Times*, *Petroleum Review* and *Petroleum Press Service* (later *Petroleum Economist*). *Offshore Services* was reviewed for the years 1972–5 and *Offshore Engineer* from its start in January 1975.

2. The only stories to be found in the press prior to the creation of the IMEG study group were articles (few in number) about the growing business opportunities for British companies.

3. The two leading journals in this area in the United States, *Offshore* and *Ocean Industry*, started publication in 1954 and 1960.

4. See Andrew Graham, 'Industrial Policy', and Roger Opie, 'Economic Planning and Growth' in W. Beckerman (ed.), *The Labour Government's Economic Record: 1964–1970* (London: Duckworth, 1972). Also, T. Smith, 'The United Kingdom' in R. Vernon (ed.), *Big Business and the State: Changing Relations in Western Europe* (London: Macmillan, 1974).

5. See Young with Lowe, *Intervention*, chs 11–13.

6. See, for example, MacKay and Mackay, *The Political Economy of North Sea Oil*; and M. Saeter and I. Smart (eds), *The Political Implications of North Sea Oil* (London: Royal Institute of International Affairs, 1976). For more recent reviews, see C. Robinson and J. Morgan, *North Sea Oil in the Future* (London: Macmillan, 1978); and A. Hamilton, *North Sea Impact: Offshore Oil and the British Economy* (London: International Institute for Economic Research, 1978).

7. See First Report from the Committee of Public Accounts, *North Sea Oil and Gas*, HC 122, Session 1972–3, esp. the DTI's memorandum to the Committee entitled 'Arrangement for the Exploitation of Petroleum and Natural Gas within Great Britain and the Continental Shelf', pp. 23–34. Government was anxious, however, for British firms to participate in the consortia searching for oil during the 1964–72 period.

8. Ibid., paras 92–5 of the report.

9. Hodges, *Multinational Corporations*, ch. 4.

10. Ibid., pp. 164, 166, 174, 177.

11. Ibid., pp. 158, 170.

12. Ibid., p. 164.

13. Ibid., pp. 165, 168.

14. Ibid., pp. 175–6.

15. As signified by the lack of political discussion of the issue.

16. Hodges, *Multinational Corporations*, p. 140.

17. Other criteria applied to proposals designed to encourage public-sector participation (i.e. the Gas Council and the National Coal Board).

18. House of Commons, *Debates*, 21 July 1965, col. 1580.

19. HC 122, Session 1972–3, p. 53.

20. Interview with a civil servant at the Department of Energy.

21. HC 122, Session 1972–3, p. 51.

22. The Department conducted its first survey of offshore purchases for the Committee's hearings, and the results are discussed in HC 122, Session 1972–3, pp. 51–2.

23. Interview with a senior American oil executive, London, 14 Nov 1975.

24. See ch. 2.

25. UK Atomic Energy Authority, *Proceedings of the Conference on the Technology of the*

Sea and Seabed held at AERE Harwell, 5–7 April 1967, AERE R. 5500, 3 vols (London: HMSO, 1967).

26. Ibid., vol. 1, p. 1.
27. Ibid., vol. 1, p. 2.
28. D. C. Watt, 'Britain and the North Sea: Policies Past and Present', *Political Quarterly*, XLVII, no. 4 (Oct–Dec 1976) p. 384.
29. *Report on Marine Science and Technology*, Cmnd 3992 (1969).
30. Ibid., p. iii.
31. Ibid., para. 50, p. 13 (my emphasis).
32. Ibid., pp. 38–9.
33. Watt, in *Political Quarterly*, XLVII, no. 4 (Oct–Dec 1976) p. 384.
34. Cmnd 3992 (1969), p. iii.
35. Select Committee on Science and Technology, *Sea-Bed Engineering: Minutes of Evidence*, HC 41 i–iv, Session 1973–4, pp. 21 and 28.
36. Ibid., p. 66. Memorandum to the Committee from the SMTRB.
37. Ibid., p. 79.
38. *Research and Development in Marine Technology*, CMT Publication no. 8, May 1972.
39. Young with Lowe, *Intervention*, ch. 13.
40. *The Times*, 18 Nov 1971; *The Scotsman*, 25 May 1972. See also 'Early Prizes Could Go to Supply Companies', *Investment Review*, 24 Mar 1972, p. 51; 'North Sea Oil Could Spell Gold for BSC', *The Engineer*, 18 Nov 1971, p. 9.
41. 'Exciting North Sea Oil Prospects', *Trade and Industry*, 9 Dec 1971, p. 504.
42. Scottish Council (Development and Industry), *Oil and Scotland's Future*, p. 158.
43. Ibid., p. 155.
44. The changes were an attempt by the Conservative Government to introduce more business-oriented management techniques into civil-service operations. Interview with Rt Hon. C. Chataway, former Minister at the DTI, London, 1 Aug 1975.
45. Interview with a senior civil servant, Department of Industry.
46. Ibid.
47. Ibid.
48. Ibid., interview with a senior civil servant at the Department of Energy.
49. Interview, as note 45.
50. Correspondence between author and the editor of the IMEG Report, 18 Mar 1976.
51. 'Government to Finance Study of Industrial Benefits of Offshore Oil and Gas Developments', *Trade and Industry*, 1 June 1972, p. 383.
52. IMEG correspondence.
53. Interview, as note 48.
54. IMEG correspondence.
55. IMEG Report, p. 6.
56. Ibid., p. 6. The consultants warned, however, that British firms should remain free to establish themselves in world markets without limitations arising from the foreign partners' interests.
57. Ibid., p. 6.
58. Ibid., p. 7.
59. Ibid., pp. 12–13.

60. Ibid., p. 13.
61. Ibid., p. 77.
62. Ibid., p. 77.
63. Ibid., p. 14.
64. Ibid., p. 14.
65. Ibid., p. 14.
66. Ibid., p. 16.
67. Ibid., p. 81.
68. Ibid., pp. 17–18.
69. Ibid., p. 5.
70. Ibid., p. 11.
71. Ibid., p. 13.
72. IMEG correspondence.
73. Interview, senior civil servant, Department of Trade.
74. Interviews, as notes 45 and 73. According to officials, there were discussions in government at the time of the commissioning of the report about the need for some type of agency to deal with the issue of the engagement of UK industry, but there was no view on what type of body it should be.
75. Interviews as in notes 45, 48 and 73.
76. When published, the report had been in the hands of ministers for about four months.
77. See the *Financial Times* leading article, 'Concentrating Resources', 17 Jan 1973, and the editorial in *Offshore Services*, Feb 1973, p. 55.
78. 'The IMEG Report – An Appraisal', *Petroleum Review*, Mar 1973, p. 106.
79. *Offshore Services*, Feb 1973, p. 3.
80. Ibid., p. 53.
81. *Financial Times*, 17 Jan 1973.
82. *Petroleum Review*, Mar 1973, p. 107.
83. One manifestation of this was that apparently the consultants gave little attention to the impact of their proposals upon other areas of government policy. For example, officials expressed concern that the report contained no mention of the effect of some of the financial assistance proposals upon Britain's GATT obligations.
84. See, for example, *The Economist*, 27 May 1972, p. 111, 'North Sea Oil Ought to be Our Jam'.
85. Officials were also anxious that British industry should assist, as far as possible, in ensuring adequate rates of field development so that security of supply would be guaranteed and revenues to the Exchequer maximised.
86. On this see Maurice Wright, 'Ministers and Civil Servants: Relations and Responsibilities', *Parliamentary Affairs*, xxx (Summer 1977).

CHAPTER 4
1. For a similar view on this issue, see Young with Lowe, *Intervention*, ch. 15.
2. 'New Reports on Offshore Oil and Gas Show "Tremendous Opportunities"', *Trade and Industry*, 25 Jan 1973, p. 176.
3. Ibid. For a full description of the elements of the Conservatives' regional policy, see *Industrial and Regional Development*, Cmnd 4942 (1972).
4. *Trade and Industry*, 25 Jan 1973, p. 176.
5. The tendency to favour independent executive agencies over additions to line

departments was characteristic of the 1964–70 Wilson Government (e.g. the transformation of the Post Office into a corporation) and continued during the Conservative period in office (e.g. the creation of the Manpower Services Commission).

6. See ch. 3.
7. *Trade and Industry*, 25 Jan 1973, p. 176.
8. Interview, Rt Hon. C. Chataway, London, 1 Aug 1975.
9. 'Director of Offshore Supplies Office Appointed', *Trade and Industry*, 1 Feb 1973, p. 240. See also D. Suffern (ed.), *Who's Who in World Oil and Gas, 1975–76* (London: Financial Times Ltd, 1975) p. 147.
10. 'DTI Supplies Chief Named', *Financial Times*, 26 Jan 1973.
11. *Trade and Industry*, 25 Jan 1973, p. 176.
12. 'DTI Supplies Chief Named', *Financial Times*, 26 Jan 1973.
13. 'Gibson Answers IMEG Critics', *Offshore Services*, Apr 1973, p. 42.
14. Ibid.
15. 'DTI Supplies Chief Named', *Financial Times*, 26 Jan 1973.
16. Chataway interview.
17. The IDU and OSO were designed to be more entrepreneurial than most departmental divisions, and there was an emphasis on individual accountability.
18. 'The UEG Comments . . . and One from ABOI', *Offshore Services*, Feb 1973, pp. 53–5.
19. 'Opportunities Being Missed', *The Economist*, 20 Jan 1973, p. 38.
20. Lord Rothschild, 'The Organisation and Management of Government R and D', in *Framework for Government Research and Development*, Cmnd 4814 (Nov 1971) (the 'Think Tank' Report). See also the White Paper of the same title as the 'Think Tank' Report, Cmnd 5046 (July 1972).
21. Department of Trade and Industry, *Observations by the Secretary of State for Trade and Industry on the 2nd and 3rd Reports from the Select Committee on Science and Technology, HC 294 and 302, Session 1971–72*, Cmnd 5176, (1972), paras 34–5.
22. Select Committee on Science and Technology, *Minutes of Evidence*, HC 41 i–iv, Session 1973–4, p. 33. (Hereafter referred to as HC 41 i–iv, Session 1973–4.)
23. Ibid., p. 2.
24. Ibid., pp. 5–6.
25. Ibid. In some of these areas (i.e. platform construction, diving) particular attention was given to research on safety.
26. Of the eight industry members, four were from shipbuilding and shipping companies, one was a professor of marine architecture, one from a marine electronics firm, one from the engineering department of an oil company and one from a private-sector research laboratory. See HC 41 i–iv, Session 1973–4, pp. 6–7.
27. Ibid., p. 28.
28. Ibid., p. 30.
29. Ibid., pp. 46–7.
30. Ibid., pp. 46–67.
31. C. Chataway, 'British Industry and North Sea Oil' in *North Sea Conferences 1 and 2* (London: IPC Industrial Press, 1973) pp. 99–101.
32. HC 41 i–iv, Session 1973–4, p. 14; interview with a former senior civil servant at the Department of Energy.

33. Department of Employment, *Education and Training for Offshore Development: Report of an Inter-Departmental Task Force*, Aug 1973.
34. For details concerning how the centre was structured, funded and run, see Petroleum Industry Training Board, *Annual Report, 1974–75*, p. 14.
35. Department of Employment, *Education and Training*. For a brief summary of the Government's initiatives in the area of training, see Manpower Services Commission, *Annual Report, 1975–76*, p. 20.
36. HC 266, Session 1974, p. 474.
37. HC 41 i–iv, Session 1973–4, pp. 2–3.
38. Ibid., p. 50. For a full copy of the report of the working party, see Select Committee on Science and Technology, *Report*, HC 313, Session 1974, pp. 43–50.
39. The method of constructing concrete platforms involves a slip-forming technique in which sections of the walls are built up using a method similar to that used when building tower blocks. However, deck installation requires that the platform be ballasted and sunk so that only the top protrudes through the water; this process demands sites with unusually deep channels.
40. For a discussion of the problem of orders for concrete production platforms going abroad see 'Norway Scores Again', *The Economist*, 24 Nov 1973, pp. 91–2; and 'Mobil's Order for Concrete Platform Could Be Major Breakthrough', *Financial Times*, 23 July 1973. See also HC 41 i–iv, Session 1973–4, p. 61.
41. See 'Offshore Oil Platform Builders Face Vital Inquiry Today', *Financial Times*, 12 Nov 1973; 'DTI "Exerting Pressure Over Oil Platforms"', *Financial Times*, 14 Nov 1973; 'DTI "Wanted Scottish Site for Oil Rigs"', *Guardian*, 14 Nov 1973.
42. HC 41 i–iv, Session 1973–4, p. 60.
43. Ibid.
44. Ibid., pp. 60–1.
45. See, for example, 'Offshore Supply: Realism Needed to Back up Oil Search', *The Times*, 31 Oct 1973. See also special supplements in the *Financial Times* entitled 'Offshore Exploration' on 19 and 20 March 1973; 'North Sea Oil Boom for Plant Manufacturers', *Petroleum Press Service*, June 1973; 'The Boom Begins in Scotland's Northern Isles', *Petroleum Times*, 14–28 Dec 1973; 'Offshore Opportunities', *Petroleum Press Service*, Feb 1973.
46. *Industry Act 1972, Annual Report*, HC 339, Session 1974, p. 13.
47. When a foreign supplier imported his goods into the UK for subsequent shipment to the North Sea a Customs pull-back could be obtained after the date of the second shipment. The penal action, therefore, can only be regarded as the interest on the money deposited against the customs tariff.
48. House of Commons, *Debates*, 6 Nov 1973, written answers, col. 119.
49. See, for example, 'Urgent Government Study on Increasing Oil Flow', *Financial Times*, 28 Dec 1973.
50. Chataway interview.
51. Interview with a senior civil servant, as in note 32.
52. See 'North Sea Slow to Yield', *Petroleum Economist*, Jan 1974.
53. 'Urgent Government Study . . .', *Financial Times*, 28 Dec 1973.
54. 'One Year Old and the Energy Department Proves Its Worth', *Financial Times*, 6 Feb 1975.
55. For some typical examinations of the oil-related issues in the February 1974

election, see 'How Will the North Sea Cake be Divided?', *Sunday Times*, 17 Feb 1974; 'General Election: Getting a Fair Share of the Profits for Britain', *The Times*, 22 Feb 1974.

56. Department of Energy, *U.K. Offshore Oil and Gas Policy*, Cmnd 5696 (1974).

57. House of Commons, *Debates*, 2 Apr 1974, cols 1107–9.

58. 'Enlarged Offshore Supplies Office to Play Key Role in Securing North Sea Oil Benefits', *Trade and Industry*, 25 July 1974, pp. 159–60.

59. House of Commons, *Debates*, 2 Apr 1974, col. 1107.

60. Ibid., col. 1108.

61. *Trade and Industry*, 25 July 1974, p. 160.

62. Select Committee on Science and Technology, *Offshore Engineering Minutes of Evidence*, HC 107 i–x, Session 1974, pp. 367–8 (emphasis added). (Hereafter referred to as HC 107 i–x, Session 1974.)

63. Interview with a civil servant at the Department of Energy.

64. OSO press note, 'Offshore Oil and Gas Production Platforms', 25 July 1975, p. 1.

65. Ibid.; interview with a civil servant at the Department of Energy. It could be argued that both the platform sites policy and monitoring also assisted industry by increasing the numbers of platform sites and platform designs available to the oil companies and by improving the delivery performance of British firms, two things which presumably increased the commercial viability of British firms against foreign competition. However, the Government's primary object in implementing these policies was to accelerate the pace of oil-field development.

66. A similar point is made by B. W. Hogwood concerning government attitudes to support policies in the shipbuilding industry. One of the criteria evident when government was considering the provision of assistance to the industry was the degree to which the firm receiving assistance was in an area of high unemployment. When the firm was also located in an area of high political support for the government of the day, this tended to reinforce the government's propensity to provide financial assistance, although this latter determinant was not usually paramount, as is apparent from the fact that Conservative governments also provided support for the industry even though most of the shipyards assisted were in areas that traditionally vote Labour. See B. W. Hogwood, 'The Politics of Industrial Change: Government Involvement in the U.K. Shipbuilding Industry, 1959–1973' (unpublished Ph.D. thesis, University of Keele, June 1977) pp. 416–20.

67. See, for example, 'U.K. Contractors Missing Out on North Sea Work', *Chemical Age*, 8 Feb 1974; 'Can U.K. Depose U.S.A. as King of the Rigs?', *The Engineer*, 18 July 1974; 'Time Slips by for U.K. Builders: Concrete Platforms', *Offshore Services*, Sep 1974; 'U.K. Must Increase Share of North Sea Supplies Trade', *Financial Times*, 28 June 1974; 'One Rig in Ten is British Built', *Guardian*, 17 Oct 1974; 'No Easily Attainable Pot of Gold', *Financial Times*, 11 Oct 1974; 'North Sea Oil: Less than a Drop in the Ocean for British Industry', *The Engineer*, 18 July 1974.

68. The evidence covered three volumes, HC 41 i–iv, Session 1973–4; HC 107 i–x, Session 1974; and HC 266, Session 1974.

69. HC 313, Session 1974.

70. See the Committee's justification of this in its report, ibid., p. 12.

71. Ibid., paras 86–7.
72. Ibid., pp. 28–9.
73. Ibid., pp. 32–3.
74. Ibid., p. 33.
75. Ibid., p. 35.
76. Ibid., p. 35.
77. Ibid., p. 37.
78. Ibid., p. 38.
79. Department of Energy, *Select Committee on Science and Technology, Government Observations on Report Session 1974, Offshore Engineering*, Cmnd 6060 (May 1975).
80. Ibid., p. 7.
81. See 'Men and Matters' column, 'Offshore R and D', *Financial Times*, 7 May 1975. Interview with a civil servant at the Department of Energy.
82. Since this chapter was written, there has been a further reorganisation of the OSO. The character of this reorganisation and the reasons for it are discussed in Chapter 9.
83. In 1975 the Labour Government did extend the nature of the auditing process. However, this was only an extension of the existing framework established under the Conservative Government in 1973, and no further policy instruments were introduced. See Chapter 8 for further details.

CHAPTER 5

1. Stephen Young in Young with Lowe, *Intervention*, ch. 2, describes the range of policy instruments that have been employed in industrial policy over the last fifteen years. The term 'orthodox' is used to designate a policy instrument which is historically conventional in this sense.
2. Department of Energy, 'Offshore Supplies Interest Relief Grants Scheme', Explanatory Notes, no. 1 (mimeo., n.d.).
3. Interview with civil servants at the Department of Energy, 1976.
4. Department of Energy, 'Offshore Supplies Interest Relief Grant Scheme', Explanatory Notes, no. 1 (mimeo., n.d.).
5. Interview, as in note 3.
6. However, the audit engineers, in pressing the oil companies to use UK suppliers, will insist that the IRG be deducted from the UK bid. Hence, domestic suppliers do have *some* 'direct' benefit from the scheme, although of a minimal kind.
7. See 'Britain's Naughty North Sea Handouts', *The Economist*, 22 May 1976, pp. 63–4, for a full background description.
8. Interview, as in note 3.
9. See House of Commons, *Debates*, 15 June 1977, cols 492–5 and 'EEC Challenge to British Aid for Offshore Suppliers', *Financial Times*, 29 July 1978.
10. House of Commons, *Debates*, 15 June 1977, cols 485–6. The next largest grants were as follows: Burmah consortium (Thistle Field) £18m.; BP (Forties Field) £10m; Shell–Esso (Brent Field) £9m.; Total consortium (Frigg Field) £9m. Grants to other consortia developing fields are under £5m. each.
11. Field development costs provided by oil company sources.
12. See ch. 2.
13. See ch. 8.
14. See questionnaire results presented in ch. 6.

15. Department of Energy, *Offshore Supplies Office*, Sep 1975, p. 9.
16. 'Research Management: The System Adopted by the Department of Energy', *Offshore Research Focus*, no. 1 (Mar 1977) p. 2.
17. This approach was recommended to the Board by the OSO.
18. Department of Energy, *The Offshore Energy Technology Board: Strategy for Research and Development*, Energy Paper no. 8 (London: HMSO, 1976) pp. 11–12.
19. Ibid., pp. 4–5.
20. Ibid., p. 5.
21. Interview with a civil servant at the Department of Energy. In fact, no appeal had been made by a sponsoring organisation as of the end of 1976.
22. Department of Energy, *The Offshore Energy Technology Board*, p. 1. Official representatives on the Board included the Department of Energy's Chief Scientist as Chairman, a member of the Department's Petroleum Engineering Division and the Director-General of the OSO. In addition, there were representatives from the Departments of Trade and Industry and the Ministry of Defence. Finally, the non-industry membership was completed by a representative from the Harwell Atomic Energy Research Establishment and an academic from Heriot-Watt University.
23. Interview, civil servant, as in note 21.
24. Department of Energy, *The Offshore Energy Technology Board*, p. 11 (emphasis added).
25. The oil companies have always been reluctant to accept risks on new technology, partly because they have become accustomed to a slowly evolving technology (see ch. 2) and partly because of the magnitude of the losses that might be engendered in using unproven technology.
26. According to a senior official, at least one major oil company in the North Sea tends to encourage duplication of R and D work amongst several suppliers, some of them foreign.
27. These potential areas included the following: deep drilling capacity; submersibles; inspection and non-destructive testing; underwater maintenance and repair; underwater tools and power sources; diving; pipe-laying; systems for marginal fields; subsea completions and sea-bed production; positioning, mooring and anchoring systems; single-point moorings; tethered buoyant platforms. For an independent assessment of the OETB's R and D strategy, see *Offshore Oil and Gas Technology – Strategy for Research and Development* (London: Royal Society, Feb 1977).
28. Interview, as in note 21.
29. For example, those firms involved in the more advanced forms of underwater work using submersibles, etc., and those firms manufacturing subsea completion systems.
30. Department of Energy, *Report on Research and Development 1975–76* (London: HMSO, 1976) p. 7.
31. Interview, as in note 21.
32. For an example of such delays, see HC 313, Session 1974, para. 94; HC 266, Session 1974, Appendix 15, pp. 450–8.
33. For a discussion of the nature of exhortation and some examples, see Young with Lowe, *Intervention*, pp. 21–2.
34. See, for example, 'North Sea Oil – a £1,500 Million Market for British Goods

and Services', *Trade and Industry*, 17 Aug 1972; 'North Sea Oil – a Major Success Story', *Trade and Industry*, 28 Sep 1972.

35. Interview, civil servant, Department of Industry; see also 'Offshore from Onshore', *Trade and Industry*, 16 July 1976, pp. 178–9, for a description of the work of the liaison officer in the West Midlands Regional Office of the Department of Industry.

36. NEDC/DToI, *Oilfield* (Newcastle: NEDC/DToI, published annually).

37. Correspondence, senior civil servant, Department of Energy.

38. Interview, as in note 35.

39. 'Offshore from Onshore', *Trade and Industry*, 16 July 1976, pp. 178–9.

40. A 'turnkey' contract is one which is awarded to a company to manage the overall design and procurement process for a large project. Contracts of this kind are usually awarded to large engineering consultancies to manage large-scale civil engineering projects or the building of complex integrated production or processing facilities, e.g. petroleum refineries, etc.

41. Ian Watson, 'Why Whitehall Would Like an Oil Rig Cartel', *Sunday Telegraph*, 21 Mar 1976.

42. Interview with a senior civil servant at the Department of Energy.

43. Watson, in *Sunday Telegraph*, 21 Mar 1976. There are indications that the Wilson Government chose to use export credits in innovative ways in other policy areas, for example, in incomes policy (witness the case of James Mackie and Son's loss of export credit facilities over a pay award; see 'Mackie Losses Export Guarantees', *Financial Times*, 23 Sep 1977).

44. There are indications that a similar policy has been followed in a bid made by British industry for a major contract in Brazil. See 'Ministers Try to Gain More Offshore Work Abroad', *Financial Times*, 7 Sep 1976; 'Bright Outlook for British Exporters', *Financial Times*, 20 Sep 1976; 'Wide Interest in British Offshore Equipment', *Financial Times*, 23 Sep 1976; 'U.K. Chases £100m Oil Rig Order From Brazil', *Guardian*, 11 Sep 1976; 'Brazil in the Market' in 'Offshore Oil Survey', *Guardian*, 30 Nov 1976.

45. Department of Energy, 'A Strategy for Oil Platforms' (12 Aug 1974) para. 4.

46. Only on the west coast of Scotland are there the fjord-like harbours with very deep channels which enable platform building to be accomplished in protected waters.

47. Interview with G. A. Mackay of the North Sea Oil Study Group, Department of Political Economy, University of Aberdeen, 9 Nov 1976.

48. 'The Demand for Production Platforms and Platform Sites 1974–80', North Sea Oil Project – Working Paper no. 11 (Apr 1974), Department of Political Economy, Aberdeen University.

49. Scottish Council (Development and Industry), *United Kingdom Offshore Oil and Gas: An Assessment of the Expected Production from Existing Finds in Scottish Waters* (Aberdeen: Scottish Council, 22 Apr 1974).

50. A senior official noted that the Department's forecast was based on *orders* for platforms placed by 1980, whereas other reports were based on platforms under construction by 1980.

51. OSO press release, 'Offshore Oil and Gas Production Platforms', (mimeo., 25 July 1975).

52. Ibid.; see also '£11.5m Site Boost for Oil Platforms Project', *The Times*, 26 July 1975.

53. 'Demand for North Sea Oil Platforms Will Fall, Report Warns', *Financial Times*, 10 Mar 1975.
54. 'University Group Takes Optimistic View of U.K. Platform Orders', *Petroleum Times*, 21 Feb 1975, p. 9. There was concern in the Government during this period that higher levels of Scottish engagement in North Sea work did not appear to be having significant employment-creation effects on Clydeside, hence the desire to open platform building sites around the Clyde. See 'Manning the Platform Business', *Financial Times*, 10 July 1974.
55. Interview with a civil servant at the Department of Energy.
56. HC 41 i–iv, Session 1973–4, pp. 62–3.
57. Interview, as in note 55. The Government has used the term 'nationalise' to describe the takeover of the platform sites. In fact, it was a special form of compulsory purchase order granted to the Government under the Offshore Petroleum Development (Scotland) Act.
58. See, for example, the Chairman of Shell's comments in 'Clyde Oil Platform Site "An Albatross"', *Financial Times*, 14 June 1975. Recently a government advisory body has issued a report recommending the closure of the two government-sponsored yards; see Oil Development Council and Scottish Economic Council, *Scottish Industry and Offshore Markets* (London: HMSO, 1977).
59. The Andoc group was a consortium of Dutch and British interests; their first order for a concrete platform (a special hybrid design) for the North Sea had been built at a yard in the Netherlands.
60. Usually concrete platforms are built, using a slip forming process, to their final height in a sheltered bay. They are then taken out to a sheltered deep water area and submerged so that the deck and modules can be easily mounted on top of the platform. Once attached, the platform is refloated and towed out to the oil site for final placement.
61. Interview, as in note 55.
62. Interview with a civil servant at the Department of Energy.
63. While there was some acceleration in offshore work in the first half of 1977, new orders for production platforms are likely only to be sufficient to occupy the existing yards, and are unlikely to benefit the two government-financed yards.
64. The Department of Energy has proved reluctant to discuss this function in any great detail. The only published material on OSO monitoring appears in a Department of Energy information folder, *Offshore Supplies Office*, p. 8, para. 9 (Sep 1975). Interviews with civil servants at the Department of Energy.
65. Interviews, as in note 64. Liaison can involve local government agencies.
66. Interview, as in note 64.
67. In some cases the 'honest broker' role has been undertaken at the ministerial level. Ministers may assist firms by making representations to oil companies in an effort to overcome any reservations which oil executives may have concerning the performance of UK firms (see, for example, the efforts by ministers concerning the Texaco Tartan Field platform order, 'U.K.–French Discord over Tartan Order', *Financial Times*, 17 Sep 1977). On some occasions ministers also call in UK suppliers to criticise their delivery performance; see 'Offshore Suppliers Rebuked by Mabon', *Financial Times*, 22 July 1977.
68. See B. W. Hogwood, 'Monitoring of Government Involvement in Industry:

The Case of Shipbuilding', *Public Administration*, LIV (Winter 1976) pp. 418–23.

69. See Department of Energy, *Offshore Supplies Office*, p. 9, for an official description of the venture managers' work. Interviews, senior civil servants, Department of Energy.

70. According to venture managers, the OSO had a substantial role to play in encouraging a number of consolidations in the ownership structure of UK diving firms. See 'The Big Diving Take-Over', *Offshore Services*, June 1975, p. 42.

71. *Annual Report, Industry Act 1972*, HC 619, Session 1975–6, p. 14; see also the 1975 Annual Report, HC 620, Session 1974–5, p. 14.

72. Interview with a civil servant at the Department of Energy. This information is also based on access the author had to departmental flow charts describing the decision paths involved in Section 8 assistance within the OSO.

73. Ibid.

74. See 'Government Refuse Help to Collapsed Oil Venture', *The Scotsman*, 2 July 1975; 'MOIRA Shakes Business Confidence: Nationalisation a Solution?', ibid., 19 July 1975; 'Inquiry Call Over Failure of Rig Repair Scheme', ibid., 26 July 1975. On the failure of the company making oil flow meters, see R. Mugal, 'Receiver for Oil Tool Specialist Group', *Guardian*, 29 Oct 1976.

75. See Hodges, *Multinational Corporations*, ch. 4.

CHAPTER 6

1. For a list of the trade associations with an interest in the industry, see Department of Energy, *Offshore Supplies Office*, pp. 26–8.

2. Confidential trade association figures. See ch. 2.

3. Interview with a civil servant at the Department of Energy, 1976.

4. See, for example, '£100 Million Plan Urged to Promote Microelectronics in Industry', *Financial Times*, 19 Sep 1978. The plan is based, in part, upon the work of the Advisory Council for Applied Research and Development (ACARD). See ACARD, *The Applications of Semiconductor Technology* (London: HMSO, 1978). Other European governments have also recently acted in this field; see, for example, 'France's Electronics Strategy', *The Economist*, 18 Nov 1978, p. 119.

5. See 'A Giantkiller versus the US and Japan', *Financial Times*, 19 Sep 1978. The four major US firms in the field controlled about half of the world market in semiconductors in 1977.

6. See, Pounce, Upson and Walker, in *Trade and Industry*, 14 May 1976. For an earlier report on the survey, see Department of Industry, *Scottish Economic Bulletin*, no. 7 (Feb 1975).

7. The 1973 Census of Production provides figures for the size of plants in manufacturing industry as a whole. About 94 per cent of all manufacturing firms employ fewer than 500 people, and 98 per cent fewer than 1000. Thus, the present group of respondents appears to have a greater than average number of large firms (as measured by employees) when compared with manufacturing industry as a whole. Whether this is characteristic of the offshore supply industry in total is not known. See Central Statistical Office, *Annual Abstract of Statistics, 1976* (London: HMSO, 1976) Table 165, p. 169.

CHAPTER 7

1. Hodges, *Multinational Corporations*, p. 19.
2. For an early survey of the literature available in the field, especially with respect to LDCs, see D. Burtis *et al.* (eds), *The Multinational Corporation – Nation State Interaction: An Annotated Bibliography* (Washington: Foreign Policy Research Institute, 1971). See also Sanjaya Lall, *Foreign Private Investment and Multinational Corporations: An Annotated Bibliography* (London: Praeger, 1975).
3. Published in English as *The American Challenge* (London: Hamish Hamilton, 1968).
4. *The American Take-over of Britain* (London: Frewin, 1969). A recent account of UK policies on multinationals is Hodges, *Multinational Corporations*; in general, see R. Black *et al.*, *Multinationals in Contention* (New York: Conference Board, 1978).
5. See R. Vernon, *Sovereignty at Bay: The Multinational Spread of U.S. Enterprises* (New York: Basic Books, 1971) esp. ch. 5. Also J. N. Behrman, *National Interests and the Multinational Enterprise: Tensions Among the North Atlantic Countries* (Englewood Cliffs, NJ: Prentice-Hall, 1970); R. Vernon (ed.), *Big Business and the State: Changing Relations in Western Europe* (London: Macmillan, 1974).
6. Servan-Schreiber, *Le Défi américain*, chs 2–4; see also J. H. Dunning, 'Technology, U.S. Investment and European Economic Growth', in J. H. Dunning (ed.), *International Investment* (Harmondsworth: Penguin Books, 1972).
7. Department of Energy, *Offshore Supplies Office*, section 4, pt 9.
8. Department of Energy, *Development of the Oil and Gas Resources of the United Kingdom 1976*, Appendix 2. Since 1976 several new oil fields have been discovered and at least two new oil companies have become operators with commercial discoveries which are being developed (Texaco and the British National Oil Corporation). For the most recent up-to-date information on oil-field developments, readers should consult the Department of Energy publication, *Development of the Oil and Gas Resources of the United Kingdom*, which is updated and published annually.
9. W. G. Nightingale (ed.), *Oil and Gas International Year Book, 1974* (London: Financial Times, 1974) pp. 595–6.
10. With the exception of Hamilton Bros, all the companies have substantial interests in Europe as well as in North America. Most also have substantial investments in Australasia and in the Middle East.
11. The four being Shell, BP, Mobil and Chevron. The remaining three are Gulf, Texaco and Esso; both Texaco and Gulf are extensively involved in the southern North Sea gas fields, and Texaco has made a number of oil discoveries in the North Sea, one of which is now being developed (the Tartan field). Esso is a joint partner with Shell in many of the larger North Sea oil fields, although Shell is the operator for all oil fields found by the partnership. For a description of the characteristics of the 'Seven Sisters', see A. Sampson, *The Seven Sisters: Great Oil Companies and the World They Make* (London: Hodder and Stoughton, 1975).
12. In order to obtain some idea of the relative commercial strength of these oil companies, see the chart attached as an appendix to this chapter which gives

their comparative size within their own national business communities.

13. British Petroleum Ltd, Briefing Note, BP Public Affairs Department, Mar 1975 (mimeo.) p. 5.

14. Most of the financing for North Sea developments is provided by consortia of banks on an international scale; only by virtue of large size and financial resources are the oil companies able to use these financing arrangements. While oil companies do devote substantial resources of their own to oil field investment, the sums are becoming so large that even the largest companies are forced to seek outside financing. See the following articles for a detailed discussion of this subject: 'Providing the Finance', FT Survey, *Financial Times*, 23 Apr 1975; 'Alternatives for North Sea Financing', *The Times*, 5 Feb 1976; 'Finance for Offshore Developments', *Financial Times*, 15 Sep 1975. See also 'Finance for North Sea Oil', *Petroleum Review*, Sep 1972; 'Development Financing: Details of North Sea Loan Arrangements', *Petroleum Times*, 10–24 Aug 1973; 'Provision of Finance for Development of North Sea Oil and Gas Fields', *Petroleum Times*, 15 Nov 1974; A. H. A. Dibbs, 'The Growing Involvement of British Banks in Financing North Sea Oil Development', *Petroleum Review*, Sep 1973.

15. See 'Urgent Government Study on Increasing Oil Flow', *Financial Times*, 28 Dec 1973, for an example of Conservative Government attitudes, and 'Benn Wants to Speed North Sea Oil', *Financial Times*, 2 Oct 1975, for an example of Labour attitudes to the problem.

16. See, for example, BP's comment on this problem in its memorandum to the Select Committee on Nationalised Industries: First Report of the Select Committee on Nationalised Industries, *Nationalised Industries and the Exploitation of North Sea Oil and Gas*, HC 345, Session 1974–5, pp. 101–2 (hereafter referred to as HC 345, Session 1974–5). See also Amoco's memorandum submitted to the Committee, ibid., p. 224; Conco's memorandum to the Committee, ibid., p. 206; and 'Too Few Skilled Oil Men for the North Sea', *Financial Times*, 24 July 1975.

17. Interview with an energy consultant for Hambro's Bank, Manchester, Aug 1975.

18. See 'Where to Go, Who to Contact', *Offshore Services*, Apr 1973, pp. 29–37, for a good survey of the differences between the purchasing organisations of the various oil companies working in the North Sea.

19. See a special investigative report on this problem entitled 'Selling Offshore', *Offshore Services*, Aug 1974, esp. pp. 27, 29–30, 35.

20. Interview with senior official of Mobil Oil North Sea, London, 28 Nov 1975.

21. IMEG Report, p. 8.

22. Ibid., p. 29.

23. Attempts were made to gain access to data relating to individual companies which is held by the OSO. However, this information was not made available, on the grounds that it was submitted by the oil companies in commercial confidence, and therefore could not be released to any third party.

24. Prices vary; concrete platforms tend to be more expensive than steel platforms, as they are generally contracted for complete, whereas steel platform prices usually only refer to the actual steel support structure (termed a jacket) which is placed in the water. See also *Offshore Engineer*, Sep 1975, p. 54.

CHAPTER 8

 1. IMEG Report, p. 6.
 2. Ibid., pp. 8, 13.
 3. Ibid., pp. 6, 13.
 4. As noted in ch. 3, this was not the first instance in which administrative pressure had been brought to bear on the oil companies to purchase British goods and services.
 5. Interview with a former senior oil company executive.
 6. Interview with a civil servant at the Department of Energy.
 7. Department of Energy, 'Confidential Quarterly Analysis of Orders by Operators on the U.K. Sector of the Continental Shelf', OSO Document OSO/35/57/01, p. 1.
 8. Interview, as in note 6.
 9. Ibid.
10. Ibid. See also OSO Document OSO/27/57/25, 'Staff Chart Audit Engineers and "Extra-Mural Activities of the Audit Engineers"'.
11. Interview, as in note 6.
12. '"Buy British", Oil Men Told', *Financial Times*, 8 Aug 1975.
13. Interview, as in note 6.
14. These are two certifying organisations in the United States (the American Petroleum Institute and Underwriters Laboratories) which vet equipment against industrial or safety standards.
15. Interview, as in note 6. See also 'Here's the Selling Routine', *Offshore Services*, Apr 1973, pp. 24–5, for similar examples. Note that these specific abuses were also mentioned in provisions of the Code of Practice (see below). See Section 1, subsections (a) – (j) and Section 2, subsections (a) – (d), in Department of Energy, *Memorandum of Understanding Between Department of Energy and United Kingdom Offshore Operators Association Ltd*, 3 Nov 1975, Annex, pp. 1–2. (see pp. 216–19.)
16. Interview, as in note 6; interview with G. A. Mackay, Scottish Office North Sea Study Group, Department of Political Economy, Aberdeen University, Aberdeen, 9 Nov 1976.
17. HC 41 i–iv, Session 1973–4, p. 55.
18. Interview, as in note 6.
19. Interview, as in note 5. See also 'U.K. Government Proposals for Offshore Oil and Gas', *Petroleum Times*, 4 Oct 1974, for the first indication that this subject might be included in legislation.
20. The UK Offshore Operators Association was created as a formal organisation in 1973, succeeding the informal Offshore Operators Committee, which had been functioning since 1964. The companies decided to form an association to handle their relationships with the Government with respect to all types of offshore matters, as this provided the necessary legal framework so that the oil companies could hire staff (five in 1977) to manage their relations and carry out the corresponding administrative work.
21. Interview, as in note 5.
22. Ibid.
23. '"Buy British" Oil Men Told', *Financial Times*, 8 Aug 1975.
24. Interview, as in note 5.
25. Ibid. This was also incorporated into the Code of Practice.

26. Department of Energy, *Memorandum of Understanding between Department of Energy and United Kingdom Offshore Operators Association Ltd*, 3 Nov 1975. See also R. Dafter, 'The Significance of that "Buy British" Agreement', *Financial Times*, 21 Nov 1975.

27. Department of Energy, *Memorandum of Understanding*, p. 1, para. 2.

28. Ibid., p. 1, para. 1.

29. Department of Energy, *Code of Practice for Purchasers of Goods and Services for Oil Related Activities on the U.K. Continental Shelf*, November 1975, Section 1 (i) and Section 3. The memorandum and Code of Practice appear as Appendix I of this book.

30. This procedure is still evolving, as a result of OSO attempts to implement to Code of Practice. Interview, as in note 6.

31. Interviews as in notes 5 and 6; interviews with senior oil company officials, November 1975.

32. Interview, as in note 6.

33. The figure for 1974 was £1280 million and for 1975 £1185 million: Department of Energy, *Offshore 1975: An Analysis of Orders Placed* (London: HMSO, 1976) p. 9.

34. Interview, as in note 6.

35. Confidential source.

36. Ibid.

37. However, Phillips Petroleum, in developing the Frigg field in Norwegian waters, had steel platforms built in the United States and shipped over to Europe. While the distances involved make platform-building abroad uneconomic, this does not, however, mean that the UK is the area with the only geographic advantage for North Sea work; many European yards are just as close to the North Sea oil fields, and some, such as the concrete yards in Norway, possess greater geographic advantages.

38. Interview, civil servant, as in note 6.

39. See Department of Energy, *Offshore 1975*; Department of Energy, *Offshore Oil and Gas: A Summary of Orders Placed by Operators of Oil and Gas Fields on the U.K. Continental Shelf During 1974* (London: HMSO, 1975); Department of Energy, *Offshore 1976: An Analysis of Orders Placed* (London: HMSO, 1977); and Department of Energy, *Offshore 1977: U.K. Goods and Services for Developments Offshore* (London: HMSO, 1978).

40. 'Implementation of the IMEG Proposals', Appendix 20 in HC 266, Session 1974, p. 473.

41. Interviews with senior oil company executives.

42. First Report of the Committee of Public Accounts, *North Sea Oil and Gas*, HC 122, Session 1972–3.

43. See, for example, Lord Balogh, 'Still Time to Retrieve the Great North Sea Losses', *Sunday Times*, 4 Mar 1973; A. Hamilton, 'U.K. Tax Terms and Policies Attacked', *Financial Times*, 2 Mar 1973, and R. Vielvoye, 'Lining Up the North Sea Oil Tax Agenda', *The Times*, 8 Mar 1973.

44. Department of Energy, *U.K. Offshore Petroleum Production Licensing, Fifth Round: A Consultative Document* (1976) p. 1, para. 6.

45. Single-point Mooring Buoys (SBMs) are complex loading devices which allow oil tankers to take on crude oil from offshore production platforms without having to come too close to the platform itself – thus allowing reasonable

loading times even in rough weather. SBMs are expensive items costing several millions of pounds.

46. Interview with senior oil company executives.

47. R. Vielvoye, 'Political Pressures Decide Placing of Orders', *The Times*, 31 Oct 1973.

48. 'U.K. Loses £2.5m Oil Rig Deal', *Financial Times*, 3 Dec 1975.

49. Vielvoye, in *The Times*, 31 Oct 1973. See also 'Mobil's Order for Concrete Platform Could be Major Breakthrough', *Financial Times*, 23 July 1973.

50. See C. Baur, 'North Sea Platform Demand Forecasts Too High', *Financial Times*, 5 Mar 1975; W. Gillen, 'Oilmen Hold Back Platform Orders', *The Times*, 28 Apr 1975. By the autumn of 1975 it had become clear that a slackening of orders was occurring which would have serious implications, not just for the new yards built with government financial aid, but also for established yards. See R. Drafter, 'Platforms of Discontent', *Financial Times*, 27 Nov 1975.

51. House of Commons, *Debates*, 7 Nov 1975, cols 337–8; 5 Nov 1975, cols 186–7.

52. 'Ninian Group Urged to Decide Soon on Third Oil Platform', *Financial Times*, 21 July 1975.

53. 'North Sea Platform Orders Disappointing, Says Benn', *Financial Times*, 8 Nov 1975. See Also 'North Sea Orders Plea Rejected', *Guardian*, 8 Nov 1975.

54. See R. Dafter, 'Lack of Orders Worries Platform Builders', *Financial Times*, 26 Feb 1976.

55. R. Dafter, 'Oil Platform Yards Run Out of Work', *Financial Times*, 28 May 1976.

56. See R. Dafter, 'UK – French Discord over Tartan Order', *Financial Times*, 17 Sep 1977, and R. Dafter, 'Compromise over Tartan Platform', *Financial Times*, 28 Sep 1977.

57. Department of Energy, *Offshore Supplies Office*, p. 7, para. 3.

58. Department of Energy, *Memorandum of Understanding*, para. 6.

59. 'OSO Accused of Unfair Trading Practice', *Offshore Engineer*, Mar 1976, p. 9.

60. This issue has received wide discussion in Canada, for example. Certain writers have discussed harnessing multinationals in the development of industrial strategies for several industries; see J. Fayerweather, *Foreign Investment in Canada: Prospects for National Policy* (Toronto: Oxford University Press, 1974) esp. ch. 5; see also, *Foreign Direct Investment in Canada* (Ottawa: Government of Canada, 1972).

61. See, for example, Young with Lowe, *Intervention*, pp. 16–28.

62. For a discussion of official and ministerial attitudes to the oil companies see Hodges, *Multinational Corporations*, ch. 4.

63. Interview with senior civil servant at the Department of Energy.

64. See ch. 9.

65. See p. 175 of this chapter.

CHAPTER 9

1. Young with Lowe, *Intervention*, pp. 184–6.

2. Ibid., pt II and pp. 185–6.

3. Some of these points were made in correspondence from a senior official who was involved in steering the production of the IMEG Report.

4. Hodges, *Multinational Corporations*, p. 286.
5. Other European governments are also involved in this type of anticipatory policy making. A few weeks after the nationalisation of the major British airframe manufactures the French Government *de facto* nationalised the French aircraft industry for similar reasons.
6. Young with Lowe, *Intervention*, ch. 2.
7. Ibid., p. 208.
8. Information on the process whereby Statoil encourages the purchase by the oil companies of Norwegian goods and services was obtained through confidential interviews between the author and Statoil executives, civil servants in the Ministry of Industry and executives with private oil companies working in partnership with Statoil. See M.J.Jenkin, 'British Government and the Offshore Industry, 1964–1977' (unpublished Ph.D. thesis, University of Manchester, October 1977) Appendix D, pp. 351–79.
9. Previous oil-field developments in which Statoil did not have a 51 per cent stake are governed by a 1972 Royal Decree stipulating the use wherever possible of Norwegian goods and services; see *Lovgivning vedrørende den norske kontinentalsokkel*, 4th edn (Oslo: Royal Ministry of Industry and Handicrafts, 1973) pp. 155–7. For some surveys of Norwegian oil policy in general, see K. W. Dam, 'The Evolution of North Sea Licensing Policy in Britain and Norway', *Journal of Law and Economics*, XVII, no. 2 (Oct 1974); Bjørn Skogstad Aamo, 'Norwegian Oil Policy: Basic Objectives', and Louis Turner, 'State and Commercial Interests in North Sea Oil and Gas: Conflict and Correspondence', in M. Saeter and I. Smart (eds), *The Political Implications of North Sea Oil and Gas* (Guildford: IPC Science and Technology Press, 1975); *Petroleum Industry and Norweigian Society*, Storting Report no. 25 (1973–4); and *Natural Resources and Economic Development*, Storting Report no. 50 (1974–5).
10. Correspondence with a senior Statoil official, 25 July 1977.
11. HC 345, Session 1974–5, para. 148.
12. Ibid., para. 152.
13. In the case of Norway and the UK this has resulted in the establishment of a joint Co-ordinating Committee between the two governments to assist in, amongst other things, the sharing-out of work between the two countries' offshore supply industries in fields straddling the median lines between the two countries' North Sea zones and seeking a potential common export strategy for other offshore markets. See 'U.K., Norway Co-operate on North Sea Development', *Financial Times*, 11 Sep 1976, and 'Offshore Notes: Bright Outlook for British Exporters', *Financial Times*, 20 Sep 1976.
14. The present study might profitably be complemented by an investigation of the manner in which government intervention in the oil industry has affected executive commitments and organisation within the oil multinationals. For example, there is reason to believe that oil companies which have extensive foreign operations, and have also had to cope with a wide variety of regulatory and political circumstances, are more willing to accept, and work in, an environment characterised by substantial state involvement (e.g. the presence of a state oil company or regulations relating to compulsory state equity participation in oil-field development). A study of the processes whereby these companies have accommodated government involvement with the oil

industry (including some indication of the limits of that accommodation) would constitute a useful contribution to our understanding of multinational enterprise.

Index